VICTORY

SPIRITUAL WARFARE
—— *for the* ——
LAST GENERATION

LUIS LOPEZ

Copyright © 2020 Luis Lopez.

All rights reserved. No part of this publication may be reproduced, distributed, or transmitted in any form or by any means, including photocopying, recording, or other electronic or mechanical methods, without the prior written permission of the publisher, except in the case of brief quotations embodied in critical reviews and certain other noncommercial uses permitted by copyright law. For permission requests, write to the publisher, addressed "Attention: Permissions Coordinator," at the address below.

Scripture taken from the New King James Version®. Copyright © 1982 by Thomas Nelson. Used by permission. All rights reserved.

ISBN: 978-1-7358737-0-1 (Paperback)
ISBN: 978-1-7358737-2-5 (Hardcover)
ISBN: 978-1-7358737-1-8 (E-book)

Front cover image by Cristina Tănase.
Book design by Infinite Designs.

First printing edition 2020.

www.harpublishing.net

*Father Elohim, Lord Yeshua,
May the power of your Word demolish strongholds and
release those who read It from bondage.
To You the glory.*

*To my loving parents,
my sisters Alma, Marivel, and Jackie
for their unconditional support.*

*And to Stacey,
thank you for never doubting.*

CONTENTS

PART I SPIRITUAL WARFARE

Introduction 11

Encounter #1: The First Time 13

Chapter 1: The Invisible War 15

Encounter #2: Slammed 23

Chapter 2: Know thy Enemy 25

Encounter #3: Smile 41

Chapter 3: Enemy Tactics 43

Encounter #4: Hound 65

Chapter 4: The Armor of God: Belt of Truth 67

Chapter 5: The Armor of God: Breastplate of Righteousness ... 75

Chapter 6: The Armor of God: Feet Prepared with the
    Gospel of Peace 81

Chapter 7: The Armor of God: Shield of Faith 85

Chapter 8: The Armor of God: Helmet of Salvation 91

Chapter 9: The Armor of God: Sword of the Spirit 95

Encounter #5: Vortex 101

Chapter 10: Command the Battlefield 103

Encounter #6: Balloon 109

Chapter 11: Finish the Fight 111

PART II THE LAST GENERATION

Introduction 125

Chapter 12: Signs of the End 127

Encounter #7: The Shadows 143

Chapter 13: The Seven Churches...145

Chapter 14: Harpazō...159

Encounter #8: 3 A.M..171

Chapter 15: The Breaking of the Seals..173

Chapter 16: The 144,000...181

Encounter #9: Pink Sky...187

Chapter 17: The Sounding of the Trumpets......................................189

Encounter #10: NO!..203

Chapter 18: The Antichrist Revealed...205

Encounter #11: The Man in Black...217

Chapter 19: The False Prophet...219

Chapter 20: Mark of the Beast...227

Encounter #12: Laughter..241

Chapter 21: The Wrath of the Bowls...243

Encounter #13: The Man in White...249

Chapter 22: The Fall of Mystery Babylon...251

Encounter #14: Victory...263

Chapter 23: Glorious Coming..265

Chapter 24: Judgement Day...271

Encounter #15: I am His...291

Chapter 25: Eternity Fulfilled...293

Conclusion..305

About the Author..306

Notes..307

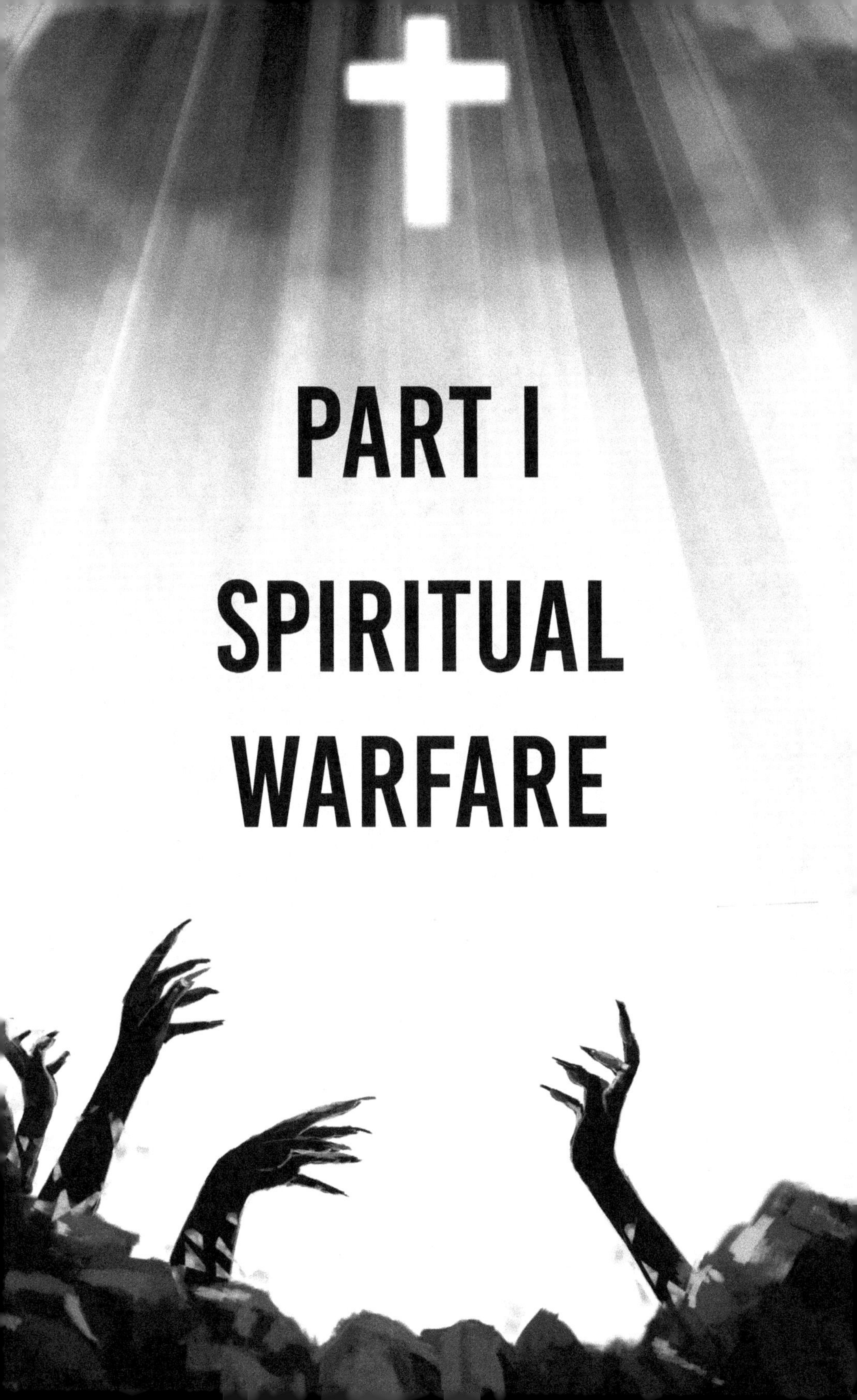

PART I

SPIRITUAL WARFARE

INTRODUCTION

If you've picked up this book, then you have had some experience or interest in what many deem unknown. A taboo subject, the existence of spiritual enemies is often a thought redirected to the subconscious; only to activate when someone brings it to the forefront or when you experience it yourself. From childhood all the way to adulthood, people from all over the world have had some experience with unknown entities and moments that some dare share and many keep secret. Today, you have taken the first step into delving in the truth about what is out there in the unknown realm. If you choose to, today becomes the marker into finally knowing the truth about ghosts, apparitions, sleep paralysis, and all other supernatural activity. Even better, today becomes an opportunity for you to stand up and fight those unseen enemies and eliminate them from your life. I provide a caution though. Be prepared. Spiritual warfare is not for the weak; and there is no turning back. Once you read, not my words, but those dictated by your Creator, then you are now fully responsible for the choice you will make hereafter. The time has come. Will you succumb to defeat or will you fight for victory?

ENCOUNTER #1
THE FIRST TIME

I opened my eyes and saw a large face staring back at me. I couldn't move my body or turn my head, but I somehow knew I was awake and in my room. Laying on top of me was an unfamiliar body with a face larger than that of a human, but definitely male. I was confused and felt a strange sensation around my body. I was in my room, but also not there at the same time, as if reality had somehow warped and part of me was in another place. I remember wondering if I was dreaming.

While I tried to make sense of what was going on, I was also feeling something else, something incredibly perverse and violating. Someone was sexually violating me. I was paralyzed and confused, yet I could feel everything. I could feel every detail of the violation all while the face was staring back at me.

This was my first demonic attack.

Chapter 1
THE INVISIBLE WAR

For though we live in the world, we do not wage war as the world does. The weapons we fight with are not the weapons of the world. On the contrary, they have divine power to demolish strongholds.

2 Corinthians 10:3-4

Being attacked and prodded by demons was my darkest kept secret. I didn't even know if what was happening to me was real. I was a college student living in Long Beach, California, trying to keep up with the fast-paced world I was living in. From sleep paralysis to out of body and sexual violation experiences, every day got harder to keep going. To the world, I was a joyous and happy person, but inside I was depressed and oppressed. I couldn't sleep. I didn't want to eat. And waking up every day was an uphill battle.

Music was all that kept me going. Every day, as I would commute to work and walk to class, I had my headphones on listening to my favorite music. One day, as I walked to class along a student-filled walkway, I was stopped by a fellow student. He tapped me on my shoulder and said something I couldn't hear through my music. I took off my headphones as the flow of student traffic kept moving around us.

He said to me, "Hi…I'm sorry, but I had to stop you and ask—can I pray over you?" I was stunned and perplexed because I did not know this guy at all, and I hadn't made any contact with him to precipitate him talking to me. "I just feel that I need to pray for you right now," he continued.

My mind raced for what seemed an eternity, trying to reason out what was happening. I didn't have any friends, so I welcomed the gesture and agreed that he could pray over me. He prayed for me amongst the sea of students without any shame, and then he said goodbye as I continued to walk to class. I couldn't believe it. How did he know? Out of the mass of students walking to class, how had he signaled me out? Who told him? I felt like he could see right through me and knew the pain I was in.

I share this story because this believer in Christ saw what I could not. He saw the invisible war. Looking past the flesh and the physical reality, this young man was able to see a human under spiritual attack. Thanks to his prayer and his biblical insight, he planted the seed that allowed me to discover God and gain victory against the evil that had been oppressing me for so long. So, too, can you release yourself from bondage and win the war for eternity. But first, you must know what this war is and how is it you were enlisted.

The First Sin

The invisible war dates back before the beginning of time. While many attribute the first sin to be that of Adam and Eve's disobedience, it is not so. The first sin was committed in Heaven by Lucifer—once God's highest ranked angel. According to Isaiah 14:12-14, he was cast down to earth after proclaiming and attempting to be higher and more powerful than the Creator. Pride was the origin of sin.

Once time and earth were created, Lucifer redirected his anger and resentment against God to His creation: your ancestors, Adam and Eve. When the serpent (now cast down to earth) deceived Eve, all of us succumbed to the effects of sin and death. What was paradise and perfect was no longer so. Our relationship with God was severed, and under a fallen world, the sins and eternal consequences of humans continued.

From Cain's murder of Abel to the immorality of the cities of Sodom and Gomorrah, God's creation became a target and an asset for the enemy to use against God. Lucifer, utilized human beings as vessels to tempt us to sin in order that we ourselves would destroy the ability to restore our relationship with the Most High and separate us from Him forever. Cutting us off from our Redeemer is the motive for why this war exists. So, yes, you are part of this war of souls. You enlisted the second you drew breath at birth. By lineage and ancestry, the enemy has targeted you. Your eternal soul is the method the enemy uses to deceive you into eternal separation from God. We can see a previous attempt to do this in the story of Noah.

Despite the common disbelief that Noah built an ark to shelter his family and all the different kinds of animals in preparation of a global flood, there is no denying the more than 200 global flood mythologies (according to The Ark Encounter) that exist in cultures throughout history. I can spend hours in conversation and debate to attest to the validity of this event, but I will not. I will focus on the cause for this event as it is a demonstration of the enemy's motive to destroy us all.

The flood took the lives of not millions, but of every single living thing on earth that did not board the ark. What caused such a global judgement? What did we do as humans do to deserve extinction from God? The gravity of unrighteousness against God's law is something the enemy knows very well. Unlike us, demons have no means of redemption. Through temptation and deceit, they lure us into sin against our Father and separate us from Him.

The inhabitants on earth during the time of Noah committed sin so greatly that it caused God regret that He had ever created us in the first place. This is the reason for the flood. As a collective, our unrighteous sins soared to the heavens and angered God. When we realize how grave our sins really are against God's holy presence, we can begin to understand why the enemy is so restless and determined to lead us into destruction.

Just as in the past, temptation is the catalyst the enemy uses in order for us to commit sin today. The serpent was not able to sin on Eve's behalf—just as the enemy is not able to sin on our behalf. We are the vehicles the enemy uses to influence our actions. This contradicts the way many of us perceive ourselves to be. We tend to consider ourselves progressive, modernized, and civilized. We think we are much more intelligent than mankind used to be, so therefore, we are no longer capable of being deceived like Eve was. The enemy uses this faulty thinking to his advantage by catering to our elevated perception of ourselves. This was evident in my life before I found Christ.

I was egotistical and placed value in academia and education as a means to prove that I was superior to others. It should come as no surprise that this perception peaked when I declared myself an atheist during my teenage years. The enemy was clever to use my arrogance and unbelief to disguise his hand on my life. I believed assuredly that I had control of my life. My decisions were mine to make. If I succeed, it was only because of me and no one else. The enemy didn't need to lift a finger, just let me continue living blindly until the day I died.

So you see, even though thousands of years have passed, the enemy uses the same methods to deceive us. Whatever chink is in your armor—knowingly or unknowingly—be assured, the enemy will use temptation to crack it if you are caught unaware.

The temptation Eve underwent continues to exist in our world today for both Christians and unbelievers. For Christians, the enemy tries to make you doubt your relationship with God with questions and fears: Why have I been afflicted with cancer? Does God not love me? Why would God cause me harm? These dangerous questions challenge God's integrity. For unbelievers, the enemy will stay dormant and simply watch you. All the enemy needs is for you to live your life according to your own desires and ensure that you never think about your Creator until you draw your last breath.

The Invisible Realm

"For our struggle is not against flesh and blood, but against the rulers, against the authorities, against the powers of this dark world and against the spiritual forces of evil in the heavenly realms."

Ephesians 6:12

In his letter to the Ephesians, Paul was clear to inform them of the enemy's identity and location. Heavenly realms or "places" is the location in which the war is fought. Even before delving further, you know of this. I'm sure you've felt evil presences at night or suffered from sleep paralysis where you couldn't move your body.

Indeed, some of you have seen dead people or shadows. Some of you have felt the chill and eeriness of a cemetery, dark forest, or been afraid of horror movies. And those who have not experienced such things are well aware of what exorcisms look like or how demon possessed persons behave.

Regardless of your experience, you have sensed or felt that there is something unseen in this world…because there actually is. We have evidence of this in Genesis 1 when it is noted that God created the heavens and the earth. The plurality of heavens indicates there are more than one. We know that there is a third heaven (2 Corinthians 12:2) and that God resides in heaven (Revelation 11:19). We can infer that there are up to three heavens—the third being most likely where God resides (we residing not in heaven, but on earth). The second heaven is the universe (or outer space) and the first heaven is the atmosphere that we see everyday. But where do angels and demons reside? We know that fighting between angels has occurred in an unseen heaven:

Then he said to me, "Do not fear, Daniel, for from the first day that you set your heart to understand, and to humble yourself before your God, your words were heard; and I have come because of your words. But the prince of the kingdom of Persia withstood me twenty-one days; and behold, Michael, one of the chief princes, came to help me, for I had been left alone there with the kings of Persia."

Daniel 10:12-14

In the instance described in the verses above, God's messenger was held in heavy spiritual warfare against a fallen angel in the kingdom of Persia. So much so that Michael had to interfere and assist this angel in his assignment to deliver this message to Daniel.

Thanks to Ephesians 2:2, we know that Satan is the prince of the air and of this earth. He is the ruler for now and the cause for our calamities and broken world. He prowls the earth unseen to the naked eye and leads his warfare against both angels and humans. It is here where the battle for your soul is fought.

When you suffer from addiction or when you are angry and violent, when your depression makes you want to end your life, know that there are entities right there with you influencing you to die in unrepented sin. It is here in this invisible realm that your prayed reinforcements fight on your behalf. When you've prayed for protection, this is where God's angels descend and fight against those rulers and principalities attempting to take control of your life.

Please try to understand this invisible realm, because you have every reason to believe that it exists. You may not have seen it, but you have surely felt it at some point in your life. Let go of the fear and the doubt. This invisible realm is there, but it is not a place of despair because the war has already been won. The only thing remaining is on which side your soul will end up in.

The War

From the fall of man at creation to today, the war for our souls continues. The passage of time has taken many into hellfire but has also saved many into the Kingdom of God. Our time is not up, and our walk is not finished. I would love to tell you that this fight and this war with the enemy can be won with a single battle, but I cannot. The enemy will plot against you until your last breath in an attempt to keep you from the Lord, but take heart. You are not alone in this fight. Our Savior and Elohim is with us. The value of your soul is priceless and belongs to God. He doesn't separate Himself from us—we separate ourselves from Him. I cannot judge or forgive you of your sins, but I can tell you that the first step to finding redemption is confession and acknowledgement that we are in need of salvation for the sins we have committed.

Our Creator is loving. Our Creator is patient. And He is also just. We are responsible and accountable for the sins we commit. Fortunately, God has such tremendous love for us that He provided a Savior to redeem us from our sins in His Son, Jesus the Anointed One. Those saved by the blood of Jesus feel such incredible joy in the peace He gives us that we often don't realize we are prime targets for the enemy.

I didn't realize this myself when I accepted Jesus as my Savior. I was under the presumption that my life was going to be easy and God would remove all hardships and tribulations. While there is truth to that in many ways, the types of problems changed. God gave me incredible opportunities to begin molding me. However, it felt as if the enemy set his sights on me through other people. The temptation to lust, to become angry, and to doubt grew tremendously as I was ridiculed more and more by others. It is here where the war really began. As followers of Christ, we are primary targets in the spiritual war for souls. The enemy does not sleep or rest and has every intention of keeping you away from God's purpose in your life. Make no mistake. Neither Satan nor any demon can match the POWER of God. And if the enemy whispers lies into your ear, remind him that his time is short—and that the war is already won.

While we may not be in a physical war in this world, every person on earth is in a spiritual war whether you see it or not. It matters not if you don't believe in Christ. All of us are capable of suffering from addictions, relationship turmoil, stress, and depression. For unbelievers, these problems are masked by "mental health" diagnoses, but make no mistake. You are being attacked by demons and are being kept in a mental and spiritual cage in the hopes that you will die without accepting Christ as your Savior. Even those that have a formidable and pleasant life are under constant vigilance of the enemy.

For us believers, the stakes are much higher. We have a direct target on our back and the full attention of the enemy. We must be aware of his schemes and know what exactly is attempting to cause havoc in our lives. Before even lifting a finger, you must know exactly who the enemy is…and what he can do.

ENCOUNTER #2
SLAMMED

Leaving home to go to college for the first time was difficult. No longer under the covering of family and friends, I felt alone in a new city. While I was nervous about the future, I was also hopeful that a change of scenery would make the weird nightly experiences stop. One of the benefits of being a college student was having a flexible schedule during the week. Because I had work or class in the mornings, my afternoons were ideal times for naps. After a busy morning, I walked back to my dorm room and took a nap to get myself rested for my night class.

I awoke sometime after, but I could not move. Just like the first time, my body was frozen…and vibrating. I could feel and hear a buzz all over my body. I couldn't move my body, but I could see my room, nonetheless. As I was trying to understand what was happening, something slammed my head against the wall, pinning it there. I could feel an immense pressure against my trapped head. I remember looking directly at the wall. It did not hurt, but I could feel the heaviness of the pressure on my head against the wall.

I was completely confused, because my body was still laying on the bed opposite side of the wall, yet my vision was focused on the wall. I tried to fight off the pressure from what was causing this, but I couldn't. I was stuck against the wall. After some time, the pressure and paralysis left. My body was free again.

Chapter 2

KNOW THY ENEMY

Be sober, be vigilant; because your adversary the devil walks about like a roaring lion, seeking whom he may devour.

1 Peter 5:8

A 6th Century Chinese philosopher and military strategist, Sun Tzu, who authored his famous book The Art of War, states: "If you know the enemy and know yourself, you need not fear the result of 100 battles. If you know yourself but not your enemy, for every victory gained, you will also suffer a defeat. If you know neither the enemy nor yourself, you will succumb in every battle."[1] Unfortunately, many in the church today have succumbed to the latter. Many fellow Christians do not like to talk about the enemy; some due to the fear they have for him and some because they don't want to give him any attention in an effort to avoid glorifying him. It is imperative that you know the enemy if you intend to be victorious in your walk. Paul makes it clear:

Anyone you forgive, I also forgive. And what I have forgiven—if there was anything to forgive—I have forgiven in the sight of Christ for your sake, in order that Satan might not outwit us. For we are not unaware of his schemes.

2 Corinthians 2:10

Being aware of the enemy's schemes is crucial to winning any war. Even military strategists do not deny this. For example, World War II general George Patton studied the life and military philosophies of his enemy and German opponent, Erwin Rommel. Known for his clever use of limited resources and flanking maneuvers, Rommel took offensive risks to capture North African territories. Patton knew this about Rommel. Having studied him, when the time of the battle of El Guettar came in 1943, Rommel used all his men and machines to push forward in an all offensive assault. He broke the lines and ignored the flanks of the enemy outsmarting them and rushing them to victory. Patton knew that to know your enemy is to possess the power to defeat him. Members of the military who have served our country will corroborate that every strategic military invasion requires extensive reconnaissance and study of the enemy in order to achieve victory.[2] The spiritual war for your soul is no different. Knowing the enemy and his capabilities is crucial in identifying him and fighting back.

The Many Names of the Enemy

Thanks to years of mythology and media entertainment, the identity of Satan and demons has become sporadic and inaccurate. Television shows like Lucifer that depict Lucifer as a compassionate being that fights against injustice or shows like Supernatural who create a non-biblical lore using biblical names and scripture have aided in the creation of faulty perspectives of what the enemy is and what he can do. You must know the identity and the many names of the primary adversary in order to know what exactly he is capable of doing to you. He goes by many names in both the Bible and cultural history. His motive is simple: to take as many souls away from God before his time on earth is over. A dishonored angel fallen from grace, these are the names by which he goes by:

The Serpent

So the Lord God said to the serpent: "Because you have done this, You are cursed more than all cattle, and more than every beast of the field; On your belly you shall go, And you shall eat dust all the days of your life. And I will put enmity Between you and the woman, And between your seed and her Seed; He shall bruise your head, and you shall bruise His heel."

Genesis 3:14-15

As previously stated, the serpent was the most cunning of all beasts and spoke lies to deceive Eve. The serpent is the first enemy we as humans encounter in the chronology of history. There are some who believe the serpent is not Satan. However, Ezekiel 28:12 confirms that the identity of Lucifer and the serpent are the same.

Lucifer

The traditional depiction of the devil (or Lucifer) as a red horned Baphomet with hooves does not derive from scripture. We can thank those hellish depictions to Renaissance artists and poets who, through artistic portrayal and poems, characterized the animalistic nature of Lucifer as a deformed monster. For example, the goat horn and hooves originated from early Christians living in the Roman world during the first century. Romans believed and worshipped the pagan god Pan, who was half-goat and half-man who was given characteristics of lust and musical talent. Early Christian theologians like Eusebius, then began to utilize the pagan image as the enemy or "adversary."[3] It is important to note that these depictions are not biblical, but instead are what many Christians and non-believers perceive and fear in Lucifer.

Luckily, our Father God has given us an understanding of Lucifer through his prophets Isaiah and Ezekiel:

> *This is what the Sovereign Lord says:*
> *You were the seal of perfection, full of wisdom and perfect in beauty. You were in Eden, the garden of God; every precious stone adorned you: carnelian, chrysolite and emerald, topaz, onyx and jasper, lapis lazuli, turquoise and beryl Your settings and mountings were made of gold; on the day you were created they were prepared. You were anointed as a guardian cherub, for so I ordained you. You were on the holy mount of God; you walked among the fiery stones. You were blameless in your ways from the day you were created till wickedness was found in you. Through your widespread trade you were filled with violence, and you sinned.*
>
> Ezekiel 28:12-14

So you see, Lucifer is not a goat-horned, hooved, Baphomet as the world illustrates him to be. On the contrary, he is described as the embodiment of perfection. Even in comparison to other angels, he was perfect in beauty and wisdom. Adorned with the most precious of stones and anointed with the highest of positions in heaven, he resided near God in the Third Heaven. It's difficult for many to remember or believe that our primary enemy against us is beautiful. It is much easier to detest a grotesque monster or abomination, but we must always remember that Lucifer remains a fallen angel who was created in perfection and beauty. He lost it all in his pride and desire to be like the Most High. Isaiah notes this and describes his sinful character:

How you have fallen from heaven O' Lucifer, son of the morning! You have been cast down to the earth, you who once laid low the nations! You said in your heart, "I will ascend to the heavens; I will raise my throne above the stars of God; I will sit enthroned on the mount of assembly, on the utmost heights of Mount Zaphon. I will ascend above the tops of the clouds; I will make myself like the Most High." But you are brought down to the realm of the dead, to the depths of the pit.

Isaiah 14:12-15

Notice that Lucifer says, "I will," a total of five times, speaking to his self-centeredness, arrogance, pride, and desire to be worshipped as God. This, in combination with his beauty, is important to note because he can appear as an angel of light as opposed to a monster. It takes sharp discernment to unmask him or the rest of the fallen angels if they are ever in your presence.

Satan

The term "Satan" means "adversary" or "the adversary" in Hebrew. A total of 52 times, Satan is mentioned in the Bible in both the Old and New Testament as the identified fallen angel and ruler of the world:

One day the angels came to present themselves before the Lord, and Satan also came with them.

Job 1:6

And the Lord said to Satan, "The Lord rebuke you, Satan! The Lord who has chosen Jerusalem rebuke you! Is this not a brand plucked from the fire?"

Zechariah 3:2

But He turned and said to Peter, "Get behind Me, Satan! You are an offense to Me, for you are not mindful of the things of God, but the things of men."

Matthew 16:23

Again, the devil took Him up on an exceedingly high mountain, and showed Him all the kingdoms of the world and their glory. And he said to Him, "All these things I will give You if You will fall down and worship me." Then Jesus said to him, "Away with you, Satan! For it is written, 'You shall worship the Lord your God, and Him only you shall serve.'

Matthew 4:8-10

Similar to the names "serpent" and "Lucifer," Satan has another name that differentiates him from the other fallen angels. This further affirms that Satan was indeed the leader and primary influencer who drove a third of the angels to rebel and commit sins on earth. True to its meaning, Satan is an adversary against God and against you.

Devil

The name "Devil" derives from the Greek word "diabolus" and is another name given to the adversary. The Greek usage of the word refers to a slanderer or one who slanders. The term Devil is only found in the New Testament and is one of the most common descriptors for Lucifer. Jesus uses the term devil specifically when referring to the enemy:

Why do you not understand My speech? Because you are not able to listen to My word. You are of your father the devil, and the desires of your father you want to do. He was a murderer from the beginning, and does not stand in the truth, because there is no truth in him. When he speaks a lie, he speaks from his own resources, for he is a liar and the father of it.

John 8:43-44

Now when the devil had ended every temptation, he departed from Him until an opportune time.

Luke 4:13

And said, "O full of all deceit and all fraud, you son of the devil, you enemy of all righteousness, will you not cease perverting the straight ways of the Lord?"

Acts 13:10

In these verses, we get a closer look at the nature and ability to lie and deceive. You have often heard that he is the "father of lies" and here John 8 confirms it. He is opportunistic and thrives in perverting God's righteousness through lies and deceit.

Ruler of Demons

But the Pharisees said, "He casts out demons by the ruler of the demons."

Matthew 9:24

The Pharisees accused Jesus of delivering people from evil spirits by the authority of pagan (and most definitely satanic) Beelzebub. As Jews, this is the highest of blasphemies, because Beelzebub is equivalent to all things satanic. We can assume that, when facing Jesus, they alleged that the ruler of demons was the adversary. This also further infers the hierarchy of his demonic kingdom in which Satan rules over all demons.

Dragon

And war broke out in heaven: Michael and his angels fought with the dragon; and the dragon and his angels fought.

Revelation 12:7

Finally, the dragon is the final descriptor of the adversary. We know who he is because Revelation directly confirms it:

The great dragon was hurled down—that ancient serpent called the devil, or Satan, who leads the whole world astray. He was hurled to the earth, and his angels with him.

Revelation 12:9

Satan's Army

Now that you understand the identity and the many names of the enemy, let's delve into the reality of his army and what it is. Satan has an army of demons at his command.

Then He healed many who were sick with various diseases, and cast out many demons; and He did not allow the demons to speak, because they knew Him.

Mark 1:34

And He was preaching in their synagogues throughout all Galilee, and casting out demons.

Mark 1:39

And demons also came out of many, crying out and saying, "You are the Christ, the Son of God!" And He, rebuking them, did not allow them to speak, for they knew that He was the Christ.

Luke 4:41

When He had come to the other side, to the country of the Gergesenes, there met Him two demon-possessed men, coming out of the tombs, exceedingly fierce, so that no one could pass that way. And suddenly they cried out, saying, "What have we to do with You, Jesus, You Son of God?

Have You come here to torment us before the time?"
Now a good way off from them there was a herd of many swine feeding. So the demons begged Him, saying, "If You cast us out, permit us to go away into the herd of swine."

And He said to them, "Go." So when they had come out, they went into the herd of swine. And suddenly the whole herd of swine ran violently down the steep place into the sea, and perished in the water.

Matthew 8:28-32

One of the many great and healing works that Jesus did was deliver people from demons. Mary Magdalene was possessed of seven at her time of deliverance, while the possessed man at Gerasenes had a legion (about 6,000) in him!

Origin of Demons

Like many other topics among Christendom, the origin of demons is often debated. However, the origin is quite clear across the Bible beginning with Genesis 6:

Now it came to pass, when men began to multiply on the face of the earth, and daughters were born to them, that the sons of God saw the daughters of men, that they were beautiful; and they took wives for themselves of all whom they chose.

And the LORD said, "My Spirit shall not strive with man forever, for he is indeed flesh; yet his days shall be one hundred and twenty years." There were giants on the earth in those days, and also afterward, when the sons of God came in to the daughters of men and they bore children to them. Those were the mighty men who were of old, men of renown.

Genesis 6:1-4

Many claim that the term "sons of God" is synonymous with "men of renown" and refer to kings or men of high positions or memorable deeds. However, this is not likely due to the cross referencing of the term "sons of God" throughout the Bible. The term is always referenced in the Old Testament as pertaining to supernatural beings: angels (Job 1:6, Job 2:1, Psalm 29:1, Deuteronomy 32:8).

The sons of God mentioned in Genesis 6 did something specific that enforced God's severe punishment upon them (2 Peter 2:4, Jude 1:6). Specifically, they had sex with women that resulted in children being born. A common assumption is that these hybrid children from angels and humans resulted in the giants of those days. There are a few markers that lead to this assumption. First, the capability of angels having sexual intercourse is possible as it is documented that angles appear fully human. When the angels went to Sodom to save Lot, the men of the city, young and old, demanded that Lot release the two men to them so that they could be sexually abused (Genesis 19). Another example of angels masquerading in human bodies can be found in Hebrews:

Do not forget to entertain strangers, for by so doing some have unwittingly entertained angels.

Hebrews 13:2

Secondly, the existence of giants or "Nephilim" as the original Hebrew word describes is out of the ordinary in itself. Deriving from the Hebraic root naphal or "fallen," Nephilim is commonly referred to large giants. The non-canonical book of 1 Enoch for example describes the size of these giants to reach a height of three thousand ells or 4,500 feet (nearly a mile) tall. However, it is worth noting that Enoch 1 is erroneous since it depicts Enoch as the "Son of Man." Numbers gives us a closer look at these Nephilim:

And they gave the children of Israel a bad report of the land which they had spied out, saying, "The land through which we have gone as spies is a land that devours its inhabitants, and all the people whom we saw in it are men of great stature. There we saw the giants (Nephilim) (the descendants

> *of Anak came from the giants (Nephilim)); and we were like grasshoppers in our own sight, and so we were in their sight."*
>
> Numbers 13:32-33

Regardless of the byproducts of the interaction between the sons of God and women, these "Nephilim" were a pollution of wickedness and to God's prime creation; so much so that they brought fear and destruction to the human population. One can speculate that after sinning, the fallen angels did this intentionally for one reason: to pollute the bloodline of Christ. Knowing the prophecy given to Adam and Eve in Genesis 3, they knew that a messiah would be born to humans and crush Satan and all his angels on the day of judgement. Knowing Satan and his determination for self-preservation, one wouldn't be surprised he would go through these lengths to prevent his own destruction. In any case, the hybrid children born from angels and humans are the demons of old and today. Their characteristics demonstrate why.

Demon Characteristics

The main characteristic that separates demons from humans and angels is that demons don't have physical bodies. They are constantly desiring and searching for bodies to possess or inhabit. Matthew 8:30 tells that the demons called Legion begged Jesus to allow them to transfer themselves to a herd of pigs after being commanded to leave the man they possessed. One can definitely see that they were terrified Jesus would cast them out into the abyss right then and there, but one can also speculate that a transfer to animals (and not humans) was the only escape they could see from this worse fate.

Regardless, it is clear that they don't have bodies in which they can roam freely on earth. This weakened state of being fuels their motives and explains their parasitic and vulturous behavior toward humans. Through possession and deceit, human beings serve as fodder for their methods of attack. Demons are the primary entities that will attack you here on earth. This is what demons can do and these are their characteristics:

Demons Have a WILL

"When an unclean spirit goes out of a man, he goes through dry places, seeking rest, and finds none. Then he says, 'I will return to my house from which I came.' And when he comes, he finds it empty, swept, and put in order. Then he goes and takes with him seven other spirits more wicked than himself, and they enter and dwell there; and the last state of that man is worse than the first. So shall it also be with this wicked generation."

Matthew 12:43-45

Besides fulfillment from inflicting harm on people, demons prioritize finding self-relief. Seeking rest in human vessels takes precedence above all else in their efforts to accomplish their own selfish desires. Even in cases where someone has been delivered and freed of them, they will return to the same person and in greater numbers. Unfortunately, this can be catastrophic for people who are caught off guard and unable to discern their return. Remember, their desire to cohabitate in a person is all consuming. This is their motive.

Demons Have the Ability to SPEAK and Have SELF-AWARENESS

Jesus asked him, saying, "What is your name?"
And he said, "Legion," because many demons had entered him. And they begged Him that He would not command them to go out into the abyss."

Luke 8:30

This may not sound surprising, but many horror movies today portray demonic entities that whisper or speak to protagonists. Biblically speaking, demons can indeed speak and respond to people, but only through human vessels on this earthly plane. Games like the Ouija board are such an example of demons needing humans for communication. With that said, this doesn't mean that you should talk or initiate a dialogue with them.

Practicing deliverance is dangerous because it requires strong faith on behalf of the Christian. For example, follower of Christ and deliverance expert Russ Dizdar has delivered hundreds if not thousands of people across the globe from demons. In many instances, the demons talk back to him and even know him by name. He immediately takes command

and shuts their mouth, because he is not interested in anything they have to say.[4] After all, they are all liars. Whether it is through other people or through spiritual mediums, do not be surprised if you ever hear voices or hear a response from an entity in your life. They can do this, and you can usually confirm that it is indeed a demon communicating with you.

Demons Have UNDERSCORE{UNDERSTANDING}

Now there was a man in their synagogue with an unclean spirit. And he cried out, saying, "Let us alone! What have we to do with You, Jesus of Nazareth? Did You come to destroy us? I know who You are—the Holy One of God!"

Mark 1:23

I personally have the tendency to mock demons and think of them as the laziest beings in existence, but I must acknowledge that they are not entirely stupid. They understand very well what they are doing and Who reigns supreme. As Mark informs, the unclean spirit in the man at the synagogue knew exactly Who Jesus was and what He could do to them. They have full knowledge of their history and their future—perhaps the latter is a reason for their unrepentance (not that repentance would do any good anyway).

Be sure that they understand you very well. They don't eat. They don't sleep. And they will watch and learn your habits for as long as they need in order to keep you away from God. If you ever encounter them directly, you should realize that they know you very well and will make every attempt to inflict fear, falsehoods, and guilt upon you. Remind them that you also have understanding and know that they have no redemption and will suffer the judgement laid upon their master.

Demons Have DOCTRINES

Now the Spirit expressly says that in latter times some will depart from the faith, giving heed to deceiving spirits and doctrines of demons,

1 Timothy 4:1

The most deceptive action a demon can impart is false doctrine. What makes this so dangerous is that these doctrines can take numerous forms. A false religion, self-worship, false moral laws…the list is endless. Modern doctrines of today, like scientology, prosperity gospels, and new age religions, are some of the many forms that demons indoctrinate millions of people across the world. Paul is correct when he says that people will depart from the faith during the last days as a result of these doctrines. In order to identify these doctrines, you need an intimate knowledge of the Bible. After all, how else are you supposed to differentiate the truth from a lie if you don't know God's Word? Ask yourself this today: does what you believe about God today come from the Bible or from demonic doctrines?

Demons Have Controlling Power Over Those They OCCUPY

Then the man in whom the evil spirit was leaped on them, overpowered them, and prevailed against them, so that they fled out of that house naked and wounded.

Acts 19:16

You have probably already seen a few exorcist movies or heard stories from priests who perform exorcisms to know about the power that the demons can manifest in a person. An uncanny ability to have brute strength and do things unimaginable with the human body are illustrations of what can happen when a demon occupies a person completely. In such cases, this is mostly true. Acts 19 serves as an example of a demon in one man who overpowered multiple Jewish exorcists. So, too, the demon possessed man in Mark 5:4-5 who broke free from chains and shackles with demoniac strength. Occupation is dangerous because the person is no longer in control. Many have succumbed to psychiatric diagnosis like schizophrenia, paranoia, or drug addiction, but be assured that this is demonic occupation.

Demonic possession also leads to the worst fate in a person: suicide. The ultimate cost in a person is worth executing even if demons know they will need to find a new vessel. They would rather you go to hell even if it means some discomfort for them while they roam for their next victim.

This isn't limited to today either. Mark 9:22 illustrates this when the father of a demon-possessed boy tells Jesus that the demon makes the boy fall into fires and water in an effort to kill himself. This type of possession is the easiest form of identification when it comes to a demonic presence or the presence of a group of them. A possessed person requires a believer in Christ to deliver them.

Expose the Darkness

So you see, demons are entities capable of speech, control over the human body, awareness, and an intent to deceive on behalf of their master. To know them is to begin unlocking the truth in defeating them. This is the first step in overcoming any fear you have of the enemy. There is nothing to fear from them. They are nothing and are not able to do anything without your consent.

The next step in delivering yourself from them will require some reflection on your part...to analyze if they are inside you now.

KNOW THY ENEMY

ENCOUNTER #3
SMILE

As I entered my final year of college, things seemed to be looking up. I was getting good grades and was working three jobs. While the stress of a constant busy schedule made me unhappy, I found hope and positivity in Christian radio stations. Listening to them on my way to work and class made me feel hopeful that God existed and was going to see me through all of it. This immense worldly pressure will pass soon, I thought. One day, after a long three-hour class, I was relieved to go home because I would finally be able to stay up late and sleep in for the weekend. After going to bed, I awoke sometime in the early morning.

My body began vibrating, so I already knew I was going into sleep paralysis, but this time, it was different. I was paralyzed, yes, but something evil was right next to me. I have never felt such evil or malice in my life. I was terrified and began to panic.

As I was becoming more aware of what was happening, the evil presence was forcing an evil grin to spread across my face. It was as if the evil had gotten inside me and was controlling me, making me grin the most demonic grin I could ever make. I fought with all the energy I had until I could finally move my head a little (this usually helped me snap out of it). When I regained control of my body, I was sweating and immediately grabbed my phone and turned on the light to drive some of the darkness back. It was around 4 a.m. on Saturday as I was sitting atop my bed… panting.

This was the first time I was afraid to go to sleep.

Chapter 3

ENEMY TACTICS

One day the evil spirit answered them, "Jesus I know, and Paul I know about, but who are you?" Then the man who had the evil spirit jumped on them and overpowered them all. He gave them such a beating that they ran out of the house naked and bleeding.

Acts 19:15-16

Now that you understand the identity of the enemy, it is imperative that you are able to recognize if he or his legion is present in your life. Just because you are consciously aware and are in full control of your body does not mean you do not have demons inside or near you. For example, a person that suffers from depression is usually diagnosed under the lens of mental health. However, this is a concealed attack of oppression on a person.

Former U.S. Senator George McGovern's describes his daughter Terry's dual depression and alcoholism in his 1997 book, Terry. He wrote, "(Terry) was dealt a double cruel hand: the companion demons depression and alcoholism. They were demons that warred ceaselessly against the other aspects of her being-a warm and sunny disposition."[5] He uses this language for a reason. Any person close to someone who suffers from this or the victim themselves know how horrific and demonic depression can be.

Typically, the victim is able to mask the signs and hide their depression from the world while the demons hollow them inside out. This can even lead to the worst of outcomes that even some believers in Christ face. For example, mental health advocate and megachurch pastor of Harvest Christian Fellowship church Jarrid Wilson committed suicide in 2019. Not only was he a brother of Christ but he was also a powerful leader for many. He was so tormented by the enemy that it ultimately led him to end his life, leaving his wife and two sons behind. There is no doubt that his torment was an attack from the enemy. While everyone believed he was living his best life, he was having an internal battle with the enemy that he, unfortunately, lost.

I myself went through something similar when I underwent depression as an unbeliever. I could not identify why everything in my life was going wrong. Everything led to bad luck or misfortune, but never to an invisible enemy. Had I not seen the demons myself (eventually), I never would have believed they were hard at work in me. These silent attacks are only a fraction of the abilities these demons can perform in our lives. Their arsenal is varied and their attacks vast, depending on how much we let them in.

Before delving into the various type of attacks we can face, I must make a disclaimer that it is my interpretation and belief that a follower of Christ who has the Holy Spirit in him or her is not capable of suffering from high level demonic attacks. The enemy will attack a follower of Christ, no doubt, but a true Christian cannot suffer from demonic possession as an example.

The degree to which type of attack you are susceptible to will vary depending on your relationship with God and if you have a relationship with Jesus the Christ. I can attest to this because, although I became a Christian six years ago, my relationship with Jesus was weaker and I was not fully committed to Christ as I should have been during my early years. As I write this now, I remember Jesus' words when He says we cannot serve two masters and that He will spit out those who are lukewarm (Matthew 6:24 and Revelation 3:16). I see why today.

Early in my walk, there were times I unsuccessfully tried to rebuke the enemy when I was attacked. It isn't enough just to say words when you are full of fear and uncertain of the power of Jesus' name. There were some attacks where the enemy laughed at me during my attempts to liberate myself—as if they could see the fear behind my bold facade. I tell you, friend, if you suffer from demonic attacks and want to deliver yourself from them on your own, it is going to require full faith in Jesus on your part to expel them. Jesus gives us evidence of this when He healed a demon-possessed boy:

When they came to the crowd, a man approached Jesus and knelt before him. "Lord, have mercy on my son," he said. "He has seizures and is suffering greatly. He often falls into the fire or into the water. I brought him to your disciples, but they could not heal him."

"You unbelieving and perverse generation," Jesus replied, "how long shall I stay with you? How long shall I put up with you? Bring the boy here to me." Jesus rebuked the demon, and it came out of the boy, and he was healed at that moment.

Then the disciples came to Jesus in private and asked, "Why couldn't we drive it out?" He replied, "Because you have so little faith. Truly I tell you, if you have faith as small as a mustard seed, you can say to this mountain, 'Move from here to there,' and it will move. Nothing will be impossible for you."

Matthew 17:14-21

After reading this, you may be wondering why it took me so long to believe or even why the disciples didn't have enough faith. After all, didn't they cast out other demons under Jesus' permission? I hate to say this, but for many of us, it is easier said than done. These demonic experiences are some of the most terrifying and frightening experiences any person can have. When demons manifest themselves in their horrid forms and torment you, fear takes over your entire soul and keeps you from thinking of anything that can save you from it.

In my case, I grew so accustomed to demonic attacks that I lost the fear through time and a closer relationship with God. Reading the Bible opened my eyes to the authority I have over them in the name of Jesus. This helped me activate my faith and fully believe to finally achieve victory and freedom. While I'm glad I don't suffer from these attacks anymore, I am wary of the doors that can reopen, inviting even worse demons and in larger numbers.

Open Doors

At some point you may wonder why I was attacked by demons and not you. Admittedly, it was my fault. I gave entry to the enemy in a variety of ways. I opened doors through lust, fornication, atheism, pride, and occultism in Egyptian mythology and astrology. It is difficult to identify which of these doors allowed the physical manifestation of demons, but my instincts tell me that it was astrology and fornication. These practices are "open doors" that allow the enemy to not only come into your life but also to inhabit and latch on to you. There are a variety of doors that you can open for the enemy without even realizing it.

Occult Doorways

Astrology, Mediums, Witches, and Wizards

Seeking those who practice occult arts is one of the quickest and easiest doorways to invite the enemy, mostly because you are actively inviting them to communicate with you. Whether it is a medium connecting you with "passed loved ones" or "familiar spirits" or practicing White or Black magic, the Bible is very clear about warning those who practice these arts:

When you enter the land the LORD your God is giving you, do not learn to imitate the detestable ways of the nations there. Let no one be found among you who sacrifices their son or daughter in the fire, who practices divination or sorcery, interprets omens, engages in witchcraft, or casts spells, or who is a medium or spiritist or who consults the dead. Anyone who does these things is detestable to the LORD; because of these same detestable practices the LORD your God will drive out those nations before you. You must be blameless before the LORD your God.

Deuteronomy 18:9-13

Do not turn to mediums or seek out spiritists, for you will be defiled by them. I am the LORD your God.

Leviticus 19:31

I used to study and practice astrological readings via personalized horoscopes and birth charts. I didn't just practice the standard astrological horoscopes that you see on newspapers or apps. I knew planetary degrees in relation to the solar system and lived my life according to what those alignments (and other astrologers) predicted. I was fascinated by the prospect of knowing the future (ironic since the Bible literally shows you the future down to the end of the age). I would live my life according to my personalized horoscopes and, worse yet, attempted to influence others to do the same.

Even as a young Christian, I did not see anything wrong with this, and when I read that it is a sin to practice the occult arts, I refused to classify what I did as occultism. Unknowingly, I did not realize I was opening doors to the enemy. I was allowing the enemy to take a hold of my life and to come close and inhabit me.

Personally, I believe this is the reason why my demonic attacks were much more pronounced than for other people. I let them in and gave them permission. I think this because of the many testimonial accounts of ex-witches, new agers, and Satanists. They experienced similar resistance when they were coming to Christ because the doors to the enemy were so freely opened that the enemy had a greater hold and stronger power over them.

For example, ex-Satanist and Santeria practitioner John Ramirez had literal physical resistance from demons in the form of choking, bed shaking, and levitation after accepting Christ.[6] Had I read my Bible, I would have seen that Leviticus 19:26, Leviticus 20:6, 27, II Kings 21:6, Isaiah 8:19, Isaiah 47:13-14, Daniel 2:27, and Daniel 4:7 all warned and condemn astrology and occult arts.

Case Study: A Ouija Story

The Ouija, or the talking board, has long been a medium to communicate with "spirits." While the board as we know it today became a commercial product in 1890, use of a planchette or Ouija board dates as far back as AD 1100 in China. To utilize the board, the user places their fingertips on the planchette over a board containing an alphabet, "yes," "no," "hello," and "goodbye." The user begins and asks the board a series of voluntary questions. If successful, the planchette moves by itself, revealing answers, letter by letter, to the user without the user's intervention. Most people are aware of this occultic practice due to the mystery and intrigue that centuries worth of stories surrounding this board have generated.

One of these stories occurred to my very close friend Gloria. Gloria was in high school when she first used the Ouija board. Things were a lot different in the 1980s. Teenagers didn't have a phone or have instantaneous availability of entertainment that network streaming provides the youth today. Having already given up on organized religion, Gloria was curious and unafraid to try the board so many people had questions about.

She, her best friend, and cousin got together and purchased the board from the local Toys R'Us and opened it up immediately. The three sat close with Gloria as the user and began to ask questions. In a test of faith in the board, Gloria asked what nobody knew…including herself, "Who is my father?"

Gloria was not prepared for what happened next. You see, she never knew her biological father. Her mom kept everything about him secret and the topic was off limits. You can imagine her surprise when the board not only revealed the location of her dad but also his full name. After this, Gloria went straight to her mom to confirm it, and sure enough, it was true. Her dad resided in Mexico and his name was the one revealed by the board.

This revelation encouraged Gloria to continue, and not just with her friends. She began to use the board by herself and ask questions from the most mundane to complex mysterious ones in order to navigate her life accordingly. The entity controlling the board never disclosed its name, but told her that they were friends before in another lifetime and that they were united for a reason.

As time went on, her relationship with the entity changed. Gloria would hear pops in her television at night. This too had an answer from the entity though. It told her that a "little boy" was infatuated with her and making the sound. Growing more and more convinced, Gloria became more open to using the board with her friends. One of them, Carlos, was not a believer in the board and mocked it when they would hang out together. The entity showed its first sign of aggression and refused to play, telling everyone he had to leave. Because of this, Gloria became confined to using it without them. This is when the problems began.

The entity became very personal and hostile. Gloria remembers that the board would make her cry, telling her awful things about herself. The entity became more aggressive and controlling, sparking fear in her. She felt she was losing control of the situation so she threw the board in the trash outside her home. She thought about burning it but decided to leave it in the trash and to just forget about it.

When reflecting on her experience, she believes the entity used her insecurity and vulnerability to isolate her. She confirms that the entity definitely communicated with her about things nobody else knew, and she thinks that her life might have taken a dark turn if she had continued. Today, she continues to have paranormal sightings and dreams and wonders if the entity is still around her.

Stories like these demonstrate the ingenuity of the enemy. They know your weak points and will use them to manipulate you into remorseful action. Appearing harmless, the entity used Gloria's thirst for revelation to begin to build a relationship with her, deceiving her in order to further torment her. It is likely that the entity wanted to lead her toward possession or cause her to end her life. There is no doubt in my mind that this was a satanic and occult attack, but it came when Gloria opened the door, allowing this entity into Gloria's life. The Ouija board is only one of many open doors: astrology, idolatry, fornication, pornography, magic, drugs, and many more exist and give the enemy permission into your life.

Now you must ask yourself which doors have you opened.

New Age Doorways

Meditation, Yoga, Spirit Guides, Astral Projection

New age practices like yoga, meditation, and transhumanism are on the rise and more popular than ever. While seeming harmless, these practices are dangerous and the most deceptive of all. Under the guise of self-love and self-improvement, these actions invite demonic activity and demons themselves into the lives of the participants—typically without the user knowing it.

For example, many people exercise using yoga in their homes, gyms, or schools and see nothing wrong with it. Even questioning its safety is ludicrous to them. It's just exercise, they believe. Many do not know the origin or what they are actually doing. The yoga practiced today is perceived as just bodily exercise, but it derives from one of the earliest scripts in ancient India, dating to around 1500 BC: the Vedas.[7]

These writings are some of the oldest Hinduism and Sanskrit literature, and as such, carry pagan origins of worship. Why is this satanic? Its practice achieves the goals of actualization and self-realization themes that Hinduism requires. Personally, any Christian that practices this is highly questionable, because a follower of Christ follows Yeshua and no other. You do not want to meddle in the occult. They are nothing more than false religions.

Even after this, many will argue that those who do yoga today don't do it for these Hindu principles, but only for exercise. There is a common saying, "There is no yoga without Hinduism, and no Hinduism without Yoga." You cannot separate the two. Additionally, Hindus believe that there is a coiled serpent asleep within each person that needs to be awakened. This serpent, or "kundalini," is known as wisdom, knowledge, or power. As you already know, the serpent is an obvious reference to the serpent in Genesis who promised Eve the same wisdom, knowledge, and power that kundalini promises.

If you remain unconvinced, former students of Indian Yoga teacher Sri K. Pattabhi Jois Guy Donahue and Eddie Turner quote, "His (Sri K. Pattabhi Jois) philosophy is that yoga would take you automatically to the meditative state you see…that's how it will draw you into the spiritual path. See that's why he says the yoga asanas are important—you just do it. Don't talk about the philosophy—99 percent practice and 1 percent philosophy, that's what he taught. You just keep doing it, keep doing it, keep doing it, then slowly…it will start opening up inside of you…"[8]

Even the movements, asanas from the practice, are invocations to gods (based on the pose). The sun salutation, for example, is a symbolic ritual of devotion to the sun god Surya (Sanskrit for Supreme Light). I bring these examples forth because yoga represents one of the many doors that are opened unknowingly by people. Many times, these doors offer the opportunity for those committed to dedicate themselves fully to the practice and thus fully deceiving the passionate. Those who delve further actually contact entities that masquerade as passed spirits, angels, or spirit guides. They eventually practice astral projection.

Case Study: Astral Projection

Astral projection, or astral travel, is the experience of coming outside of your body, known as an out of body experience (OBE). This is done with the understanding that your soul projects beyond while your physical body remains intact on earth. Seemingly adventurous and enlightening, astral projection practitioners tell of encounters where they meet spiritual guides or their guardian angels and are able to travel all over the world in the spiritual plane.

While this may seem harmless, it is devastating for any person who willingly seeks it. Ex-Santeria and former Satanist John Ramirez reveals the true forms and activity that occurs when one travels in the spirit realm. John grew up in the occult. Coming from a lineage of witches and warlocks, John's father exposed him to the occult early on. His mother, influenced by Santeria, took him to a tarot card reading as a child. The psychics warned him that if he did not do a particular ceremony within thirty days, he would be blind. They inserted him into a bowl with herbs and performed incantations over him, and after that day, his life completely changed.[9]

Soon he was being formally trained by high ranking devil worshippers, and he delved deep into devil spiritualism. So much so that he recalls retrieving blood from gang murders so he could use it for witchcraft. After suffering abuse from his father, he now felt powerful, under a new given authority. When his father was murdered in a bar, he credited Satan for relieving him and his mother's pain. John claims that Satan became the father he never had. As time went on, John became a high priest of "palo mayombe," a form of African black-magic, and served Satan by targeting Christians. This is when he began astral projecting.

Under instruction from Satan, John traveled outside his body to different cities, neighborhoods, states, and even countries in search of Christians he could prey upon. As his soul hovered over these areas, he would speak curses onto them and things he wanted to happen. In some instances, John remembers small groups of Christians praying in homes or on the streets, but in those areas and neighborhoods, he recalls he could never accomplish anything there. He said, "You just couldn't touch it. But other neighborhoods, yes."

Luckily, things took a turn after meeting his now Christian wife. Reluctant to leave his life of Santeria and Satan worship, John reached a turning point that changed everything. After agreeing to attend Sunday church services to please her, something happened. He began to change his mind. On a morning just like the others, the pastor gave an open altar call. John stood up and went forward. Feeling protected in a room full of Christians and in front of the pastor, he was sure Satan couldn't hurt him.

As soon as he came to stand in front of the pastor, he became demon possessed, grabbed the pastor by the throat, and lifted him up. John then said, "I came for you." Immediately, a group of men came forth and tried to restrain him, but John was out of mind and focused...ready to kill. He was not prepared for what happened next. All the people in the congregation, about two hundred in number, raised their hands and began praying over him—praying ardently over a person who would have killed them all in a heartbeat.

John gets emotional as he remembers this moment, because this was the day he saw the power of God—in that church. He remembers the men close to him whispering, say "Jesus is Lord, say Jesus is Lord. Say it. Say it!" He gathered the strength to fight and shout the words, "JESUS IS LORD!" And in that instant, the devil left. John is now a warrior for Christ and publicly exposes the evil and deception of the occult.[10]

I share this testimony from John Ramirez and encourage you to read his full testimony in his book, *Out of the Devil's Cauldron*, because he practiced and was fully knowledgeable of astral projection. There is no benefit to it. It is evil, and demons roam through this practice to seek and destroy those who they can prey on. John was a human volunteer to aid them in their destruction. I can attest to this because I had several astral projections myself.

Unlike John, my astral projections were not voluntary. I never understood why I came outside my body. Eventually, I learned from deliverance practitioner, Russ Dizdar, that I was being intentionally tormented by demons. Like John describes, it is true. You have the ability to hover, walk, and travel from place to place—just as in real life.

I remember living in Arcadia, California, when I was immediately transported outside my house. It was eerie because the colors were different and there was no moonlight. I could only see darkness in what I knew was a park a block from where I stood. I stood in the middle of the street in utter silence—no noise of cars or any sounds from the neighborhood. I began to see shadows moving from the darkness of the local park, and I began walking into my house. As soon as I opened the door, I saw a black entity at the stairs waiting for me.

Without warning, it began dragging me to my room as I fought and fought to break free. With as much energy as I could possibly muster, I hit the bed and came back to reality. I will never forget this experience, because of how vulnerable I felt. I usually feel safe in my day to day, but here…it was different. I was somewhere else. I didn't know the rules and I didn't know who was there with me. Regardless of intent, be advised: New Age meditations and practices bring you close to astral projection. And none of it is good.

Musical Doorways

Satanism in the Music Industry
Music is one of the greatest mediums in existence to ventilate human emotions and is able to manipulate it's full range from the most extreme happiness to the most heartfelt sadness. The vast majority of people on earth listen to music without much thought, and sadly, they are completely unaware of the true meaning of lyrics, music videos, performances, and the effects they have on listeners—particularly satanism Hollywood. What is referred to as the "Top 40" of music and artists, all contain references to either satanism, sex, the occult, or other masonic and spiritual symbolisms.

Deemed as conspiracy theory, many brush this notion off, viewing it as ludicrous and insane, but that is simply not the truth. The biggest and most popular artists are involved, and some have spoken out about it while others have been killed for it. Because there are so many examples of Satan's grand scheme, it is hard to know where to begin. So, I will use real quotes, imagery, and events to give you a small taste of just how demonic the music industry is.

You might already be aware of the secret society conspiracy known as the illuminati that use masonic shapes like the all-seeing-eye and the pyramid. Whether you believe or not, what is fact is the masonic imagery used in music videos. For example, the all-seeing-eye references of Rihanna's "Where Have You Been" and Katy Perry's "Dark Horse" music videos are clear. Or what about the black and white tile floors of Cardi B's "Money" and Kesha's "Praying" music videos? The list is endless, and the examples are so many that you could write an entire book on it.

Regardless, I want to highlight this because the imagery that used to be so sub-textual is now in the forefront for all to see. What used to be hidden is now in plain sight. This is very clear in the works from new artists like Billie Eilish, who uses graphic satanic imagery in her videos "Bury a Friend" and "All the Good Girls Go to Hell" (where she is literally depicted as a black fallen angel on earth) and artists like Bad Bunny who have now transitioned demonic music and visuals in his "Yo Perreo Sola" music video. When I've shown examples of this to people in real-time, I usually get a response that it's a "coincidence" that these artists use those symbols or that I am reading too much into it. However, that's only music videos and doesn't even begin to cover the extent of demonic media.

Award shows like the Grammy's are huge culprits of public demonic expression. Nicki Minaj's 2012 Grammy performance for example was a five-minute video and live performance of the self-titled "The Exorcism of Roman" (her alter ego) that displayed witchcraft ritual and levitation illusions during the performance. During the video snippet, the priest asks a Nicki Minaj that has crawled on the ceiling what its name is. To which Nicky screams, "ROMAN!" Sounds like Legion in the demoniac doesn't it?

The Super Bowls are some of the biggest culprits of satanic expression as well. In 2015, Katy Perry opened the Super Bowl Halftime Show riding on top a red-eye glowing animatronic beast enveloped in a flaming outfit. So what? Well, any person who knows their Bible understands the immediate comparison to the harlot who rides the beast in the book of Revelation. Another example is Madonna who, in 2012, opened her show with a Babylonian scenery and apparel and then closed it with a black mass to her song "Like a Prayer." It took me a while to catch these things in real-time watching them. I developed a greater sensitivity toward these things later since I worked in the entertainment industry for a few years.

I will never forget during my film study what one of my cinematography professors said: "There's always a reason for something to be on the screen. Every detail from the most minute vase to the floor and cup on the screen." He was right. Working on sets and editing footage taught me that everything you see on the screen has a reason and purpose for being there. That picture frame in the background? Production design planned and purchased it. The picture frame with a pyramid? Planned and purchased. Someone is responsible for all that you see on the screen. So, when you see it, know that it is not an accident.

I understand that this will still not be enough for some people, but take it from the artists themselves:

"Rock has always been the devil's music. You can't convince me that it isn't."[11]

David Bowie

"...what was going on in my life at 15. That's how I got introduced to the music industry, cuz I swear I wanted to be like the Amy Grant of music. But it did not work out so I...sold my soul to the devil. "

Katy Perry, TEN Live Interview

From an interview with Bob Dylan:

Interviewer: "Why do you still do it? Why are you still out here?

Bob: "Well, it goes back to that destiny thing. And I made a bargain with it. Long time ago...I'm holding up my end."

Interviewer: "What was your bargain?"

Bob: "To get where...I am now."

Interviewer: "Should I ask who you made the bargain with?"

Bob: (chuckles) "Wi...wi...with, you know? With the chief commander."

Interviewer: "On this earth?"

Bob: (laughs) "On this earth...and in a in a world we can't see."

Lies and Deception

Probably the most common ways demons attack people are through lies and deception. In fact, the 1995 film, The Usual Suspects, gave birth to the quote: "The greatest trick the devil ever pulled was convincing the world he didn't exist."[12] This is the easiest tactic. Because if you don't believe in God or if you believe in a false religion, then Satan already has you in his cage. There is no more work to be done for him and he will move on to the next soul. Similarly, if he twists scripture to have you believe that God doesn't punish certain sin or attempts to make you believe that you are a good person that God would never condemn, then he can leave you to live your life according to the lie you've bought until you draw your last breath. In my short walk so far, this is what I perceive to be the most common and effortless way the enemy attacks people. When you are so far removed from the truth, as is written in the Bible, the enemy doesn't have to lift a finger. He can just wait until you die in the lie. This almost happened to me.

For all my life, I searched for the truth in conspiracies and the unknown in an effort to have all the big questions answered. Why do I exist? Who made me? What is my purpose? From aliens to evolution, I searched far and wide for the truth. In many of my phases, the enemy left me alone to do what I pleased. I had zero demonic attacks (physical), and while my struggles were worldly, they were all self-inflicted and self-attributed. I felt power in myself and arrogance to proclaim that everything that I had was only because of me and my ability to achieve it. Had I continued or suffered death before my coming to Christ, I would have died in condemnation. When I look back at how invisible the enemy was to me, I see how clever he was to deceive me that he was actually there. In fact, demons started to manifest themselves to me only when I began reading the Bible.

My recommendation is this: For unbelievers in Christ, I tell you that I understand you. I get that you find this reasoning ridiculous and all this talk of demons and Satan juvenile and insulting to your intellect. Listen, the enemy will not present himself to you if you don't give him reason to. Getting over the lie that our Creator doesn't exist will be your biggest hurdle, but I promise you that if you trust Him, all your questions will finally be answered and your life will be transformed into a life of goodness and purpose He has marked for your life. There are no incantations or trinkets needed to take the first step. Talk to Him today. Ask Him your questions. Ask Him to present Himself to you. The enemy's lies can end today, and your name can be imprinted in the Lamb's Book of Life into eternity.

For my fellow brothers and sisters in Christ, I tell you that our walk is not over. While we have overcome the enemy's greatest lie, he will still whisper lies to make us doubt God and our salvation. Thoughts that we are not saved or that God has forgotten us will manifest, but focus on Jesus and rebuke the enemy with scripture. Be like the wise builder who built his house on rock so when the rain, floods, and winds came, the house stood firm and did not fall.

Nightmares

The second most common demonic attack is through nightmares. While less common from my own personal experience, I have family members, friends, and have heard hundreds of people online who have shared their nightmare experiences. These nightmares typically use family members or loved ones to torment the individual through sexual perverse acts or through violence.

For example, a friend of mine once shared with me that she had a nightmare in which her close relative was violating her. Instances like this are horrific and serve as a taunt and a way the enemy tortures his target. These nightmares, unlike casual dreams, are also much more vivid. These "lucid" dreams seem real to the individual, which is why they are so keen to remember them and never forget them.

Because of the nature of these types of nightmares, most people keep these experiences to themselves for obvious reasons of embarrassment, fear, or ridicule. While not common in my experience, I myself have had sexual nightmares with people I know. I am certain that these nightmares were enemy-driven since I was cautious and unwilling to partake in any of the perverse activities. I was not in control of the situation (the nightmare), but I did have some control on whether I wanted to act or not. Other nightmares are violent and can be characterized by loved ones attacking you or trying to kill you. These typically show the victim running away, attempting an escape or even actually being killed in the nightmare.

Another nightmare instance is the deception of aliens. All my life, I was allured at the prospect of alien life outside our known solar system, so it came as quite a shock to discover that aliens were demons masquerading as intelligent life forms. While I can go into great depth into the reasoning for this, I will provide two easy explanations for this assertion.

First (and the most important), all alien visitation experiences in which the victim has called on the name of Jesus has resulted in the aliens fleeing or screaming. This alone is the biggest piece of evidence to unmask their disguise. Any entity that departs or is cast out in the name of Yeshua is an enemy of the Most High. Since the enemy in this world is clearly Satan and his army, there is no doubt that these beings or apparitions are demonic.

Secondly, I had an alien demonic attack myself. While living in Arcadia, California, I had an experience where I awoke from sleep to find a grey alien face in front of me. I was confused at what I was seeing and what was occurring, and I was trying to make sense of a grey bony hand being placed over my face. At the time, I was not courageous enough to fight and was not aware that aliens were demons, so I did not fight and just kept this experience as a memory.

If you suffer from these nightmares, pray immediately and call on the name of Jesus to deliver you from them. Use this nightmare as a sign that you are being attacked by the enemy. Don't delve into the moment. Instead, redirect your fear and transform it into faith. He will deliver you if you call on Him.

Sleep Paralysis

WebMD defines sleep paralysis as the feeling of being conscious, but unable to move, and occurring between the stages of wakefulness and sleep. Symptom descriptions of pressure on the chest or a sense of choking are noted to be caused by lack of sleep or erratic sleeping behaviors[13] Reading this online was reassuring when I first began having these experiences. What WebMD was not able to explain, however, was the sense of evil that occurred when I had these experiences—much less the visual, physical, and auditory apparitions I experienced later. Most people have experienced sleep paralysis to a certain degree in their lifetime, but few actually suffer from these experiences in high frequency.

I began having these experiences in my 20s right before my commitment to Christ. They began tamely, with just me in the room, conscious of my surroundings, but unable to move. Because these experiences were so foreign to me when they began, I was confused at what I was feeling. I was dumbfounded by the faces I saw or the pressure I felt on my body. I realized my sleep paralysis was not normal when I was slammed back and forth and when I was separated from my body and could see my body sleeping. I must have had over 60 sleep paralysis experiences before I finally was delivered from them, so believe me when I tell you that these are demonic attacks.

Unlike nightmares, the enemy pulls you out of your dimensional reality so that you can experience things in a much more visual or physical way. But why? Why attack through sleep paralysis? The aim is to torture you and instill fear, but most importantly, to break you. These attacks are highly frightening for those who have experienced them. I'm sure the enemy feels joy from your torment, but I've come to find that the primary reason is to keep you away from pursuing God and keep you from achieving your purpose.

Let me explain. While I was having these demonic attacks, I was very much afraid. Afraid, but not enough to stop me from reading the Bible, praying, or attending church services. I was also not afraid to share them with my close friends and relatives. One of my relatives was highly curious of my experiences, and in her time away from home, she began to attend church on her own accord and learning about God through scripture. She began having these sleep paralysis attacks as well and was so filled with fright that, in time, she stopped attending church services altogether.

I share these examples to demonstrate that, while the enemy enjoys to torture, they also have an aim to stop your walk with God. If the fear is so extreme that the victim wants these attacks to stop at all costs (even if it means stopping prayer, reading the Bible, or attending church services), then the enemy has been effective in putting a stop to your spiritual journey. In my case, it backfired on the enemy. Because if the demons I saw, felt, and heard were real, then that meant that God, Jesus, and angels were also real.

Physical Manifestations

I am very fortunate that I never reached this stage of demonic attack. Yes, I saw, felt, and heard demons, but I was never physically marked by them. Unfortunately, this is not the case for others. Demons are able to attack you physically and leave marks or scars on your body. I will never forget a phone call I received from a friend of mine in the middle of the day. She was crying, afraid of what had just happened to her. She was frantic, explaining to me that a demon had taken the form of her son to violate her. Her concern was greater because she had awakened with marks all over her legs. I must admit that I shivered as I saw the images on my phone. There were recent scratches on her body that hadn't been there before. I tried to help as much as I could and counsel through faith and prayer, but I couldn't shake off the thought of how much more severe this type of attack was.

I was so curious that I did more research for similar testimonies so I could help her deliver herself from this. Sure enough, there were others all over the world who had suffered from these experiences...and some, even worse. These physical demonic manifestations are much closer to what the world deems as being "haunted." Things flying off the shelf, lights flickering or breaking, things moving by themselves, these are much more severe instances of demonic attack. The probable causes in these instances are certain doors opened by the victim or occultism caused at the location.

The good news, however, is that the cure remains the same. Using the authority Jesus gives you to expel these demons is the answer. It is usually tougher to execute the deliverance, however, because it requires full faith during a physical confrontation with the enemy. Don't succumb to fear though. The power behind our Savior is incomparable to anything the enemy can do. You've already won.

Demonic Possession

Possession is the highest grade of attack the enemy can do to a person. To be possessed by a demonic spirit is to lose control of your mind and body and allow the demon to inhabit you and use your body. Thanks to the 1973 film, *The Exorcist*, most people know just how gruesome and terrifying this experience can be for spectators. We can see the effects these possessions have on people by looking at the people Jesus healed from demonic possession. These people were unable to live normal lives for years before being cured by Him. Some were living in caves and in chains and others were violent, attempting suicide by drowning or burning themselves on fire. Whatever the consequence, the methodology was always the same. The victim was not in control of their mind or their body.

While possession and deliverance from these demonic spirits exist today, I must reiterate once more that I do not believe it is possible for a believer in Christ to be possessed by a demonic spirit. To be in Christ is to have the Holy Spirit in you. Yes, you can be attacked or tempted by the enemy, but by no means can an evil entity inhabit you while the Holy Spirit is in you. Having said this, possession is a real condition many suffer from.

If you or someone you know is suffering from this condition, I must advise you to be careful in how you approach deliverance. There are many brothers and sisters in Christ whose calling is to deliver people from demonic possession. Similar to the apostles in Matthew 17:19, it requires tremendous and solid faith to deliver yourself or someone from the enemy. Even the apostles in Acts 19:15 were not able to cast them out and were sent running off naked and beaten by the possessed man.

I'm sure you must be wondering why your faith isn't enough to deliver demonically possessed individuals. Remember, these demons can speak, are violent, will attack you, and will attempt to frighten you while you are in the process of delivering yourself or someone. You must be so grounded in faith and so strong in your relationship with Christ that you are completely unaffected by all the lies and violence set forth from the possessed victim. Think of *The Exorcist* in which the girl's head turns completely or she levitates from her bed. The demon did all of this to distract or break the priest from completing the exorcism.[14] In this way, possessed people are not delivered so easily. This is why not everyone is called to practice deliverance. I can attest to this as you will read later. It took complete faith in Jesus against horrible creatures for me to deliver myself from demonic attacks.

Close the Doors

Today, I am free of demonic attacks. Well, I should say that I am free from physical attacks. The attacks against me are now subversive and usually come through other people. Regardless, the doors that opened me up for visitations and manifestations are now closed. I could have saved myself much time and torment had I known this information from the beginning. Knowing what doors I had opened that allowed these entities to come into my life would have helped me know which sins to stop. Knowing what you have allowed into your life is crucial in determining which door to close. Even if you do not suffer from physical demonic attacks, do a self-analysis on which practices have exposed you to demonic activity in your life. Chances are, they're still there. Once you've identified them, get ready to fight.

ENEMY TACTICS

ENCOUNTER #4
HOUND

One of my aspirations in life was to work in entertainment. Red carpets, celebrities, the glamour...well, I wanted to be somebody important and make money to support my family back home. I got my opportunity in college interning for Viacom and 20th Century Fox; my biggest achievements at the time. After graduation, I surpassed my wildest expectations when I was offered a position as a page for NBCUniversal's Page Program.

Excited for this opportunity, I moved to Arcadia, California, as soon as I could. Living on my own once again, I focused heavily on my work while listening to Christian sermons during my long morning commutes. Now that I had this great opportunity, I wanted to focus more on God and thank Him for it. I decided to read the Bible more frequently and more seriously to learn more about Him.

After a nightly read, I went to sleep as I had done every previous day. Suddenly, I awoke in the middle of the night and saw a huge beast that resembled a large dog or wolf with two red glowing eyes staring at me. My body reacted instantly, and I jumped back as my legs tried to kick it in the face. My body was thinking way ahead of my mind and reached out for the light switch. In an instant, the light turned on and nothing was there. My lamp was on the floor and my sheets were scattered at the end of the bed. I was panicked and breathing rapidly as I tried to make sense of what had just happened. All I could remember was the face of a beast with two glowing eyes.

Chapter 4

THE ARMOR OF GOD: BELT OF TRUTH

For we do not wrestle against flesh and blood, but against principalities, against powers, against the rulers of the darkness of this age, against spiritual hosts of wickedness in the heavenly places.

Ephesians 6:12

You know the enemy. You know his tactics. Now is the time to gear up and do something about it. Many may not know that God has specifically equipped His children with a set of armor, the purpose of which is to help us to stand firm during the spiritual warfare. You are not defenseless. God knows that the enemy comes to you from a spiritual plane. Thanks to Paul's epistle to the Ephesians, we have the necessary tools to fight the enemy head on—the Armor of God. There are six pieces of armor that He provides and expects us to equip ourselves with starting with the Belt of Truth:

Stand firm then, with the belt of truth buckled around your waist.

Ephesians 6:14

Out of all the pieces of armor, Paul begins with a belt. But why? It is likely that you would think something so light would be the last thing he mentions. Similar to King David's sling, the belt carries a large significance. The belt—known as the cingulum or balteus—played a crucial role in the effectiveness of a soldier's armor. It was the belt that held the sheath, without which there would be no place to put a sword. So if you don't have a belt, you have no access to your weapon! In addition to securing your weapon, the belt also had strips of armor attached to protect the lower half of the soldier's body. The belt served as a foundation to a Roman soldier's set of armor. If the belt was not secured properly, the soldier might struggle or lose his weapon in the battlefield, which could get him killed.

More importantly though, the belt served as the first part of preparation before heading to war. You see, Roman soldiers wore a tunic underneath their armor. If unfastened, however, this tunic would fly off at the wind's first whim or be utilized by the enemy to cover or blind the soldier if picked up at the hem and placed over the soldier's head during battle. This is where the belt comes in. The soldier fastens the belt around the tunic and feels secure—ready to stand and equip the other pieces of armor.

What purpose does the Belt of Truth serve for you? Jesus lets us know in His prayer to the Creator and explains what TRUTH is in John 17:

My prayer is not that you take them out of the world but that you protect them from the evil one. They are not of the world, even as I am not of it. Sanctify them by the truth; your word is truth.

John 17:15-17

Jesus, praying to the Father, gives a clear and straightforward definition of truth: God's Word. The Holy Bible was given by inspiration from God.

All Scripture is God-breathed and is useful for teaching, rebuking, correcting and training in righteousness.

2 Timothy 3:16

The Greek expression translated "inspiration of God" literally means "God-breathed." His promises, His commands, and His Word is truth—plain and simple. We've all heard skeptics and unbelievers making the claim that the Bible was created by man, but they fail to realize that scripture Itself informs the reader that all the words are God-breathed and useful for instruction (not to mention that many of the books and letters in the Bible were written under God's instruction). As Christians, we are to test all things and then hold on only to that which is good—the truth—discarding all else. We are to be like the Bereans who searched the Scriptures daily to find out whether these things were so:

Now the Berean Jews were of more noble character than those in Thessalonica, for they received the message with great eagerness and examined the Scriptures every day to see if what Paul said was true.

Acts 17:11

That Berean spirit is what is needed to equip the Belt of Truth. Be eager and willing to ensure that you know the truth. Do not blindly take someone's word for truth or anyone that stands on a pulpit. Investigate God's Word for the truth for yourself and check that the words you read and hear are correct in scripture. After all, Paul instructs Timothy:

Study to shew thyself approved unto God, a workman that needeth not to be ashamed, rightly dividing the word of truth.

2 Timothy 2:15

It is very important to actively check that what you hear or read is the truth that Jesus tells us will set us free. It is not possible to discern truth from lie if you do not constantly examine God's Word for the truth. For example, according to the World Christian Encyclopedia, there are at least 33,000 Christian denominations across the world.[15] If there are 33,000 denominations, can they all be true? Can Catholics coexist with 7th Day Adventists in the truth of God's Word? Can Jehovah Witnesses share the Kingdom of God with Mormons? I tell you with full conviction—NO. There can only be one truth. All denominations and religions cannot be correct, especially within Christianity. Jesus came to divide family and friends, because He is the only Savior who fulfilled prophecy and paid the sins of man (Matthew 10:34-35). The Messiah has made it clear that He serves as the Head of the church and all of His followers are the body.

You are the body of Christ. Each one of you is a part of it.

1 Corinthians 12:27

As members of the Body of Christ, we are not separated by denomination. There is no arm of Lutherans, a nose of Jehovah Witnesses, and a leg of Calvinists. The body is made up by followers of Christ. It's that simple.

The truth exists in the same way, and the choice to be made is on you. This choice is crucial, but God has given you assurance in search for the truth.

The LORD is near to all who call on him, to all who call on him in truth.

Psalm 145:18

If we are not convinced that our principles and beliefs are 100 percent true, how can we expect to accomplish anything? The enemy uses this insecurity to remove your belt and leave you naked and vulnerable for attack. So… how secure is your belt right now? As Psalm 145:18 notes, truth must be bound around us and written on our hearts—our conviction must reach beyond an outward show. Arm yourself with the Belt of Truth and plant your feet strong on the ground, for the enemy draws near.

The Belt of Truth in Action

Thanks to the advent of technology, communication has become so mainstreamed that it is very easy to communicate with loved ones who are far away. This was the case for myself and my cousins who live about five hours away from me. Thanks to the voice Discord application, we were able to converse almost daily, and because of it, I was also able to meet new people who then became friends.

One of these was a young man by the name of "Vora" who came into the Discord and talked about many topics. Recently coming out of the Jehovah's Witnesses denomination, I was amazed by how well versed he was in scripture. I was not in any denomination, so contact with Bible knowing believers was very rare, especially in a Discord filled with agnostic or atheist people.

During the days of debates, he would refer to scripture to defend God or instruct my cousins on what the Bible said about certain things. Through time, I discovered that he lived through a rough childhood and suffered from a lot of self-doubt and insecurity. He was remarkable due to his ability to identify his insecurities and self-diagnose. He would tell us about his depressions and other sins. This was strange to me because it is not often that people self-diagnose their mental health (especially so accurately and eloquently).

As years went on, he would let us know his plans and ambitions to return to school, get a new job, and become an author. I thought these were great, so I encouraged him and offered assistance if he needed it. But he never moved forward. It was difficult to understand because he was a man of God. He knew scripture. I didn't understand why he was not trusting and just pushing onward. I reminded him of Philippians 4:13, gave him my personal testimony, and did all I could to encourage him until one day he told me he did not want to hear my advice anymore.

Time passed and none of his plans ever came to fruition. I share this story because it demonstrates what can happen when you haven't equipped yourself with the Belt of Truth. He knew God's Word. He said he believed it. But he didn't live in it.

Drop the Weights

Before you even decide to put on the Belt of Truth, you have to be sincere with yourself. Are you committed to victory? Are you willing to leave all your loose ends of sin behind to achieve it? If you are content with your "small sins," if you are okay with your lack of interest in prayer, if you don't mind not being interested in knowing your amazing Creator, then you are going to be a consistent loser. If this is your decision then you are an unprepared soldier in the battlefield and should be prepared to be defeated every time.

Are your ready to let go of your weights to achieve deliverance and victory? I ask because I have had to return to fasten my Belt of Truth. Not letting go of my sins was not enough to defeat demons until I made a commitment to being a soldier. Understand that's what you are. You are a soldier in this invisible war. This is who you are and what you do. You get up. Put your tunic on. You fasten your belt and you go to war because that's what you do. This is why your commitment is so important. Truly being sincere that you believe God's Word and in the fight is what will make the difference if you should stand in victory or be slain with the fallen.

If you don't believe in God's written truth, you then succumb to the lies of the enemy. He stumps you. There's nowhere to go and you don't do what God has called you to do. You can't use any of the other pieces of armor because your belt has loosened and your armor fallen. This is why it is crucial that you stand firm in God's truth. Not yours. Not man's. God's alone. Don't allow the enemy to break you with lies and doubt and make a firm commitment right now. Equip yourself firm with the Belt of Truth.

Chapter 5

THE ARMOR OF GOD: BREASTPLATE OF RIGHTEOUSNESS

…with the breastplate of righteousness in place

Ephesians 6:14

The second piece of armor Paul mentions in Ephesians 6:14 is the Breastplate of Righteousness. Why is the breastplate important—for both ancient soldiers and us? The breastplate was a central part of the Roman soldier's armor—it provided protection for the torso's vital organs like the heart, lungs, and so on. Without a breastplate, a soldier would be asking for death, since any attack could instantly become fatal. With a sturdy breastplate, the very same attacks become ineffective and useless as blows glance off the armor.

We see a lesson of this from 1 Kings 21 in the life of wicked King Ahab. Under counsel from his Sedonian wife Jezebel, this selfish leader allowed a man to be killed just so he could take the man's vineyard. This king of Israel, "who did evil in the sight of the Lord more than all who were before him" according to 1 Kings 16:30, was prophesied by Elijah that he would die in the battle described in 1 Kings 22. So Ahab decided to disguise himself to appear as a common solider while his ally, King Jehoshaphat of Judah, wore his own kingly robes:

Now the king of Syria had commanded the thirty-two captains of his chariots, saying, "Fight with no one small or great, but only with the king of Israel." So it was, when the captains of the chariots saw Jehoshaphat, that they said,

"Surely it is the king of Israel!" Therefore they turned aside to fight against him, and Jehoshaphat cried out. And it happened, when the captains of the chariots saw that it was not the king of Israel, that they turned back from pursuing him. Now a certain man drew a bow at random, and struck the king of Israel between the joints of his armor. So he said to the driver of his chariot, "Turn around and take me out of the battle, for I am wounded."

The battle increased that day; and the king was propped up in his chariot, facing the Syrians, and died at evening. The blood ran out from the wound onto the floor of the chariot.

1 Kings 22:31-35,

King Ahab was killed through an opening between his armor and breastplate. While King Ahab was served divine justice from God, even the smallest of openings in this armor can serve defeat to a soldier. That is why a soldier needs a large piece of armor to cover the whole torso.

So the Roman breastplate is a crucial piece of defensive armor. But what is the Breastplate of Righteousness? Psalm 119:172 lets us know what righteousness is:

My tongue shall speak of Your word, for all Your commandments are righteousness.

To be righteous is to do what is right in God's eyes and in His law. In contrast, lawlessness is sin, and sin is the opposite of righteousness. So to be righteous is to obey God's laws. Iniquities and sins are actions and thoughts that go against God's laws. Since sin is in conflict with God's way of living for us, it is harmful to ourselves and others. Our perfect and just God will not associate with us if we go down the path of sin and evil. Without righteousness, we leave ourselves open to certain death. We cut ourselves off from God and His protection! God's commandments are the righteousness of the breastplate. So how do we put it on? Follow and obey God's commandments. With the Breastplate of Righteousness locked in place, remind the enemy you follow God's commandments. Once you have put on the Breastplate of Righteousness, you must be sure not to remove it. Ezekiel 33:13 shows that wearing righteousness is not a one-time event; rather, it requires a lifetime of action:

Suppose I tell a godly person that they will live. And they trust in the fact that they used to do what is right. But now they do what is evil. Then I will not remember any of the right things they have done. They will die because they have done so many evil things.

One day, the war we're fighting will be over. And when it is, we are promised in Isaiah 32:17:

The work of righteousness will be peace, and the effect of righteousness, quietness and assurance forever. By faithfully living God's way and staying clear of Satan's, we will find this peace, quietness and assurance—forever.

The Breastplate of Righteousness in Action

In 2018, there was a mass shooting in a bar in Thousand Oaks, California. As I read the headlines on the news, I felt a sense of sadness of how close evil had drawn so near to my home. As the list of victims was revealed, they indicated that a Christian college student was amongst the deceased, and I was immediately troubled. I thought in my mind, "If only she wasn't there…what if she stayed in that night?" The pain her family must be going through must be unimaginable.

As believers in Christ, we must face hard truths—some we may not want to hear. Putting on the Breastplate of Righteousness means to live a life of righteousness. I cannot help but wonder what the outcome would have been if the Christian girl had not gone to the bar that night. Now I don't know if she drank or what her reasons were for going, but I do know that the enemy wants to catch us off guard. We give the enemy space to enter when we do or go to places God does not intend for us. Don't forget you have free will.

What you do and what God wants you to do can be separate things. You can be very committed and motivated to the spiritual fight and have the first piece of armor of the Belt of Truth on, but if you do not live in obedience and righteousness then trying to put on the Breastplate of Righteousness will be of no use. That breastplate will fall right off. It's a scary reality that this is possible because it can ruin years of victories and lead to destruction.

This has occurred to me in the past. My biggest weakness is lust. After seasons of successful victories against the enemy, my Breastplate of Righteousness fell off in one fell swoop of temptation. What I had on successfully for years fell off in literal seconds. Wearing this breastplate is the fulfillment of the commitment that you decided to wear with the Belt of Truth.

Even more importantly, there is no way that you can defeat demons without it. I remember the feeling when I backslid. I was powerless. It felt like God was lightyears away from me. There is no way I would dare practice self-deliverance or deliverance on others in that state. It may sound like a big ask to obey God's laws, but as you get to know God more, you begin to realize that His laws are for your own good and that you naturally will want to do them. Trust that living in His righteousness is best for you, and even if you your breastplate drops, put it on again. We are not perfect, but we must strive to live righteously if we are to be equipped with this piece of armor.

THE ARMOR OF GOD: BREASTPLATE OF RIGHTEOUSNESS

Chapter 6

THE ARMOR OF GOD: FEET PREPARED WITH THE GOSPEL OF PEACE

...and with your feet fitted with the readiness that comes from the gospel of peace.

Ephesians 6:15b

The third piece of armor goes on your feet. Shoes, like the belt, may initially seem unnecessary for a combat role, but that is not so. Imagine a fully armed Roman soldier. He has his sword, his shield, his helmet, his breastplate, and his belt...but his feet are completely bare. A shoeless soldier in the battlefield is going to contend with debris on the ground. It may be nothing more than twigs and pebbles, but to a bare foot, they can cause serious pain (anyone who's ever stepped on a Lego block can testify to the pain)—and one of the last things you want to deal with in the middle of a fight is worrying about where you step. Similarly, we are to equip our feet with the Gospel of Peace.

And Jesus went about all Galilee, teaching in their synagogues, preaching the gospel of the kingdom, and healing all kinds of sickness and all kinds of disease among the people.

Matthew 4:23

And how shall they preach unless they are sent? As it is written: "How beautiful are the feet of those who preach the gospel of peace, who bring glad tidings of good things!"

Romans 10:15

The Greek word euaggelion, translated as Gospel, simply means "good news." While it may seem that the feet prepared by the Gospel of Peace refers to evangelism, the feet laced with sandals is much more sedentary. It means standing strong in the face of an attack. Secure. Fixed in position and immovable. It is knowing that you are secure in your salvation and upon Who has redeemed you. This goes beyond a basic understanding of the Gospel. It is fully embracing it.

Unfortunately, most believers don't feel confident in the application of the Gospel of Peace in regard to their own personal salvation. This is why many Christians today fear Satan. They fear ghosts, apparitions, dark places like cemeteries, and anything that can be deemed as "spooky." This is quite simply salvation insecurity. Why? Because if your feet are prepared with that Gospel, you know very well that you are under an invincible God. No enemy can touch you or cause you to fall. The power that you receive from God comes from the Gospel and the peace you have because of the Christ who is mediating on your behalf. Think about Peter in the Garden of Gethsemane when the troops from the Sanhedrin went forward to arrest Jesus:

Jesus answered, "I have told you that I am He. Therefore, if you seek Me, let these go their way," that the saying might be fulfilled which He spoke, "Of those whom You gave Me I have lost none."

Then Simon Peter, having a sword, drew it and struck the high priest's servant, and cut off his right ear. The servant's name was Malchus.

So Jesus said to Peter, "Put your sword into the sheath. Shall I not drink the cup which My Father has given Me?"

John 18:8-11

What caused a fisherman with no combat experience to draw a sword and cut off the ear of one of the servants? Well…he had Jesus next to Him. He felt safe and secure that He could do anything if Jesus was there with him. This is what we must do when we prepare our feet with the Gospel of Peace. Have the confidence of the safety and protection you are under. Know without a doubt that Jesus is right there with you as you fight the enemy.

The Gospel of Peace in Action

During many of my nightly demonic encounters, I didn't fight back. Even as I grew in God's Word, the fear of these moments was so much that I was not able to overcome them. There were failed attempts in which I would try to cast them out in Jesus' name and could not. The demons simply laughed at me and the oppression continued. This happened because my feet were not prepared with the Gospel of Peace.

It was one thing to say that I was covered under the blood and protection of Jesus and another to truly believe it. This is a very important difference. In order to do God's will, in order to persevere, in order to defeat that demonic oppression, you must really be secure in the Gospel as it applies to you. The day I was delivered was the day I believed in the voracity of the Gospel. I knew the power that supported me and had full confidence that Jesus was with me.

No longer was demonic deliverance limited to the pages of the New Testament. I activated it by calling on Jesus and relying on His promise. I was certain He would deliver me from all those demons, and I was certain that I could command them to imprisonment under the power and authority of Jesus. So while the enemy was charging at me, I remained fixed in position.

This is how you equip your feet with the Gospel of Peace. Stand your ground and be fully convinced that you are given the authority to destroy the enemy because Jesus has granted it to you through His name and the Gospel. You received this authority the day you accepted His salvation; now stand and own it. Equipping your feet is to fear nothing and nobody and to being a fixture of confidence in the power of God.

Chapter 7

THE ARMOR OF GOD: SHIELD OF FAITH

In addition to all this, take up the shield of faith, with which you can extinguish all the flaming arrows of the evil one.

Ephesians 6:16

The fourth piece of armor is your defense against the enemy's weapons. Unlike the other pieces of armor, the shield is different. Paul tells us that the shield is something we must take up, something we are required to raise. Just strapping it to our arm won't do any good at all if we don't make the effort to hold it aloft and use it. The Roman shield—the scutum—was a tall, rectangular shield featuring at its center a large metal boss (or knob). The Roman shield was a strong and strategic piece of armor. When used collectively, Roman soldiers gathered together with raised shields covering all their sides all at once. This testudo or tortoise formation created an impressive mobile line of defense. The height of the shield, averaging three and a half feet tall and almost three feet wide, gave Roman soldiers a great deal of protection from enemy soldiers. Similarly, the Shield of Faith grants us this protection. Here is a biblical definition of faith:

Now faith is the substance of things hoped for, the evidence of things not seen.

Hebrews 11:1

Though faith is based on solid, unseen evidence, that doesn't mean it comes naturally or easily. Paul here makes it clear: You don't hope for what you already have. Faith involves a huge element of trust. We must examine the evidence and see that God has proved Himself to be unchanging and consistent, and then we must firmly believe that He will fulfill His promises to us.

How do we raise up our Shield of Faith then? We call it trust. Trust in the Lord with all your heart at all times. The enemy will shoot his darts at you. Raise your shield and trust that the Lord will defend you as you persevere in your trials and tribulations according to His Word and promises. Shadrach, Meshach, and Abed-Nego, during the Babylon captivity, are perfect examples of this faith in trust. They refused to bow down to Nebuchadnezzar's statue in front of hundreds of people and were condemned to be burned in a fiery furnace as a consequence. In the face of the enemy, they said:

If that is the case, our God whom we serve is able to deliver us from the burning fiery furnace, and He will deliver us from your hand, O king. But if not, let it be known to you, O king, that we do not serve your gods, nor will we worship the gold image which you have set up.

Daniel 3:17-18

When Satan (through Nebuchadnezzar) attacked the devotion of Shadrach, Meshach, and Abed-Nego to God, they were able to stand resolute and unwavering because of their faith. In their response, they essentially said, "God is capable of delivering us from this fate." And this is exactly what God did:

Then Nebuchadnezzar was full of fury, and the expression on his face changed toward Shadrach, Meshach, and Abed-Nego. He spoke and commanded that they heat the furnace seven times more than it was usually heated. And he commanded certain mighty men of valor who were in his army to bind Shadrach, Meshach, and Abed-Nego, and cast them into the burning fiery furnace. Then these men were bound in their coats, their trousers, their turbans, and their other garments, and were cast into the midst of the burning fiery furnace. Therefore, because the king's command was urgent, and the furnace exceedingly hot, the flame of the fire killed those men who took up Shadrach, Meshach, and Abed-Nego. And these three men, Shadrach, Meshach, and Abed-Nego, fell down bound into the midst of the burning fiery furnace.

Then King Nebuchadnezzar was astonished; and he rose in haste and spoke, saying to his counselors, "Did we not cast three men bound into the midst of the fire?"

They answered and said to the king, "True, O king."
"Look!" he answered, "I see four men loose, walking in the midst of the fire; and they are not hurt, and the form of the fourth is like the Son of God."

Daniel 3:19-25

They said, "Whether God receives our soul at the time of persecution or He delivers us from it does not matter. He gave us His commands and we are going to keep them regardless of the physical outcome. We know He is all powerful.

The Shield of Faith in Action

About two years ago, I had just completed an internship and arrived home from Israel. While I felt alive and energized, I was unemployed and in need of work. I was confident that I would find something close to home soon. As days turned to months, I began to become weary and lose motivation to do anything. I felt lost in purpose as I was halfway through the year. I began to lose patience because I had no idea where God wanted me to go. Should I look elsewhere? Does He want me in another city, state…or even country?

This period was difficult because God was silent, and I began to doubt His presence in my life. I couldn't believe that such a worldly thing could cause me to be so devoid of hope. Before I started to look elsewhere, my mom insisted I wait on God. She was certain He would find something for me near my town. And that He did. In December of that year, the job came. And not only that but the job was also better than I was qualified for.

As soon as I was about to crack, God provided. But the message here is in my wrongdoing. I needed to put on that Shield of Faith and not listen to the lies of insecurity and that God was not there for me and with me. God provided for me in less than one year, but think of Joseph. How long did he wait in prison (wrongfully accused) before God freed him and gave him the highest of purpose for all of Egypt and his family?

The Shield of Faith protects you from doubt and temptation under mundane circumstances. When you get that medical diagnosis, when you just lost your job, or when a loved one passes, these are moments in which you are vulnerable. The enemy attacks you and asks you to doubt God's goodness. The enemy wants you to question why God would put you in that circumstance. Having full trust that He has reason and purpose for you is the first step in equipping this shield.

When Satan tempted Jesus in Matthew 4, he was offering Him the option to distrust God. "Look at what your Father is doing to you in this desert. He offers you no food and wants You to starve and die." To these implications, Jesus responded, "It is written, 'Man shall not live by bread alone, but by every word that proceeds from the mouth of God.'" Jesus trusted in God's Word and refuted Satan's attack immediately. So, too, shall we disperse the enemy's temptations.

The Shield of Faith is your line of defense and what you use to quench the fiery darts of the enemy. If the enemy can't get close to you, then he resorts to firing these darts from far off. You must still defend yourself and equipping the Shield of Faith is how you do it. When the lies and temptations hit your shield, don't allow them to whisper and linger in your ear. Do not distrust God. On the contrary, nullify the temptations with faith. Faith in God's Word and His promises is what extinguishes those flaming arrows.

So when the enemy affects your life, when you stress over money, lose your job, suffer loss or disease, then equip yourself with the Shield of Faith and trust Him. Trust that whatever the outcome, you will not serve pagan gods or follow doctrines of demons. You serve the Most High and Yeshua the Christ, and your name is written in the Book of Life.

Chapter 8

THE ARMOR OF GOD: HELMET OF SALVATION

Take the helmet of salvation and the sword of the Spirit, which is the word of God.

Ephesians 6:17

The fifth piece of armor provides confidence. The Roman helmet, like helmets today, protected the head from the attacks of the enemy. The head is an important area to protect. As we know today, our cranium protects the brain, an integral vital organ in our body. Our mind is the key to our survival and we therefore give it utmost importance. After all, if your conscience becomes affected adversely, then your body is unable to function. But what does a helmet have to do with salvation? Salvation is simple and clear in John's famous passage known to all the world:

For God so loved the world that He gave His only begotten Son, that whoever believes in Him should not perish but have everlasting life. For God did not send His Son into the world to condemn the world, but that the world through Him might be saved.

John 3:16-17

And what is this everlasting life that John refers to?

Now I saw a new heaven and a new earth, for the first heaven and the first earth had passed away. Also there was no more sea. Then I, John, saw the holy city, New Jerusalem, coming down out of heaven from God, prepared as a bride adorned for her husband. And I heard a loud voice from heaven saying, "Behold, the tabernacle of God is with men, and He will dwell with them, and they shall be His people. God Himself will be with them and be their God. And God will wipe away every tear from their eyes; there shall be no more death, nor sorrow, nor crying. There shall be no more pain, for the former things have passed away."

Revelation 21:1-4

This is the prize we are fighting for—to enter this glorious Kingdom! Never lose sight of this. This coming Kingdom, with its eternal peace and prosperity, makes every price in this life worth paying. We can receive tremendous hope and comfort by focusing on the incredible sacrifice Christ gave to save us and the amazing Kingdom that is the goal of our salvation. This hope works like a helmet to protect our minds from the discouragement and despair in this world.

I do not pray that You should take them out of the world, but that You should keep them from the evil one. They are not of the world, just as I am not of the world.

John 17:15-16

Christians have been called out of this world. Though we remain in it, we are not of it and remain separate. Our way of living and even of thinking should differ from the world's. We are to develop the mind of Christ (Philippians 2:5), and as we have seen, that means having God's laws written on our hearts and minds so we can remember to always obey God.

Be sober, be vigilant; because your adversary the devil walks about like a roaring lion, seeking whom he may devour. Resist him, steadfast in the faith, knowing that the same sufferings are experienced by your brotherhood in the world

1 Peter 5:8-9

Our enemy hates that we have chosen this path and will stop at nothing to destroy us because of it. Just as the helmet protects the vital but vulnerable head from otherwise fatal blows, the hope of salvation can protect our thoughts from our enemy's attacks and temptations to disobey God.

Now he who received seed among the thorns is he who hears the word, and the cares of this world and the deceitfulness of riches choke the word, and he becomes unfruitful.

Matthew 13:22

Without the helmet of salvation, we will be unprotected from the "cares of this world" that bombard our thoughts and feelings every day. No matter what comes, no matter how vicious the attacks our enemy land on us, we know that as long as we remain with God, we are moving slowly but unstoppably toward an eternal victory with the Helmet of Salvation on.

The Helmet of Salvation in Action

During college, I did not have the typical collegiate experience. I didn't go to parties, I didn't join fraternities, and I didn't join many clubs or have friends. I was so busy all the time. Taking an overload of five classes, having three jobs, and being in a Mexican Folklorico company took up all my time. Unfortunately, I reduced my time reading the Bible. I went through a period of months without touching it, thinking, I listened to Christian radio today or I'm too tired today. Eventually, the days piled on and I lived without reading the Bible. I was a baby believer, focused only on completing my daily worldly activities.

What I did not know was that this was causing me to be a bitter and angry person. I was somehow stressed and frustrated with everyone in my world. I was judgmental and angry that I had to do so much while others lived happily. How is a newfound believer in Christ a person like this? This is what happens when you don't pair the Helmet of Salvation with the Sword of the Spirit. The focus on the non-important cares of the world cloud your vision and priorities. The Kingdom of God is the priority. Your salvation is the priority. This is why this piece of armament is so important. Keep your head straight. Place your priority in Christ.

Chapter 9

THE ARMOR OF GOD: SWORD OF THE SPIRIT

Take the helmet of salvation and the sword of the Spirit, which is the word of God.

Ephesians 6:17

Now the final piece of spiritual equipment: The Sword of the Spirit. Notice that every other piece that has been mentioned has been armor. The Sword of the Spirit, however, is your weapon. It is as clear as it can be. The Word of God is the sword. The Book, the Bible, is the sword against the enemy that will defeat him. In fact, Hebrews 4:12 states:

For the word of God is living and powerful, and sharper than any two-edged sword, piercing even to the division of soul and spirit, and of joints and marrow, and is a discerner of the thoughts and intents of the heart.

Remember when Jesus was tempted in the wilderness by Satan? How did Jesus rebuke him? Through the Word.

Then Jesus was led by the Spirit into the wilderness to be tempted by the devil. After fasting forty days and forty nights, he was hungry. The tempter came to him and said, "If you are the Son of God, tell these stones to become bread." Jesus answered, "It is written: 'Man shall not live on bread alone, but on every word that comes from the mouth of God." Then the devil took him to the holy city and had him stand on the highest point of the temple. "If you are the Son of God," he said, "throw yourself down. For it is written: "'He will command his angels concerning you, and they will lift you up in their hands, so that you will not strike your foot against a stone." Jesus answered him, "It is also written: 'Do not put the Lord your God to the test.'" Again, the devil took him to a very high mountain and showed him all the kingdoms of the world and their splendor. "All this I will give you," he said, "if you will bow down and worship me." Jesus said to him, "Away from me, Satan! For it is written: 'Worship the Lord your God, and serve him only.'" Then the devil left him, and angels came and attended him.

Matthew 4:1-11

Did you catch that? Jesus used scripture to resist and rebuke Satan! He could have defeated Satan a million ways, smite him on the spot, cast him into Sheol, have the ground eat him up, but no. He used God's Word as the truth and the weapon against Satan's lies. And more than that: notice that Paul only gives us one weapon. We could have had a bow, a javelin, a mace, but no. Just one sword, one weapon, because that is all we need. God's Word is all you need to attack the enemy.

I cannot stress this enough. You must know the Word of God to fight the enemy! How are you going to rebuke him if you don't know the Word? When I delivered myself from a large group of demons and sent them into the abyss, I did not do so on a whim. I had read God's Word before and understood that the abyss was a prison specifically where demons resided until the day an angel opened it. Can you imagine if all people who suffered from demonic attacks knew that they could get rid of them by casting them out into the abyss under Jesus' name and authority? Lives would be changed! Faiths would be strengthened!

In 2016, a video began circulating the internet of underground Chinese Christians receiving a luggage case filled with Bibles. When the luggage was opened, a multitude of people ran and reached out desperately to touch a copy of the Bible. It was as if they were reaching out for food and water. Once they got their hands on one, many of them kissed it and hugged it tightly. How is it possible that we, who live in free countries with religious freedom, ignore the Bible we already own? It is a shame that many Christian Americans today do not read their Bible when they have such an opportunity to do so. Worse, there is a danger to not knowing the Word, for God has made it clear:

> *My people are destroyed from lack of knowledge.*
>
> Hosea 4:6

I implore you, that if you get anything out of this book, that you equip yourself with the Sword of the Spirit. Pick up your Bible. You can do it! Forget about yesterday; you have the breath of life in you today. Turn the first page if you haven't done so and have God's Word at the ready so when the enemy comes, you can, just like our master Jesus did, rebuke him with God's Word.

Lastly, the Sword of the Spirit calls for prayer:

And pray in the Spirit on all occasions with all kinds of prayers and requests. With this in mind, be alert and always keep on praying for all the Lord's people.

Ephesians 6:18

Prayer is the means in which you access your resources. You have an arsenal of power behind you. In a single prayer, God can send angels to protect you. In a single prayer, you can unleash a torrent of power against the enemy. This is critical because, as believers, we are each other's support system.

I am beyond grateful for the close connection of believers in my life today. They have prayed instantly for me in my times of need and the results of the power of prayer have shown. Unfortunately, I have a family member who suffers from alcoholism. During times in which he drinks, he becomes violent against the family—to the point of even physically attacking his dad. When this happens though, I've asked for immediate prayer from my friends. They literally drop everything and pray in that moment, and within minutes, the event de-escalates. He leaves the house or goes to his room, but everyone is safe, and peace is restored.

Prayer is not to be underestimated. In another case, missionary John Patton resided in New Hebrides Islands along with his wife and children. One night, hostile natives surrounded John and his family with the intention of killing them. John prayed to God fervently for their deliverance. At dawn, they were surprised to be alive and find that the attackers had left. One year later, the chief of that once hostile tribe became a believer in Christ. Curious, John recalled that night and asked him why he and the other natives had not killed him and his family that night. The chief responded, "Well, who were all those men that were with you there?" John was perplexed because there had been no men with John and his family that night. "What are you talking about?" John replied.

The chief then said, "Well, we were afraid to attack because we saw hundreds of big men in shining garments with drawn swords. So we turned back."[16] This is the power of God. It is not limited to history. It is alive and powerful today. Don't ever doubt the power of prayer. Use it to protect yourself and others. Remember, the Sword of the Spirit can help your loved ones too.

The Sword of the Spirit in Action

Nothing compares to the feeling of discovering Jesus. I was ecstatic and so hopeful the day I accepted Christ. There was a skip to my step, and I felt like there was nothing that I couldn't do now. During this happiness, the enemy attacked me with sudden and negative thoughts that God didn't love me. I remember thinking specifically, "You really think God would ever forgive you after all you did?" At the time, I assumed these thoughts were mine, doubting my newfound salvation. I kept it a secret, but they continued on as the years went by.

It was not until I knew God's Word that a sense of security began to build. As I was walking around my local park one day, a thought came into my head, "God will never forgive you." Angry, I yelled, "STOP! That is not true! If we confess our sins, He forgives us and makes us new!" While I did not get the scripture from 1 John 1:9 completely accurate, this moment was the beginning of my fight back against the enemy. This is the first time I used the Sword of the Spirit. Eventually, as I grew more in God's Word, the fight became easier, because I now had more of God's Word to pull from.

Gear Up

These six pieces of armor make up the whole Armor of God. This is your uniform and the weapon for which you defend yourself from the merciless attacks of the enemy. Each piece, when secured, equips you with all the strength of our Creator firm on the ground with full force of faith. Nothing on this earth or on the spiritual planes can overthrow you when you are complete in His set. You are a warrior of God. Stand up and gear up. The time is now to take command of the battlefield.

ENCOUNTER #5
VORTEX

Living in Arcadia, California, was a turning point for me. The more I read the Bible, the less I was interested in working. I felt conflicted and could not explain it. It wasn't laziness, but more lack of ambition. The frequency of attacks and out of body experiences was getting stronger too, so it was hard to pretend like everything was okay at work.

As this was happening, I remember being outside of my body one night. I was pinned down and being bitten all over by many black shadow beings. I could feel their bites as I was surrounded by a huge vortex of red-orange fire. It was like a tornado made of fire with a large white light at the top. I did not know what was happening or where I was, but I remember chanting, "JESUS IS LORD!", over and over again as I was looking up.

After the experience was over, I felt calm and reflected on what had just happened. To this day, I still don't know exactly why this happened or where I was, but I am definitely sure of one thing: If those things were not pinning me down, I would have floated uncontrollably like a balloon to the top of that white light.

Chapter 10

COMMAND THE BATTLEFIELD

They shall be like mighty men, Who tread down their enemies In the mire of the streets in the battle. They shall fight because the Lord is with them, And the riders on horses shall be put to shame.

Zechariah 10:5

This is the answer you've been searching for. This chapter teaches you how to fight and get rid of any demons in your life. You know the enemy. You know his tactics. You've put on the Armor of God. Now is the time to do something about these attacks and deliver yourself from the enemy. The answer is simple, but it can be difficult to execute if you are not grounded in your faith. Do not fear. Whatever you face does not compare to the mighty power of God and the resources he places at your disposal. You are His warrior. Now fight!

Renunciate the Enemy

To fight is to be active. Being a Christian is not an adjective; it's a verb. Be vocal and command the enemy to defeat. Remember, just because you don't see the enemy directly does not mean that they are not there. You might be wondering what this looks like. It looks exactly as it sounds. Speak it. Say, for example, "I renounce all addiction to drugs, alcohol, or any legal or illegal substance that has bound me in the name of Jesus." Or say something like, "You have no authority over me in the name of Yeshua the Christ."

The words are the easiest part because there are no magic spells, no trinkets, or incantations. You are simply telling the enemy you know Whose you are from and that you will not partake in their games any longer. There's a caveat to this though and that's your faith. You will not be successful if you are not grounded in faith.

There have been times when demons are harassing people (myself included) and we invoke the name of Jesus to no avail. Why is that? Remember Acts 19:15 where the traveling Jews attempted to cast out demons and were overpowered by them? You require true faith to deliver yourself or someone.

If you are not currently suffering from physical manifestations, then delivering yourself from demons might be easier since you are not seeing the enemy directly. If you need privacy, close yourself in a room and take time to renounce the enemy in Jesus' name. Believe it. Trust in Him with full conviction. Use scripture from the Bible and refute the enemy's lies. If an evil thought or lie is whispered in your ear, act on it immediately.

Sometime ago, while commuting to work, I was enjoying a song or a sermon on Christian radio when suddenly a horrible thought crossed my mind: I'm not saved! Jesus doesn't love me! I remember yelling at the enemy in my car, rebuking his lie with John 3:16. I'm not sure what this must have looked like to the drivers that were next to me, but I didn't care. I refuse to let the enemy lie and deceive me into depression. Taking command of the battlefield means to engage. Use the Bible as your resource.

Example Prayer:
"I am strong in the LORD and in the power of His might" (Eph. 6:10).

Take ownership of your faith and activate it whenever you receive temptation, feel anger, resentment, or hear a lie from the enemy. This is how to attack the enemy. Use God's Word to rebuke them. Do not allow their lies to inhabit your mind. Be unashamed and speak it.

If you are suffering from physical manifestations (sleep paralysis, nightmares, visions, out of body experiences, shadows, possession, and so on), then know that your fight will be much more at the forefront. You and the enemy see each other face to face. This can be terrifying. These entities are horrid and a vivid reminder of hell's existence. Fear shoots up through your body as you literally see monsters. This is where true faith comes in.

In spite of the monstrosity that you see, you, like King David, must ground yourself in faith and know with all your heart that Jesus has power over them and will decimate them under His covering. This is your moment. Look at them in the face and take command of them.

You will see near the end of the book exactly how I managed to liberate myself from these demonic forces and fight them. It was very specific. I gave them direction knowing and believing full well in the authority that Christ gives me on His behalf. Whatever your circumstance is, the fight remains the same. You must face them head on and invoke the power of Jesus. Remember, they cannot hurt you if you are a believer in Christ. They have no power. They are eternally condemned and will be thrown in the lake of fire along with their master. There is nothing to fear from them.

Resistance

When you give the enemy "permission" into your life, whether through drugs, alcohol, sex, witchcraft, or other sinful practices, you are opening doors for the enemy. You are giving them access to affect all aspects of your life. Depending on which door you've opened, will determine the severity and type of attack you receive. Meaning, the more you delved into those doors, the more resistance you are going to get when you try to close them.

For example, John Ramirez's deliverance was much more violent and aggressive than for many others. After he decided to follow Christ, the enemy didn't make it easy for him. For a total of one month, he was under spiritual attack every single night, ranging from demons trying to strangle him to demons shaking the bed intensely and levitating him. Not being able to speak and fully paralyzed, John was helpless and at the mercy of the enemy. He had made commitments to them and they were not going to let him go.

It took a full affirmation of faith and commitment to Christ that finally allowed him to get rid of them. This happened to me as well. My demonic attacks grew in intensity the closer I got to Christ, but it took a full grounding of faith to finally expel them. Regardless of what doors you opened, when you are ready to fight, expect resistance from the enemy. They are not going to let you go easily. They will reveal themselves in full and try to cripple you with fear. Do not give in! Fight! Whatever they do or say believe that you serve the Most High and are protected by the blood of Jesus. They are nothing. Let them know their place and tell them to send them a message to their master: his time is short.

Make Your Choice

Something you must consider is the cost of what you are about to do and what you just did. Getting rid of the demons inside or around you requires something from you that changes your life forever. You see, keeping the enemy at bay means that your lifestyle will have to change. The sins you commit freely and the life that you live must be Christ-centered; after all, faith in Jesus is what delivers you from demons. This is probably the most difficult choice an unbeliever can make. Being a follower of Christ means following His teachings and instructions.

I once received a phone call from my friend who had just suffered from a demonic attack. I helped as much as I could, but deep down, I felt sorrow, knowing the choice she would have to make. It isn't enough to deliver yourself from the enemy and then continue living a lifestyle of sin. Jesus is so specific about the difference between the world and that of someone who picks up their cross. This choice doesn't ask you to be perfect. We are not called for perfection, but for repentance. I have fallen during my own walk and made plenty of mistakes, but that does not mean that I give up. You must get up and try to do better by Christ until your race is finished.

Consider this before you make your choice. A life free of demonic oppression is a life dedicated to our Messiah. The choice changes your life for the better, but know that you will have to change the way you live if you want to continue to be free.

Fight to the End

Remember to Whom you belong and Who has given you the strength to be victorious. As this life continues, our mind and bodies become tired, become diseased, and our flesh withers. Do not allow these circumstances to defeat you. Renew your strength in the Lord. It matters not if you are 19 years old or 99 years old. The Word of God carries the same strength It always has. Use it! Call upon it in your time of need.

Feel tired? Open your Bible to Matthew 11:28. Feel depressed? Turn to John 16:33. God is ready and willing to meet all of our needs; all you need to do is seek Him whole-heartedly, and He will speak to you directly.

We know the end of this story. The victory of this war belongs to God. And every single one of us has a part in this fight. So wrap around you the Belt of Truth, put on the Breastplate of Righteousness, slip on your feet the Gospel of Peace, raise up your Shield of Faith, secure your Helmet of Salvation, and grasp your Sword of the Spirit! You are a warrior of God and you have a fight to finish.

ENCOUNTER #6
BALLOON

I don't go out much, so in my free time, I usually stay home and rest. On an Arcadian Saturday, I took a nap as I usually did on my weekends. At some point during the nap, I floated up on the air to the ceiling in my room. I was calm, but perplexed, because I didn't know what was happening. I looked down and saw myself sleeping. I did not panic, but I was confused. The real me was invisible on the ceiling, but my body was down on the bed. Am I down there or am I up here? The more I began to actively think about these questions, the faster I returned to my body. When I went back to my body, I awoke and sat up in the silence of the room.

Chapter 11

FINISH THE FIGHT

For I am already being poured out as a drink offering, and the time of my departure is at hand. I have fought the good fight, I have finished the race, I have kept the faith. Finally, there is laid up for me the crown of righteousness, which the Lord, the righteous Judge, will give to me on that Day, and not to me only but also to all who have loved His appearing.

2 Timothy 4:6

A battle won is a time for celebration, but it is not the end of the fight. Deliverance from demons and the enemy marks only one victory of long-lasting battles to come. This fight continues until the very end of your life. The enemy does not sleep. The enemy does not rest. And the enemy will never give up on you. He will wait patiently if it means dragging you to hell with him. Each battle will be different, but they will be fights with the potential of victory nonetheless. Some of the earliest disciples and apostles knew this very well. In a letter to his mentor, the apostle Paul captured this sentiment and described the believer's journey to a race and a hard-fought fight.

For those who may not know, Paul was a mentor to Timothy (pastor of the church of Ephesus) for over a period of twenty years, and in this epistle or letter that dates back to about AD 67, Paul writes to Timothy a final piece of advice and a request to someone whom he sees as a son. His advice was to stay strong and endure in faith from the coming persecution. His request was for Timothy to come to Rome quickly, as Paul foresaw his upcoming death. In the letter, Paul used his life to illustrate for us a comparison of what it means to persevere and finish well. To help drive home the point, he included a precautionary depiction of what it is like to not finish the race at all:

> *Be diligent to come to me quickly; for Demas has forsaken me, having loved this present world, and has departed for Thessalonica*
>
> 2 Timothy 4:9

Here we have Paul and Demas, both believers and evangelists of the Gospel. One persevered and finished strong to receive the crown of righteousness and the other deserted his mentor for the love of the present world. While we don't know if Demas ever repented and continued on in his race or completely abandoned it, we do know that even a believer in Christ can abandon the race set forth for him by God.

When I first read these words from the apostle Paul to Timothy, I was astounded at Paul's confidence that he had finished well. I did not feel that way, so how could he? And when I talked about this with my family and friends, they would tell me not to worry so much about it—that I was young. The time to worry, they said, was when I was older. But you see, that is not true. Hebrews 9:27 tells us that we are all appointed to die once, and age is not a discriminating factor. I am not promised tomorrow, or next month, or next year. It can be disheartening to think of our race ending uncompleted or earlier than we hoped, but there is a comforting thought that Paul gifts to us: we are not alone in our race. In 1 Corinthians 15, Paul attributes his victory to the grace of God:

> *But by the grace of God I am what I am, and His grace toward me was not in vain; but I labored more abundantly than they all, yet not I, but the grace of God which was with me.*
>
> 1 Corinthians 15:10

You see, the grace of God is what allows us to be victorious in our race. And every believer in Christ is equipped with that grace to achieve the impossible and cross that finish line strong. In thinking of what it takes to finish the race well, just as Paul did, I thought of four things we can do to cross that finish line strongly: Have daily communion with God, put our faith into practice, render ourselves as a living sacrifice, and stand strong in the faith.

Daily Communion

Make God a part of your daily life. This is a simple thing to do that can sometimes be forgotten by the worries and duties of our everyday life. I used to think that God lives in a building, but remember, God is omniscient and omnipresent. I can call out to God anytime and anywhere! In fact, Jesus instructs us in Matthew 6:6 to pray in a private, secluded room!

We are not waiting on God; it is God who is waiting on us. Do you have a busy lifestyle? Put on Christian radio on your commute and spend a few minutes before work to pray. I put forth a challenge that you spend at least five minutes with God every day of the week. This is important, because spending time with God will keep you aligned in your race so when the enemy comes to you with deception, you are at the ready because you have a clear line of communication with God. Indeed, trust and believe that God hears and listens:

Now this is the confidence that we have in Him, that if we ask anything according to His will, He hears us.

1 John 5:14

He does hear us.

Application of Faith

Daily appropriation of the Gospel. What does that mean? First, we need to understand that the Gospel applies to all sinners. That's you and me. As Christians, we sometimes forget and assume that the Gospel is only for unbelievers, but that is incorrect. The Gospel is not for the righteous, but for sinners. Having understood that, we can apply our faith by activating our access to God because it is through Christ that we have access to the Father!

For through him we both have access to the Father by one Spirit.

Ephesians 2:18

How do we activate our faith then? We do it by putting it into practice. How many times have you been irritated or angry at your husband, wife, brother, or sister? You feel that anger build as it rises all the way up until words you wish you could take back come out of your mouth. If we had applied our faith in Christ as soon as we felt the first pinch of anger, we could have prevented hurting someone and become an example of the patience that God has for all of us.

How about worry? I was in McAllen, Texas, on vacation and the weather prognostic for the day of my flight was severe thunderstorms. Worry came in fast because I just knew that my flight was going to get cancelled and I didn't know what to do if it did. Were they going to give me a hotel? So many questions assaulted me at once, and then I remembered: it's okay. God is with me. He is in control.

At one point, I lived in Dallas, Texas, while doing some time for an internship opportunity. I didn't take my car, so every day, I would wake up before dawn to take the bus to get to work. After driving constantly for years, it was a very humbling and grateful experience to use public transportation. It was on the bus that I encountered an elderly mute woman who rode with me every day. While we never formally met, she was always kind and always smiled at me, and sometimes she even saved me a seat when the bus was full.

As a Californian in an entirely new state and city, I was not prepared for Texan thunderstorms. After leaving work one day, a big thunderstorm occurred and caused a traffic jam that deviated the bus from the original route. As the bus went off into unknown streets, I began to panic. I had no idea where I was. There was crazy thunder, rain and lightning everywhere. It got so bad that my landlord was worriedly messaging me, asking where I was so she could pick me up.

It was obvious that I was worried, because that mute woman caught my attention and did a motion with her hands I will never forget. She pushed both her hands down slowly, motioning me to relax, telling me that everything was going to be okay. In that moment, I immediately remembered my identity—whose I was. As a child of the Most High, I am always under His protection; I need not worry. I get emotional remembering her, because her simple motion and her kindness reminded me to apply my faith. I have access to God through Christ Jesus who is always with me in the midst of all my thunderstorms in life. All I need to do is activate my faith. We can all do this and apply the Gospel by:

PRAYING DAILY

Talk to God. It's that simple. As a new Christian, I didn't know how to pray. I didn't know if I should be reciting prayers from books, using objects, or using others to do it for me. Jesus makes it so simple to pray and instructs us to spend personal private time in prayer. I understand that our lives can become very hectic with very busy schedules. We work, we have families, we indulge in activities for entertainment, and I admit that I am culpable in this, but if we spend just five minutes in the morning and at night—shutting off the television and setting the phone aside—praying to God, your focus will redirect back to our Creator and, in turn, align you to the race track.

PARTICIPATING IN FELLOWSHIP

This is a big one. I spent the majority of my Christian life alone, exploring many churches and leaving them for what I deemed unbiblical doctrine. It is a very lonely and challenging road this way. Ecclesiastes 4 tells us that:

Two are better than one, because they have a good return for their labor: If either of them falls down, one can help the other up. But pity anyone who falls and has no one to help them up.

Ecclesiastes 4:9

I experienced true fellowship for the first time when I joined a local congregation called Orcutt Christian Church. After years of searching, I finally decided to try and attend one of their services. I will never forget my first day because of the amount of love I received from strangers who had just met me. The unconditional love that I didn't deserve was a clear reflection of God's love for us. I felt right at home.

I remember a beautiful sister in Christ, Heather. Her joy and excitement to see me and her warm embrace really captured a sense of unity and home that I was looking for. Through time, my pastor and the members of the church aided me in my times of need and prayed over me when I was in need. That support is like no other. I cannot tell you how many times God has used the members of this church to speak to me directly when I needed it. This is why fellowship is so important to the Gospel. We are each other's support so that when we fall or deviate from our path, we are there to pick each other up and continue in the race.

READING THE BIBLE

Reading the Bible can be daunting, because there is a misconception that the Bible is difficult to understand. Remember the grace of God that Paul mentioned? It lives in you! Reading the Bible is an active practice because God is talking to you as you read it. In my biggest troubles, a specific verse that I was casually reading was the answer I was looking for. A chapter a day or a one-year Bible plan are great ways to begin reading and getting to know God directly from His Word.

Render Yourself as Sacrifice

There are times in your race when your flesh will rebel to what God's will is for you. It is natural for human beings to be afraid, apathetic, and unwilling to move forward into the unknown. While my time as a follower of Christ seems short at six years as of this writing, I can tell you that I was very guilty of this fear and apathy early in my walk. God would place me in situations that I did not want to be in.

I remember feeling relief after graduating from Long Beach University. To finally go home with my family is what I had always wanted—no more driving in Los Angeles traffic, no more isolation! I would get to be with my friends! Well, God had a different plan for me.

I had applied to NBC Universal's Page Program, and after a grueling three interviews, I remember walking out of that building knowing with absolute certainty that I had gotten the job, but I felt completely unwilling to do it. I remember thinking, "God don't make do it! I want to be home, not here." What could I possibly do in that city where people have grown so cold? So what ended up happening? I learned the biggest lessons in my life while working there and grew to know God more than I had ever before. I got to publicly share my testimony with my friends and loved ones. Remember that isolation? I was able to read the Bible in its entirety for the very first time. And I learned to forgive others and my past. All of that was only possible because of that decision to do what I did not want to do.

You see, the most monumental moments of our lives come through unfamiliarity, change, and delving into the unknown. Surrender your will to God who knows and wants the best for you and for others. This is confirmed in 2 John 6:

This is love, that we walk according to His commandments. This is the commandment, that as you have heard from the beginning, you should walk in it.

2 John 6

We surrender our lives as a sacrifice by obeying God's commands. The next time you feel that surge of fear or rebellion of something you feel inside your bones that God wants you to do, just release your will and give it God. Take a breath. Envelop yourself in His wisdom and obey. Take the leap and jump. For Jeremiah 29:11 tells us:

"For I know the plans I have for you," declares the Lord, "plans to prosper you and not to harm you, plans to give you hope and a future."

Jeremiah 29:11

Remember this:
I can **TRUST** in His promises.
I can **OBEY** in His commands.
I can **RECEIVE** in His blessings.

We are in good Hands!

Stand Strongly in Faith

Lastly, in order to finish well, you must stand strongly in the faith. There have been and will continue to be times in which you will have to defend your identity in Christ.

But in your hearts revere Christ as Lord. Always be prepared to give an answer to everyone who asks you to give the reason for the hope that you have. But do this with gentleness and respect.

1 Peter 3:15

There are two things Peter means by being prepared to give an answer:

Defend the FAITH

While it is impossible to know everything as it pertains to God and His creation, there is a vast amount of information that we can still learn. Pastor John McArthur said, "You are the only Bible that some unbelievers will ever read." I have found this to be true. To many people, you are a walking Bible and a point of contact should they ever have questions about Christianity.

Much of my time these past few years have been spent answering questions from unbelievers. While not an expert, I have gained a passion and admiration for apologetics, because the evidence that atheists ask for has fortified my faith. For example, thanks to technology, I've communicated with my cousins through an online voice chat server for about three years now. This communication was slowly becoming a daily practice, and the taboo that was my Christian testimony was finally discussed when one of them asked me about it.

This sparked endless hours of discussion and conversations, many of them having questions about the Bible, God, and Jesus. While some have remained in their atheistic views, one of them now believes in God. Why? Because after a myriad of questions and discussions about topics even some Christians deem taboo—creation, the flood, the authenticity of the resurrection, and the Bible—they have come to a greater understanding of the Bible and God because they asked a Christian.

While I don't have all the answers (and I admit it can be difficult sometimes when the questions come at you faster than you can explain them), I am able to share evidence for my faith, because I too was once curious about the authenticity of God's truth. Reflect on which questions you have today and seek answers. We have a myriad of resources online, videos, audio sermons, and each other.

Use Your LIFE as Evidence

We are the biggest advocates for Christ. Our lives are reflections of the Messiah who lives in us. In college, I was always suspicious of Christian students. Why were they talking to me? Why were they so nice? I want to be like that! Our lives are a testament to the existence and goodness of God's love for His children. It is a heavy responsibility, but a perfect tool to share the Gospel to others. Defending the faith and using your life as evidence builds perseverance. And trust me, we will need it as we continue in our race. And always remember: Be UNASHAMED of the Gospel!

Conclusion

With the full Armor of God on you and your sights set to the finish line, let's reflect on what you can do to finish well:

1. Daily Communion with God
2. Application of the Faith
3. Render Yourself as Sacrifice
4. Stand Strongly in the Faith

We are all at different points in our race. If you've been running long and have grown tired, have been praying less, have been reading the Bible less, have been missing church, leave it in the past. It's okay! You are alive today. You have the breath of life as you are reading this! Get that second wind in you and finish strong so that as we near our last breath and are close to that finish line we can be confident like Paul was almost 2,000 years ago and say, "I have fought the good fight. I have kept the faith!" In 1 Corinthians 9:24, we read:

Do you not know that those who run in a race all run, but one receives the prize? Run in such a way that you may obtain it.

1 Corinthians 9:24

And what a prize it is that we strive for! How amazing it is to think of the day when we cross that finish line, when Jesus places a crown on your head, and says to you, "Well done!" He is faithful to His promise!

His lord said to him, "Well done, good and faithful servant; you have been faithful over a few things, I will make you ruler over many things. Enter into the joy of your lord."

Matthew 25:23

What a wonderful day it will be when we hear those words!

Some of you may be thinking, well Luis, I am not saved. I am not a believer, and I'm not sure I believe in this prize. I tell you today is the day of salvation! What is it you need or are waiting for? I offer my life as testimony to the goodness that God has done in me. Is my life not better for my faith? Am I not healed from fear and sadness? I extend to you an invitation into eternity with our Savior who lived a sinless life and took upon Him the horrible death of crucifixion to absolve us of our sins. Receive the love that God has for you and begin your conversation with your Father today.

I want to reassure you that while the spiritual fight continues until your death, so does the presence of God in your life. We are not alone in our race. Though the body ages and weakens, our faith grows and becomes stronger with every battle won alongside Jesus. Let's finish the fight. Get up and move forward. We may not cross the finish line together, but we will see each other on the other side and share eternity together.

FINISH THE FIGHT

PART II

THE LAST GENERATION

INTRODUCTION

"Now learn this parable from the fig tree: When its branch has already become tender, and puts forth leaves, you know that summer is near. So you also, when you see these things happening, know that He is near—at the doors! Assuredly, I say to you, this generation will by no means pass away till all these things take place. Heaven and earth will pass away, but My words will by no means pass away."

Mark 13:28-30

Now that you understand spiritual warfare in your life today, it is time to understand what is coming for the last generation. Through God's will, you have been selected to live as the last generation. You get to live out the final pages of the Bible and have a front row seat at the events that bring in the long awaited return of Messiah. Whether you like it or not, the world as you know it will change and you will have to make definitive choices on earth that will affect your eternity. Unlike your previous fight in the invisible realm, spiritual warfare during the last generation is different. Living during this time will require you to make choices that might cost you your life or that of your loved ones on earth. Living in the last pages of the Bible means the war comes to the physical world. The barriers are gone and the Day of the Lord has come. Brace yourself and gear up for the end of the age. Jesus is here.

Chapter 12

SIGNS OF THE END

As Jesus was sitting on the Mount of Olives, the disciples came to him privately. "Tell us," they said, "when will this happen, and what will be the sign of your coming and of the end of the age?

2 Corinthians 10:3-4

As a child growing up, I was always afraid of the world ending. The process of dying was confounding and despairing as it was, so the thought of the entire world as I knew it coming to a catastrophic close terrified me to my core. Seeing the news headlines and reports in the 1990s all seemed conclusive that the world was in degradation. I would often hear conversations among my parents and family members that often included the casual, "the world is ending," tagline that sent shivers down my spine.

Even though I didn't know that God was there, I was afraid of His creation. The sound of thunder or the power of the windstorms that hit my bedroom window—a sudden reminder of a much greater being in control of the world—were all fearful signs of the inevitable. As time went on, I weighed the cultural events around the world and observed the reactions of people to them. The failures of Y2K, the 2012 Mayan prophecy, and even Nostradamus' writings all gave certainty to the arguments by many that despite every generation's claim that they are the last, the world was not going to end.

I will never forget reading the New Testament for the first time, because I finally received an answer and timeline of what was to come. My understanding of Jesus' second coming was nothing like what I read in the Scriptures. The signs. The events. These were all simple to understand, just like the coming of a season.

Even learning this though, I never imagined I would live in the last generation—the generation that would suffer through the Great Tribulation, that would see the breaking of the seals, the trumpets, and the bowls—all for one glorious conclusion: to see Jesus descending from the clouds and collecting His remnant. I must admit that even as a believer, I was fearful because the coming times are not only cataclysmic for unbelievers but will also be some of the most trying times for us Christians.

Many of us will be designated for execution, persecuted from a tyrannical global government, or afflicted by starvation. Despite how grim the times will be, the Hope that is coming trumps all feelings of despair. We are living in the last pages of the Bible, and for me, it is not a time of fear, but of faith.

Brothers and sisters in Christ, now is the time to demonstrate our faith. It is our time to proclaim His name to a world seeking answers. The harvest is ripe, and the time we've been waiting for is near. Just as Jesus has said, "Look up…for your redemption is near."

Directly from the Source

As I write this, it seems the world is in turmoil and disorder. Quarantine during the global spread of the Covid-19 Coronavirus, the increase in climate change and weather phenomena, to the raging fires in California, the Amazon rainforest, and in Australia; the world seems to get worse. Just in the beginning of January 2020, the members of the Bulletin of the Atomic Scientists declared the "Doomsday Clock" at 100 seconds to midnight.[17]

Seeing the world burn and in disarray can be enough for anyone to speculate or scoff at the thought of the world ending soon. Now, I must affirm that the world will indeed end someday and very specifically. It will not happen as a result of an asteroid, a gamma ray burst, or even nuclear catastrophe like many documentaries speculate. No. The end of the age comes at the second coming of Christ in a finale of warfare with all the weapons the enemy has mustered in Megiddo and all pointing at Him in the sky. That will be the end of the age. But to know how we get to that moment requires us to discard speculation and go straight to the source: the Bible.

We are fortunate to know what signs accompany the last days before His coming, because Jesus Himself lets us know multiple times across the four Gospels and New Testament revelations. In response to his disciples regarding the signs of His second coming and the end of the age, Jesus states:

> *"Take heed that no one deceives you. For many will come in My name, saying, 'I am the Christ,' and will deceive many. And you will hear of wars and rumors of wars. See that you are not troubled; for all these things must come to pass, but the end is not yet. For nation will rise against nation, and kingdom against kingdom. And there will be famines, pestilences, and earthquakes in various places. All these are the beginning of sorrows. Then they will deliver you up to tribulation and kill you, and you will be hated by all nations for My name's sake. And then many will be offended, will betray one another, and will hate one another. Then many false prophets will rise up and deceive many. And because lawlessness will abound, the love of many will grow cold. But he who endures to the end shall be saved. And this Gospel of the kingdom will be preached in all the world as a witness to all the nations, and then the end will come."*
>
> Matthew 24:4-14

The first sentence Jesus begins with can arguably be the most important (since it is a preface to everything He is about to impart). To "take heed" or "be sure" that no one deceives you serves as a caution and a warning to be knowledgeable and discerning of what is real truth against the coming falsehood in the name and image of Christ. The second sentence goes further into this assertion by describing that many will come in His name and attempt to usurp His authority.

Currently, in my walk, I see this pattern in action today. There is no denying or debating that every single believer is the bride of Christ and that we make up the church (see 1 Corinthians 12). Yet, why do hundreds of denominations exist today? Why do Lutherans, Baptists, Jehovah's Witnesses, or Catholics exist today? Aren't (or shouldn't) we all be one unit as scripture dictates? We all believe in the One Christ, right?

This is why it is crucial that we take heed and that we are not deceived by the various interpretations of Who Christ is. When I first began to read the Bible, I was shocked at how little I actually knew about Jesus. The Jesus I thought I knew was not the Jesus that was in scripture. The more I learned, the more I began a search for the right church. Like dominoes falling one by one, I left them as soon as I discovered a contradiction of practice according to what was written in the Bible. After some time, I stopped searching because I was so discouraged at the division that I saw and experienced. More discouraging was the fact that many in those denominations were so unwilling to question or analyze what was a man-made tradition and what was actually biblical.

Today, I simply describe myself as a member of the church of Christ, because that's what I am. I believe in Jesus as the Messiah as He is dictated in both the Old and New Testament. With that said, I am not here to judge or condemn others for a selected denomination they choose to take membership in. But I do ask that you take Jesus' warning seriously and learn Who He is. Don't allow others to dictate Who He is for you. Discover Him yourself by researching and reading your Bible.

After some words of encouragement, Jesus then dictates each of the coming signs one by one. Nation will rise against nation, famines, pestilences, and earthquakes. All of these the beginning of sorrows. It goes without saying that these events are already occurring. The World Wars and the current global political instability is a vivid description of the kingdoms rising against kingdoms.

Famine ravishes countries suffering from poverty. According to Action Against Hunger, despite the fact that more than enough food is produced to feed the global population, more than 820 million people go hungry a year.[18] The current state of world hunger doesn't even account for the incoming famines projected by the United Nations. Due to the Coronavirus of 2020, the United Nations' World Food Programme has coined the term "mega-famines" as a warning if poverty level countries are not financially funded.[19] From the 2002 SARS outbreak, H1N1, the Zika virus, the 2010 Swine Flu, the Ebola virus, and to 2020s Covid-19 Coronavirus, the pestilences increase in frequency and magnitude.

So is the case with earthquakes. News headlines such as 2018 Live Science publication, "Tons of Major Quakes Have Rattled the World Recently. Does That Mean Anything?", give credence to what we all know is currently happening.[20] The US Geological Survey in 2020 cited more than 500 earthquakes near the Puerto Rico region alone.[21] These signs are easy to identify. Many people across social media masquerade their innate fear of the truth with humor by attempting to laugh at the state of the earth, but they know…they know the time they've most feared is here.

The second portion of His message is for the believer: be prepared for the tribulation and harm that will befall on you because of Him. This is an important notion to consider for a follower of Christ because this will be a personal sign that you will experience. You will be hated (or killed) for proclaiming your faith in Jesus. We've seen this shortly after the ascension of the Messiah during the persecution of the early church by the Roman empire, but we are ramping up to see the conclusion of this today. Many in our society describe Bible believing Christians as "bigots" for affirming their faith and defending God's law. Worse yet, many false prophets are indeed deceiving many today through prosperity Gospel or antichrist doctrines. Despite these troubling signs, Jesus reassures us that those who endure to the end will be saved. This, in combination with Him letting us know that these things must come to pass before His coming, is comforting. To survive or die in faith for Him is to pick up and follow our cross.

The last sign in this scripture, however, is quite interesting, because it is now very viable in our day. Before His second coming, the Gospel must be preached to all the world. The advent of the internet has made this much more possible along with hundreds, if not thousands, of missionaries that go all over the world to preach the good news to the most remote locations possible. In fact, American missionary John Chau preached the Gospel to the North Sentinel Island isolated tribe in 2018 for the very first time. This cost him his life, but he preached the Gospel to those who had never heard it, bringing us closer to the fulfillment Jesus described.

As in the Days of Noah and Lot

Jesus made references that all people understood to explain His second coming. He utilized two well-known events from Genesis to facilitate understanding for all, Noah and Lot:

As it was in the days of Noah, so it will be at the coming of the Son of Man. For in the days before the flood, people were eating and drinking, marrying and giving in marriage, up to the day Noah entered the ark; and they knew nothing about what would happen until the flood came and took them all away. That is how it will be at the coming of the Son of Man.

Matthew 24:37-39

Using a correlation to the days of Noah to an audience of Jews well aware of the event served as a vivid illustration of what the world will be like right before His coming. He notes that the majority of the human population will live according to their desires and practice their status quo until Jesus comes swiftly and quickly without warning. Comparably, Jesus also uses a similar example in the times of Lot.

Likewise as it was also in the days of Lot: They ate, they drank, they bought, they sold, they planted, they built; but on the day that Lot went out of Sodom it rained fire and brimstone from heaven and destroyed them all. Even so will it be in the day when the Son of Man is revealed.

Luke 17:28-30

If you delve deeper into what those days of Noah and Lot, you get an in-depth look into what those days really were. For that answer, all you have to do is go back to the beginning: Genesis. For Noah, wickedness was at an all-time high with humans thinking evil continually—enough for God to regret creating man. The times of Lot give a clearer picture as to the type of wickedness that Noah's time could have referred to:

Then the men rose from there and looked toward Sodom, and Abraham went with them to send them on the way. 17 And the LORD said, "Shall I hide from Abraham what I am doing, since Abraham shall surely become a great and mighty nation, and all the nations of the earth shall be blessed in him? For I have known him, in order that he may command his children and his household after him, that they keep the way of the LORD, to do righteousness and justice, that the LORD may bring to Abraham what He has spoken to him." And the LORD said, "Because the outcry against Sodom and Gomorrah is great, and because their sin is very grave, I will go down now and see whether they have done altogether according to the outcry against it that has come to Me; and if not, I will know.

Genesis 18:16-21

In context, Lot was residing in Sodom apart from Abraham, the latter having just been visited by three angels. Right away, we understand the reason for the incoming judgement on Sodom and Gomorrah. The outcry against those cities is so high and their sin so great that it was deemed a judgement of termination necessary. After Abraham pleads with God to save the righteous (if any) that live in that city, God sends two angels to fulfill Abraham's request:

The two angels arrived at Sodom in the evening, and Lot was sitting in the gateway of the city. When he saw them, he got up to meet them and bowed down with his face to the ground. "My lords," he said, "please turn aside to your servant's house. You can wash your feet and spend the night and then go on your way early in the morning."

"No," they answered, "we will spend the night in the square."

But he insisted so strongly that they did go with him and entered his house. He prepared a meal for them, baking bread without yeast, and they ate. Before they had gone to bed, all the men from every part of the city of Sodom—both young and old—surrounded the house. They called to Lot, "Where are the men who came to you tonight? Bring them out to us so that we can have sex with them."

Lot went outside to meet them and shut the door behind him and said, "No, my friends. Don't do this wicked thing. Look, I have two daughters who have never slept with a man. Let me bring them out to you, and you can do what you like with them. But don't do anything to these men, for they have come under the protection of my roof."

"Get out of our way," they replied. "This fellow came here as a foreigner, and now he wants to play the judge! We'll treat you worse than them." They kept bringing pressure on Lot and moved forward to break down the door. But the men inside reached out and pulled Lot back into the house and shut the door. Then they struck the men who were at the door of the house, young and old, with blindness so that they could not find the door.

The two men said to Lot, "Do you have anyone else here—sons-in-law, sons or daughters, or anyone else in the city who belongs to you? Get them out of here, because we are going to destroy this place. The outcry to the LORD against its people is so great that he has sent us to destroy it. So Lot went out and spoke to his sons-in-law, who were pledged to marry his daughters. He said, "Hurry and get out of this place, because the LORD is about to destroy the city!" But his sons-in-law thought he was joking. With the coming of dawn, the angels urged Lot, saying, "Hurry! Take your wife and your two daughters who are here, or you will be swept away when the city is punished."

When he hesitated, the men grasped his hand and the hands of his wife and of his two daughters and led them safely out of the city, for the LORD was merciful to them. As soon as they had brought them out, one of them said, "Flee for your lives! Don't look back, and don't stop anywhere in the plain! Flee to the mountains or you will be swept away!"

Genesis 19:1-17

Aside from the wickedness of society during Noah and Lot's time, the citizens of the earth were all caught off guard before God's judgement. This is the message that Jesus is conveying to the last generation. He will come like a thief in the night—at a time in which the world will be living their lives according to their normalcy. This is one of the most important messages Jesus has for us. Be prepared. Have your lamp lit and ready. Jesus completes his statement and concludes that their punishment will be the same as the punishment of those cities. Just like the day that Lot exited Sodom, so too shall it be at His coming. Fire and brimstone rained from heaven and destroyed them all, meaning that those unprepared will suffer the same fate.

From the Prophets of Old

One of the most incredible aspects of the Bible is prophecy. Prophecy is a prediction of a future event. Because God is eternal and created time, He knows the beginning and the end in complete accuracy. The composition of prophetic writings account for 26.8% of the Bible, resulting in 1,817 prophecies alone.[22] This demonstrates God's reliability as the only living and true God. Jesus fulfilled over 100 prophecies given before His coming that ranged from 400 to 1500 years before His birth.

One of the most incredulous prophecies was the restoration of Israel as a nation. After the dispersion or "Jewish diaspora" due to Roman wars between 66 AD to 136 AD, it seemed impossible that Jews would ever return to their homeland. After centuries of occupation from the Ottoman Empire, Britain, and Arab Palestinians, the prospects of God's promise to Abraham seemed weakened. But God prepared us and set a marker that Jesus' second coming would not occur until Israel returns to its land following exile:

This is the word that came to Jeremiah from the LORD: "This is what the LORD, the God of Israel, says: 'Write in a book all the words I have spoken to you. The days are coming,' declares the LORD, 'when I will bring my people Israel and Judah back from captivity and restore them to the land I gave their ancestors to possess,' says the LORD." These are the words the LORD spoke concerning Israel and Judah: "This is what the LORD says:

> *Cries of fear are heard—*
> *terror, not peace.*
> *Ask and see:*
> *Can a man bear children?*
> *Then why do I see every strong man*
> *with his hands on his stomach like a woman in labor,*
> *every face turned deathly pale?*

> *How awful that day will be!*
> *No other will be like it.*
> *It will be a time of trouble for Jacob,*
> *but he will be saved out of it.*
> *"'In that day,' declares the LORD Almighty,*
> *'I will break the yoke off their necks*
> *and will tear off their bonds;*
> *no longer will foreigners enslave them.*
> *Instead, they will serve the LORD their God*
> *and David their king,*
> *whom I will raise up for them.*
> *"'So do not be afraid, Jacob my servant;*
> *do not be dismayed, Israel,'*
> *declares the LORD.*
> *'I will surely save you out of a distant place,*
> *your descendants from the land of their exile.*
> *Jacob will again have peace and security,*
> *and no one will make him afraid.*
> *I am with you and will save you,'*
> *declares the LORD.*
> *'Though I completely destroy all the nations*
> *among which I scatter you,*
> *I will not completely destroy you.*
> *I will discipline you but only in due measure;*
> *I will not let you go entirely unpunished.'"*
>
> Jeremiah 30:1-11

This prophecy was fulfilled on May 14, 1948, when Head of the Jewish Agency, David Ben-Gurion, declared establishment of the state of Israel, officially joining the United Nations as a state in 1949.[23] While Israel's existence today may seem normal for us that have been alive these past few decades, Israel's return to their promised land is a monumental moment in fulfilled biblical prophecy. Never in the history of the world has a lost civilization come back from dispersion, retaining their culture, language, customs, and native identity as the Jewish people did.

More importantly, this event solidified God's Word as truth. For years, atheists used the impossibility of Israel ever returning as a nation to discredit the Bible. Preachers before 1948 had to retain their faith in believing that an event such as this would be possible in a time where it was deemed inconceivable. Under the leadership of David Ben-Gurion, this monumental moment in history became even more miraculous when Israel was attacked by Iraq, Lebanon, Egypt, Syria, and Jordan immediately following Israel's midnight declaration of independence.

Despite being outnumbered, Israel won the war and even passed the 60% proposed territory markup proposed by the U.N. settlement plan. Unable to defeat the newborn state of Israel, Egypt, Jordan, and Syria returned to attack again in 1967 in what became the Six-Day War. Using Yom Kippur, the holiest day of the Jewish calendar, the three Arab nations executed a surprise attack on Israel.[24] Egypt attacked through the Sinai Peninsula, while Syria attacked from the north. Completely surprised, unprepared, outgunned, and outnumbered, Israel counter-attacked and won against all three nations. In just three hours, the Egyptian air force was destroyed. It took two more hours to destroy the Syrian Air Force and only minutes to eliminate the Jordanians. Within the first hours of the war, Israel annihilated the airpower of its enemies. This victory allowed for the capture of the entire Golan Heights territory from Syria, the Sinai Peninsula (including the Gaza Strip) from Egypt, and the West Bank and East Jerusalem from Jordan. Now having four times the amount of territory, this should have been enough for the world to see that God's Word is incorruptible.

But what does this have to do with the last days? Well, Jesus cannot come until Israel is gathered once more as a nation. And it is now. This fulfilled prophecy now allows the sequence of events that set of the final years of the age.

To the Disciples of Late

We are fortunate to have testimonies and teachings from Jesus and His disciples in writing. Following Jesus' ascension, the disciples seemed to be on their own to evangelize the Gospel to the world, but the New Testament writings and letters offer evidence that they were truly led by the

Holy Spirit—just as Jesus had promised in John 14:26. Under direction from the Holy Spirit, the disciples were able to transcend the chronology of time and interpret to all remaining generations the things to come.

Then Peter stood up with the Eleven, raised his voice and addressed the crowd: "Fellow Jews and all of you who live in Jerusalem, let me explain this to you; listen carefully to what I say. These people are not drunk, as you suppose. It's only nine in the morning! No, this is what was spoken by the prophet Joel:

"'In the last days, God says,
I will pour out my Spirit on all people.
Your sons and daughters will prophesy,
your young men will see visions,
your old men will dream dreams.

Even on my servants, both men and women,
I will pour out my Spirit in those days,
and they will prophesy.
I will show wonders in the heavens above
and signs on the earth below,
blood and fire and billows of smoke.
The sun will be turned to darkness
and the moon to blood
before the coming of the great and glorious day of the Lord.
And everyone who calls
on the name of the Lord will be saved.'"

Acts 2:14-21

This scripture and reference to the prophet Joel not only describes the power of the Holy Spirit in the disciples but also provides a prophetic message to all living in the last generation. It's you who will receive His Spirit. Your relationship with God will allow Him to show you the things to come in prophecy, visions, and dreams. Throughout my walk, I have read testimonies and seen countless videos of babies, children, teenagers, and adults having dreams of things to come or having prophetic visions of the end. These powerful experiences should be tested with discernment, but should also be considered, as many of them are biblical. I have had a few such experiences myself during my walk.

For example, I once had a vivid dream of a city being destroyed by bombs. Another one I had was of a large tsunami engulfing a large group of people. Unlike normal dreams, these are much more vivid and memorable. You don't forget them, and they stick with you because you know deep down that these things are coming and that His return is near.

The physical signs of blood moons, strange phenomena in the sky, and the strange signs all over the world all reflect the season of the end of the age. In combination with the prophecies and visions of fellow believers, the picture becomes clear, and the time for harvest draws near.

The World Today

But know this, that in the last days perilous times will come: For men will be lovers of themselves, lovers of money, boasters, proud, blasphemers, disobedient to parents, unthankful, unholy, unloving, unforgiving, slanderers, without self-control, brutal, despisers of good, traitors, headstrong, haughty, lovers of pleasure rather than lovers of God, having a form of godliness but denying its power. And from such people turn away! For of this sort are those who creep into households and make captives of gullible women loaded down with sins, led away by various lusts, always learning and never able to come to the knowledge of the truth. Now as Jannes and Jambres resisted Moses, so do these also resist the truth: men of corrupt minds, disapproved concerning the faith; but they will progress no further, for their folly will be manifest to all, as theirs also was.

2 Timothy 3:1-9

I was living in Arcadia, California, when I first read the scripture above and was struck by how relevant it was to my time. The descriptions of people being lovers of themselves fits exactly to the culture today. Selfies, social media "likes," and the self-indulgence of today's society hit hard, especially since I was working in the entertainment industry at the time. As I kept reading, the more the reality of the time sunk in. Disobedience to parents is rampant—I have witnessed so many strangers and even children in my family outright disrespect their parents through physical violence or profanity when they spoke to them. Television shows, like *Keeping Up with the Kardashians* or *Teen Mom*, both propagate this behavior so that it feeds into the youth's culture.

When has a time so clearly reflected the prophetic words of Paul? Unthankful, unholy, unloving, unforgiving, slanderers, without self-control are all adjectives that describe the world I experienced every day. More damning is the fact that people are lovers of pleasure rather than lovers of God. This new movement of "self-love" and "my truth" all focus on the self and completely disregard our Creator. This new age religion, with celebrity advocates and many other media personalities, push forth the description of the days before the end. They have eliminated what is truth and have designated your self-defined truth as the actual truth. This all falls under the perilous times described above and the timing of the last days.

We are here. Even if some of you reading this don't believe it, you know deep in your soul that the world is falling into degradation. I felt this even as an unbeliever in my time. I knew the world was going to end even as a child. The signs are everywhere, and the hour is late. Now is the time to look up!

If you haven't received Christ as your Savior, now is the time of Salvation! Take that first step and talk to Him today. It matters not what you did in your past. He is the Redeemer and cleanser of our sins. Ask for repentance and submit yourself to Him while you still have the breath of life!

For fellow believers, it is a time for preparation and evaluation. If you call yourself a follower of Jesus, it is time to practice faith in action. But first, Jesus asks you to recognize which revelatory church you belong to.

SIGNS OF THE END

ENCOUNTER #7
THE SHADOWS

I have fond memories of Arcadia because of my time in solitude. The more isolated I am, the more I talk to God. I was lucky to live in a very affordable house in a very expensive city. My room was the size of a closet space with just a bed and a hanging closet. One night, I opened my eyes and saw black shadows amongst my hanging clothes. At first, I thought my eyes were imagining shapes amidst the darkness, but they kept moving and shifting. The more I began to focus, the clearer I saw them. They weren't just there, but they were moving closer to me. I panicked and sat up to get a closer view to make sure, and as I hit the light, there was nothing there.

Chapter 13

THE SEVEN CHURCHES

Write, therefore, what you have seen, what is now and what will take place later. The mystery of the seven stars that you saw in my right hand and of the seven golden lampstands is this: The seven stars are the angels of the seven churches, and the seven lampstands are the seven churches.

Revelation 1:19-20

Sometime around 95 AD, John was exiled to the Grecian island of Patmos, where he received a revelation of what was to come from Jesus. Now known today as the book of Revelation, these writings concerning the things to come have become synonymous with cataclysmic end of the world events that decimate the earth and its people—all leading to the second coming of Messiah Jesus. The following accounts of John's visions and conversations with angels and holies in heaven tell of what has passed, what must come to pass, and what will pass in eternity.

Jesus begins His revelation to John with an evaluation of seven physical churches located in Asia Minor (of what is modern day Turkey). In context, the messages are written to each of these specific churches and serve a specific purpose to a direct group of people. Similar to the parables Jesus gave during His ministry, He incredibly adds an entire layer of meaning that applies to every believer alive: you.

You represent one of these churches based on your current state and relationship with Jesus. As you read the following assessments from Jesus, open your heart. Let His truth sink inside you. If you feel guilty or a heavy feeling, be at ease. That feeling is a feeling of conviction in your heart and the beginning of a change in the right direction. Remember, Jesus gives these churches the opportunity to repent and change their ways. The same applies to you. So long as you are alive, the time to correct yourself and re-establish your relationship with Him is today.

The Loveless Church in Ephesus

To the angel of the church in Ephesus write:
These are the words of him who holds the seven stars in his right hand and walks among the seven golden lampstands. I know your deeds, your hard work and your perseverance. I know that you cannot tolerate wicked people, that you have tested those who claim to be apostles but are not, and have found them false. You have persevered and have endured hardships for my name, and have not grown weary.

Yet I hold this against you: You have forsaken the love you had at first. Consider how far you have fallen! Repent and do the things you did at first. If you do not repent, I will come to you and remove your lampstand from its place. But you have this in your favor: You hate the practices of the Nicolaitans, which I also hate.

Whoever has ears, let them hear what the Spirit says to the churches. To the one who is victorious, I will give the right to eat from the tree of life, which is in the paradise of God.

Revelation 2:1-7

Jesus begins His message to the Ephesian church by commending the fervor to which the church members have discerned and persevered through hardships in His name. This is impressive, since Greek and Roman culture in Ephesus around 90 AD delved greatly into pagan worship as well as in idolatry. Acts 19 gives an insight into the population Paul had to contend with in Ephesus:

"So not only is this trade of ours in danger of falling into disrepute, but also the temple of the great goddess Diana may be despised and her magnificence destroyed, whom all Asia and the world worship." Now when they heard this, they were full of wrath and cried out, saying, "Great is Diana of the Ephesians!'

Acts 19:27-28

Jesus also notes that this church also hates the practices of the Nicolaitans as He does. While there is some debate about the Hebrew and Greek compound of the term, Iranaeus, the author of *Adversus Haereses* asserts that Nicolaitans were heretical followers of Nicolaus, the proselyte of Antioch mentioned in Acts 6:5.

Despite this praise, Jesus makes a profound critique: They have forgotten their first love. What does He mean and how is it possible for such a devoted church to have fallen so greatly? The answer is in Matthew 22:

Hearing that Jesus had silenced the Sadducees, the Pharisees got together. One of them, an expert in the law, tested him with this question: "Teacher, which is the greatest commandment in the Law?"

Jesus replied: "'Love the Lord your God with all your heart and with all your soul and with all your mind.' This is the first and greatest commandment. And the second is like it: 'Love your neighbor as yourself.' All the Law and the Prophets hang on these two commandments."

Matthew 22:34-40

They forgot to love. When the church at Ephesus first began, Paul wrote to them in Ephesians:

*For this reason, ever since I heard about your faith in the Lord Jesus and **your love** for all God's people, I have not stopped giving thanks for you, remembering you in my prayers.*

Ephesians 1:15-16

Paul commended and instructed them to keep loving their brothers and sisters and speaking the truth with love (Ephesians 4:14-16). Whether the church in Ephesus got distracted in mundane teachings or if they developed hate for the pagan world they lived in, Jesus has highlighted their lack of affection and love for Him. Comparable to today, we also live in a wicked generation that deems right as wrong and what is wrong as right (Isaiah 5:20).

Many of us begin our Christian walks with an abundance of love for Yeshua and have every intention to spread the good news to everyone we know. But as we continue to spread God's Word and speak against evil, we can become combative and walk less in love. So much is your passion to speak against evil that you forget to treat others in love and share His message with love. Jesus is instructing them to repent and go back to their first days in which they loved and evangelized lovingly.

I am embarrassed to say this, but I fall under the church of Ephesus today. When I began my walk, I was so ecstatic and full of love that any loving emotion like a simple hug could bring me to tears. I was so thankful for God and all He was doing for me that I relished in learning more and more.

But as I learned more from the Bible, I became combative and debated fellow Christians and unbelievers alike. Love was becoming more and more distant in me and anger was increasing. My anger grew at false doctrines, deceit, and false prophets. While Jesus praises your fervor and faith in Him, He also expects you to love as He does. He knows you're faithful to Him. He commends you for your deeds and hard work. But if you are not walking in love as He instructed, then your faithfulness is in vain. If you fall in line with this church's error, take some time to slow down. Restart your heart and reflect on the way Jesus treated and treats sinners. It is commendable and great that you have a passion to defend Him and correct the world, but you must do so in gentleness. Continue to stand up for God's Word and continue to fight against evil, but always do it from a position of love.

The Persecuted Church in Smyrna

To the angel of the church in Smyrna write:
These are the words of him who is the First and the Last, who died and came to life again. I know your afflictions and your poverty—yet you are rich! I know about the slander of those who say they are Jews and are not, but are a synagogue of Satan. Do not be afraid of what you are about to suffer. I tell you, the devil will put some of you in prison to test you, and you will suffer persecution for ten days. Be faithful, even to the point of death, and I will give you life as your victor's crown.
Whoever has ears, let them hear what the Spirit says to the churches. The one who is victorious will not be hurt at all by the second death.

Revelation 2:8-11

As opposed to the church in Ephesus, Jesus finds no fault in the church of Smyrna. Poverty stricken and heavily persecuted, He encourages and reminds them that they are rich due to their faith. His message also serves as prophetic encouragement for what was about to occur to them. They were about to suffer prison, enslavement, physical torture, and even death for their faith in Jesus. In 155 AD, for example, Smyrnan bishop Polycarp was burned at the stake and stabbed when the fire failed to consume him.

This message applies to many Christians today. While Americans may not suffer this degree of persecution, our brothers and sisters in the Middle-East, China, Russia, and many other countries are currently suffering great persecution and are being killed for their faith in Jesus. To them (and soon the last remnant left), Jesus brings you this message: Stay strong in your faith and persevere. You are on the correct path, and while your surroundings and circumstances might not reflect it, you are beyond rich in abundance. You will not suffer from the second death and, in fact, will gain the Crown of Life (Revelation 2:10) for your endurance to the end. Pain is but an instant, but your reward is eternal.

The Compromised Church in Pergamum

To the angel of the church in Pergamum write:
These are the words of him who has the sharp, double-edged sword. I know where you live—where Satan has his throne. Yet you remain true to my name. You did not renounce your faith in me, not even in the days of Antipas, my faithful witness, who was put to death in your city—where Satan lives.
Nevertheless, I have a few things against you: There are some among you who hold to the teaching of Balaam, who taught Balak to entice the Israelites to sin so that they ate food sacrificed to idols and committed sexual immorality. Likewise, you also have those who hold to the teaching of the Nicolaitans. Repent therefore! Otherwise, I will soon come to you and will fight against them with the sword of my mouth.
Whoever has ears, let them hear what the Spirit says to the churches. To the one who is victorious, I will give some of the hidden manna. I will also give that person a white stone with a new name written on it, known only to the one who receives it.

Revelation 2:12-17

Similar to the others, the city of Pergamon was an epicenter of trade and pagan worship. With temples dedicated to Athena, Dyonisus, Temenus, and Zeus, it is of no wonder that Jesus attributes this city as Satan's throne. While not all the members of the church of Pergamum renounced their faith in Jesus, some members strayed from Jesus' teachings. Some members retained the teachings of Balaam described in Numbers 22-25, when Balak hired Balaam to draw Israelites away from God. Others also held to the teachings of the Nicolaitans. Once again though, Jesus gives them the opportunity to repent and gain His eternal reward.

Unfortunately, this message applies to many Christians today. The passage of time has given birth to numerous pastors who have compromised the Word of God for false doctrines and created man-made theologies and practices. Many of today's churches (especially the largest one's) have fallen into these traps. Because they are not reading the Bible themselves, they are blindly accepting and believing what the pastor says and does without any self-reflection and scriptural analysis. It is crucial that you read your Bible and ensure that your pastor's practices and your beliefs are scripturally sound. Make sure your faith is rooted in the Word and not on what someone has told you about the Word. Read your Bible and stay true to the faith. If you fall under the church of Pergamum, revert back to zero. Ask yourself what you believe in and if your practices and lifestyle reflect the teachings of God and Jesus as dictated in the Bible. Jesus gives you the opportunity to repent and correct yourself.

The Corrupted Church in Thyatira

To the angel of the church in Thyatira write:
These are the words of the Son of God, whose eyes are like blazing fire and whose feet are like burnished bronze. I know your deeds, your love and faith, your service and perseverance, and that you are now doing more than you did at first.

Nevertheless, I have this against you: You tolerate that woman Jezebel, who calls herself a prophet. By her teaching she misleads my servants into sexual immorality and the eating of food sacrificed to idols. I have given her time to repent of her immorality, but she is unwilling. So I will cast her on a bed of suffering, and I will make those who commit adultery with her

suffer intensely, unless they repent of her ways. I will strike her children dead. Then all the churches will know that I am he who searches hearts and minds, and I will repay each of you according to your deeds.
Now I say to the rest of you in Thyatira, to you who do not hold to her teaching and have not learned Satan's so-called deep secrets, 'I will not impose any other burden on you, except to hold on to what you have until I come.'

To the one who is victorious and does my will to the end, I will give authority over the nations— that one 'will rule them with an iron scepter and will dash them to pieces like pottery'—just as I have received authority from my Father. I will also give that one the morning star. Whoever has ears, let them hear what the Spirit says to the churches.

Revelation 2:18-29

Jesus begins His assessment of the church in Thyatira by commending their growth over time. However, He is quick to delineate the cause of His discontent: the corruption of Jezebel. While this Jezebel is not the Phoenician Jezebel that was Ahab's queen, her practices remain the same. She infiltrates the church with false gods under a false guise and interferes with the worship of the true God. You may have heard of "the Jezebel spirit" in your time as a precautionary term—and with good reason.

This evil spirit is alive and well today. For example, the singer Beyonce can be interpreted as a Jezebel. She presented herself as a Christian early in her career only to seduce and promote immorality to the masses. While I cannot quote the exact lyrics due to copyright, the voiceover "Denial" from her album Lemonade describes using sheets of a religious text as a tampon. This blasphemous statement (symbolic or not) is only one of a myriad examples of her exposed worship of Satan. Similarly, there are Jezebel celebrities who self-identify as Christians, but never profess His name and instead teach new age doctrines of "self-love" and "multiple ways to get to God." When you follow these people, they lead you astray from the faith and (as God describes) cause you to commit spiritual adultery.

Jezebels are not limited to only women though. Justin Bieber, Kanye West, and many others identify as believers of Jesus and promote anti-biblical messaging via their entertainment. If you follow any of these Jezebels, stop. Be cautious of who you follow and depart from their blasphemy. If you fall under the church of Thyatira, realize that Jesus condemns their tolerance of Jezebel. Identify if there are any Jezebels in your life and cut them out. It may seem extreme if you don't understand the message, but I assure you, Jesus expects you to be all in for Him. Remember, you cannot serve two masters.

The Dead Church in Sardis

To the angel of the church in Sardis write:
These are the words of him who holds the seven spirits of God and the seven stars. I know your deeds; you have a reputation of being alive, but you are dead. Wake up! Strengthen what remains and is about to die, for I have found your deeds unfinished in the sight of my God. Remember, therefore, what you have received and heard; hold it fast, and repent. But if you do not wake up, I will come like a thief, and you will not know at what time I will come to you.

Yet you have a few people in Sardis who have not soiled their clothes. They will walk with me, dressed in white, for they are worthy. The one who is victorious will, like them, be dressed in white. I will never blot out the name of that person from the book of life, but will acknowledge that name before my Father and his angels. Whoever has ears, let them hear what the Spirit says to the churches.

Revelation 3:1-6

Jesus gives a critique to the church of Sardis very quickly and very bluntly. They're dead. Dead of faith. Dead in action. They either don't believe anymore or their faith is completely unrecognizable. They continue to practice as a church, but they're completely dead...without strength.

Many people fall under the category of this church today. They like to identify as Christian, but nothing in their life reflects true spirituality. There is no interest or curiosity to grow and they have no problem being that way. Jesus makes sure to tell the members of this church that if they do not wake up, He will come like a thief and come for them at a time they will be unprepared.

If you fall under this church, reenergize and reboot your faith in Him. Read your Bible. Think about what will happen when you draw your last breath. Are you comfortable going to your Creator for judgement? Leave the things of this world and re-establish your relationship with Jesus today. Do not be this dead church.

The Faithful Church in Philadelphia

To the angel of the church in Philadelphia write:
These are the words of him who is holy and true, who holds the key of David. What he opens no one can shut, and what he shuts no one can open. I know your deeds. See, I have placed before you an open door that no one can shut. I know that you have little strength, yet you have kept my word and have not denied my name. I will make those who are of the synagogue of Satan, who claim to be Jews though they are not, but are liars—I will make them come and fall down at your feet and acknowledge that I have loved you. Since you have kept my command to endure patiently, I will also keep you from the hour of trial that is going to come on the whole world to test the inhabitants of the earth.

I am coming soon. Hold on to what you have, so that no one will take your crown. The one who is victorious I will make a pillar in the temple of my God. Never again will they leave it. I will write on them the name of my God and the name of the city of my God, the new Jerusalem, which is coming down out of heaven from my God; and I will also write on them my new name. Whoever has ears, let them hear what the Spirit says to the churches.

Revelation 3:7-13

This is it. This is the church we want to be a part of, and it is a personal goal of mine to reach it. He opens the door for us to enter when we remain faithful to the end. So great is Jesus' praise for this church's endurance that He promises to keep them from the hour of trial that is going to come and test all people on earth.

Some Christians interpret this to mean that He will rapture His church before the Great Tribulation. Others interpret this to mean that He will protect this church during the Great Tribulation. Whatever He means, I want this for myself and my loved ones. We kept His Word, we endured, and never forsook His name.

What do we need to do to belong to this church? Make the decision to yield to His will and fulfill your purpose. Go through that open door that no one can shut. Trust in Him and make your life a living testimony for all to see.

The Lukewarm Church in Laodicea

To the angel of the church in Laodicea write:
These are the words of the Amen, the faithful and true witness, the ruler of God's creation. I know your deeds, that you are neither cold nor hot. I wish you were either one or the other! So, because you are lukewarm—neither hot nor cold—I am about to spit you out of my mouth. You say, 'I am rich; I have acquired wealth and do not need a thing.' But you do not realize that you are wretched, pitiful, poor, blind and naked. I counsel you to buy from me gold refined in the fire, so you can become rich; and white clothes to wear, so you can cover your shameful nakedness; and salve to put on your eyes, so you can see.

Those whom I love I rebuke and discipline. So be earnest and repent. Here I am! I stand at the door and knock. If anyone hears my voice and opens the door, I will come in and eat with that person, and they with me.
To the one who is victorious, I will give the right to sit with me on my throne, just as I was victorious and sat down with my Father on his throne. Whoever has ears, let them hear what the Spirit says to the churches.

Revelation 3:14-22

Jesus' final assessment is of the lukewarm church of Laodicea. They were neither hot nor cold. According to Jesus, this state is the worst state to be in. He prefers you would be one or the other, but not lukewarm. I dare state that the majority of Christians today fall under this church. Being lukewarm today means that you believe in Jesus, but you also believe in the world. You love your faith, but you also love your worldly pleasures and ambitions. Jesus gives the example of those who love money and riches, but are poor in Spirit, pitiful, and wretched. The Laodicean church was wealthy and did not feel the church was in need of anything. Does this sound like many churches today? How many churches today are wealthy and spiritually impoverished? How many churches have succumbed to the love of the world?

I hate to say this, but this message is for so many Christians who feel they've done enough simply by going to a church service on Sundays. These people think that by going to church on Sundays they are in good standing in the sights of Elohim—when they are really poor in faith and blind. If they do not repent, He is going to spit them out.

If you are a part of this church, break the chain and activate your faith. I am not judging you. I'm only trying to tell you the truth as Jesus has declared His message to the church of Laodicea. Do not be lukewarm. If you say you are a follower of Christ, then live like it. Prove it. We are not perfect, but we are called for repentance and are expected to change our old ways. Act on it even if it takes you some time to get there. Your salvation depends on it.

Whoever Has Ears, Let Them Hear

Before Jesus delves into the coming events in His revelation, He purposefully begins with a self-evaluation for the hearer of these words. Why does He do this? Because your salvation is the most important thing to Him! The events that follow His revelation will come to pass regardless of your salvation, but entering His Kingdom is solely up to you. It is your decision and actions that will decide if your name is written in the Book of Life. A person who has said in their heart, "There is no God," has already made his or her choice. However, you—the believer—has to persevere and be correct in your faith.

Remember the preface Jesus gave before revealing the signs of the end in Matthew? Take heed to not be deceived. Just as the churches of Ephesus, Pergamum, Thyatara, Sardis and Laodicea, you can call yourself a follower of Christ and be hypocritical or wrong in your behavior. Ignorance of His instruction or of His teachings is not an excuse when the Day of the

Lord comes. On the Day of Judgement, we stand alone. So, take the first step and recognize where you are now in your walk. Open your ears to Him and allow yourself to hear. Because the question Jesus asks is for you: Which church are you?

Chapter 14

HARPAZŌ

But about that day or hour no one knows, not even the angels in heaven, nor the Son, but only the Father.

Mark 13:32

One of the most divisive and controversial doctrines amongst all Christians is the timing and existence of the rapture. The Latin word "rapturo" is derived from the ancient Greek word "harpazo," meaning a catching or snatching away. In the New Testament, the word is found seventeen times. Five of these mentions refer to the physical snatching of a human being, such as the Lord snatching Philip away in Acts 8:39 and Paul being caught up to the Third Heaven in 2 Corinthians 12:2.

The biblical concept of the rapture is widely known across the world and has even been the subject of literature and film media. So why is this event so divisive amongst Christendom? Interpretation of scripture that describes and uses "harpazo" is not clear on the timing or reliance of the event, so much so that many denominations fixate themselves exclusively to a position regarding the event.

Unfortunately, this has led to many debates and dissension between many Christians—to the point where many Christians are exiled or insulted if they don't agree to the rapture position of certain denominations. For example, the Catholic church, Lutheran, and Calvinist denominations don't believe in a pre-tribulation rapture, whereas Baptists and Pentecostals typically believe in a pre-tribulation rapture.

Regardless of your existing position on the rapture, it is of my belief that it should not be a cause of such division amongst ourselves. I, myself have a position on the topic. However, it would be dishonest of me to solely portray my viewpoint as the correct one (despite my confidence in it). Therefore, I have included all three arguments for each of the rapture perspectives in the hopes that you will delve deeper into them and decide which one you feel is scripturally accurate.

Pre-Tribulation

Those who believe in a pre-tribulation rapture believe Jesus will come before the Great Tribulation to take His church to heaven. You have probably seen renditions of this in film and television such as the *Left Behind* series, for example. The chaos and worldly disorder are usually accompanied with the reasoning that this pre-tribulation rapture triggers the final seven years of the earth. Believers in this doctrine usually attribute the following four scriptures to support their argument:

Brothers and sisters, we do not want you to be uninformed about those who sleep in death, so that you do not grieve like the rest of mankind, who have no hope. For we believe that Jesus died and rose again, and so we believe that God will bring with Jesus those who have fallen asleep in him. According to the Lord's word, we tell you that we who are still alive, who are left until the coming of the Lord, will certainly not precede those who have fallen asleep. For the Lord himself will come down from heaven, with a loud command, with the voice of the archangel and with the trumpet call of God, and the dead in Christ will rise first. After that, we who are still alive and are left will be caught up together with them in the clouds to meet the Lord in the air. And so we will be with the Lord forever. Therefore encourage one another with these words.

1 Thessalonians 4:13-18

These words spoken by Paul describe a moment in the future when Jesus will descend from heaven and raise the dead who died in Christ first, followed by those believers still living on earth. This ascension of believers is described as literally a "lifting off" into the clouds to meet Messiah. This scripture is often used as the main argument for pre-tribulation rapture because of the simplicity and clarity of the event. Evidently, this event will indeed happen, but when? Pre-tribulationists continue forward using additional scripture to sound their case.

Listen, I tell you a mystery: We will not all sleep, but we will all be changed— in a flash, in the twinkling of an eye, at the last trumpet. For the trumpet will sound, the dead will be raised imperishable, and we will be changed. For the perishable must clothe itself with the imperishable, and the mortal with immortality.

1 Corinthians 15:51-53

Not all of us will experience death. Paul reveals a mystery that provides more insight into the moment in which those dead and alive will be instantly transformed into a new body. The obvious reference to 1 Thessalonians 4:13 and Philippians 3:21 strengthens this argument because we, as believers, indeed, require a new body to coexist with the Lord. Just as Paul confirms, the perishable must be clothed in the imperishable in order to be in the presence of God. We can see examples of this in action in Exodus 33:20, 1 John 4:12, and 1 Timothy 6:16. Even the non-canonical Book of Enoch describes that angels cannot be near and behold His face in chapter 14. The fact that we need another body grants more evidence to the fact that our sin is incompatible with God's holiness.

For you yourselves know perfectly that the day of the Lord so comes as a thief in the night. For when they say, "Peace and safety!" then sudden destruction comes upon them, as labor pains upon a pregnant woman. And they shall not escape. But you, brethren, are not in darkness, so that this Day should overtake you as a thief. You are all sons of light and sons of the day. We are not of the night nor of darkness. Therefore let us not sleep, as others do, but let us watch and be sober. For those who sleep, sleep at night, and those who get drunk are drunk at night. But let us who are of the day be sober, putting on the breastplate of faith and love, and as a helmet the hope of salvation. For God did not appoint us to wrath, but to obtain salvation through our Lord Jesus Christ, who died for us, that whether we wake or sleep, we should live together with Him.

1 Thessalonians 5:2-10

The third commonly used scripture highlights Paul's encouragement to believers as evidence that God does not appoint us to wrath. This is interpreted to mean that God will not appoint believers to the wrath of the Great Tribulation.

Do not let your hearts be troubled. You believe in God; believe also in me. My Father's house has many rooms; if that were not so, would I have told you that I am going there to prepare a place for you? And if I go and prepare a place for you, I will come back and take you to be with me that you also may be where I am. You know the way to the place where I am going.

John 14:1-4

The fourth and less commonly used scripture that supports a pre-tribulation rapture is Jesus' promise for not only His return but also His taking of us. His illustration of Him preparing rooms for us also gives headway for interpretations that we will inhabit those rooms when He takes us.

These scriptural arguments are not the sole reasoning for a pre-tribulation rapture, however. A heavy argument toward this position is made from omission of the church during the Great Tribulation. Phrases such as "those in Christ," "the church," or the "Body of Christ" are not mentioned through Revelation 4-18. Only terms of "the elect" and "saints" are used. This omission is further supported by scripture that directly states that God will keep believers from "the hour of testing." This interpretation may work if one accepts the messages of the seven churches to be universal, since that was a directive message to the church in Philadelphia. Indeed, 1 Thessalonians 1:8-10 also makes a compelling case:

The Lord's message rang out from you not only in Macedonia and Achaia— your faith in God has become known everywhere. Therefore we do not need to say anything about it, for they themselves report what kind of reception you gave us. They tell how you turned to God from idols to serve the living and true God, and to wait for his Son from heaven, whom he raised from the dead—Jesus, who rescues us from the coming wrath.

1 Thessalonians 1:8-10

Finally, one of the most common and recited scriptures that favor this view is the timing of His coming:

But of that day and hour no one knows, not even the angels of heaven, but My Father only.

Matthew 24:36

Under a pre-tribulation, this scripture from Matthew is used as a precaution for solely the rapture event and NOT to His second coming. These events are seen as separate instances. However, this can be contradictory to the message contained in scripture. The next verse confirms that Jesus is talking about the "coming of the Son of Man." Another flaw is that if the rapture occurs, then all one needs to do is count seven years forward (the duration of the Great Tribulation) and estimate Jesus' return in the clouds. Also worth noting is that a pre-tribulation rapture cannot occur before "the last trump" referenced in 1 Corinthians 15:52. So while the pre-tribulation position is compelling, it is not completely foolproof.

Warfare Tip

If a rapture occurs at an unprecedented time and you are left amongst the living on earth, then use this as evidence of all that you have heard to be true. God is real. Jesus is real. Repent and accept Jesus immediately and learn as much as you can with the time and resources you have left at your disposal. Times are going to be extremely difficult for all, but especially for newfound believers. You will be persecuted severely and will be given to suffer from global judgements and a one-world tyrannical government. The decision to follow Christ in this time might likely cost you your life, but do not be dismayed. After all, remember your reward. Eternity in the presence of your Creator and the Lamb.

Mid-Tribulation

While less common, there are fellow believers that adopt the ideology of a mid-tribulation rapture—where the rapture occurs (just as it would in a pre-tribulation scenario) at the 3.5 halfway year point of The Great Tribulation. Unlike the other rapture theories, the mid-tribulation viewpoint uses an eschatological approach heavily based on the book of Daniel. Just as pre-tribulationists, both believe that they will not suffer God's wrath (as previously promised in 1 Thessalonians 5:9). Due to this critical point, a mid-tribulation argument relies on a rapture before the antichrist breaks his peaceful union with Israel, a calculation of three and a half years:

And he shall speak great words against the most High, and shall wear out the saints of the most High, and think to change times and laws: and they shall be given into his hand until a time and times and the dividing of time.

Daniel 7:25

This moment in time has also been interpreted by mid-tribulationists to be the final trumpet referenced in 1 Corinthians 15:52 and Revelation 11:15:

In a moment, in the twinkling of an eye, at the last trumpet. For the trumpet will sound, and the dead will be raised incorruptible, and we shall be changed.

1 Corinthians 15:52b

The seventh angel sounded his trumpet, and there were loud voices in heaven, which said: "The kingdom of the world has become the kingdom of our Lord and of his Messiah, and he will reign for ever and ever."

Revelation 11:15

This is a contradiction, however, because if the intention and purpose of this timeline is that believers don't experience God's wrath on earth, then the timing cannot be the final trumpet, since the sixth seal marks the beginning of God's wrath:

For the great day of His wrath has come, and who is able to stand?

Revelation 6:17

 Warfare Tip

In the event that a rapture occurs as soon as the antichrist is revealed in Jerusalem, then you have very little time left to correct your relationship with Christ. The world at that point will be brutal for those who don't worship the beast and his image—which will most likely mean your death if you choose Christ. You will need to repent and envelop yourself in Christ to get to the end. Don't be afraid of what is to come; after all, you're in good company. The early church and disciples gave their lives for their faith and now have their names sealed in the Book of Life.

Post-Tribulation

The third most common opinion regarding the rapture is a post-tribulation scenario, in which the church (both dead and living) will be raptured at the conclusion of the Great Tribulation and at the second coming of Jesus in the clouds. This post-tribulation event is unlike all other rapture theories because it is a combination of a resurrection and rapture event. Unlike pre and mid viewpoints, post-tribulationist believers use scripture that directly conflicts with the other rapture perspectives. One of the strongest scriptures in favor of this argument is Matthew 24:

Immediately after the tribulation of those days the sun will be darkened, and the moon will not give its light; the stars will fall from heaven, and the powers of the heavens will be shaken. Then the sign of the Son of Man will appear in heaven, and then all the tribes of the earth will mourn, and they will see the Son of Man coming on the clouds of heaven with power and great glory. And He will send His angels with a great sound of a trumpet, and they will gather together His elect from the four winds, from one end of heaven to the other.

Matthew 24:29-31

Clearly referring to Jesus' second coming, Matthew 24 makes a clear distinction that the angels will be sent out to gather the elect from one end of the heavens to the other after the tribulation of those days. This is further supported and described much more in depth in Revelation 14:

And another angel came out of the temple, crying with a loud voice to Him who sat on the cloud, "Thrust in Your sickle and reap, for the time has come for You to reap, for the harvest of the earth is ripe." So He who sat on the cloud thrust in His sickle on the earth, and the earth was reaped.

Revelation 14:15

Finally, Jesus confirms this in his explanation of the parable of the weeds:

He answered, "The one who sowed the good seed is the Son of Man. The field is the world, and the good seed stands for the people of the kingdom. The weeds are the people of the evil one, and the enemy who sows them is the devil. The harvest is the end of the age, and the harvesters are angels."

Matthew 13:37-39

This "gathering of His elect" occurs at Jesus' return, which means that if a pre-tribulation occurs, Jesus must come once more after the rapture. But the best evidence concerning the time of the resurrection is the book of Revelation itself. The book is dictated and presented by Jesus and John in chronological order. The seals, the trumpets, the bowls all follow a sequence of events until the resurrection of the elect at Jesus' appearing.

Warfare Tip

If you begin to see the events of the end as described in the Bible and in this book, then you will need to endure the worst time in history. Very few will be the last to survive the end of the age and be alive to see Jesus' coming, which means that many will most likely die before that via persecution, starvation, or cataclysmic catastrophe. Your faith will be tested like never before, and you will have to verbally deny your faith in Christ or suffer death. This can be a scary thought, but remember, our fellow brothers and sisters in Christ have also suffered in His name. Jesus has prepared us for this. The world hated Him and so will they hate us in His name. But don't be in distress, this time is also a time for revival. Many will seek answers for the disorder and chaos on earth, and you will be a beacon of light to many. Endure in the faith for your reward is incorruptible and invaluable.

Which One Is It?

During my first read of the New Testament, I understood that the ascension and resurrection of believers occurred at the very end. With little knowledge regarding the entire biblical context revolving around the Old and New Testament and the authorship and background of these books and letters, the scripture I had read led me to understand that those "harpazo" references pointed to Jesus' coming. In an effort to understand the truth, I researched all rapture perspectives to get a better understanding of what is to come.

Personally, I feel that God would use the time of the Great Tribulation to test our faith and use us for His glory. After all, the early church and the disciples suffered some of the worst deaths and persecution in their time. Why would we be exempt? Most of the hope that I see from pre-tribulationists seems to derive from the fear to live in those times—and who can blame them? These are literally the worst times on earth. However, I also sense a fear from many pre-tribulationists to undergo death during those times. I believe this fear is the cause for such a hope for a pre-tribulation rapture. To live in such a time means to watch your family die of starvation or murder. To live in such a time is to live on the run and starve in the wild.

But to live in this time is also the ultimate test of faith. We would all like to think that we would never deny Christ even if you had a gun to your head. But until you are in a position where you verbally have to deny your faith in Christ or face death, then the separation of real believers against the false ones occurs. I understand the ongoing desire to avoid this.

To be living in the last generation and just receive your new body and ascend to heaven is ideal. No death on earth. No hardship. But no believer should be so fixated on a rapture as a means to avoid a test of faith. While I currently hold a no rapture or post-tribulation perspective, that does not mean that I am certain or completely accurate in my position. For example, Matthew 24 describes a detailed scene of His coming that doesn't align with the final moment of the age:

But of that day and hour no one knows, not even the angels of heaven, but My Father only. But as the days of Noah were, so also will the coming of the Son of Man be. For as in the days before the flood, they were eating and drinking, marrying and giving in marriage, until the day that Noah entered the ark, and did not know until the flood came and took them all away, so also will the coming of the Son of Man be. Then two men will be in the field: one will be taken and the other left. Two women will be grinding at the mill: one will be taken and the other left. Watch therefore, for you do not know what hour your Lord is coming. But know this, that if the master of the house had known what hour the thief would come, he would have watched and not allowed his house to be broken into. Therefore you also be ready, for the Son of Man is coming at an hour you do not expect.

Matthew 24:36-44

His coming will come at an unprecedented time in which people will be living their life as they do, completely unaware of their spiritual condition. This is not possible if the final battle of Armageddon is held in Megiddo after the destruction the earth has suffered from the seven bowl judgements.

The case can be made that these descriptions are metaphorical scenarios in which Jesus illustrates scenes for His disciples to understand. Regardless if the rapture is true or not, one thing is clear: Jesus has instructed us to be ready for His coming. Through multiple parables and teachings, He repetitively emphasized the importance of preparedness.

I am saddened today to see just how divisive the rapture is across Christianity when there is no reason for it. Believing in a certain rapture interpretation does not affect your salvation. So long as you are living readily for His return, the timing of a rapture and the resurrection will not have an effect on your salvation. What is certain though is that Jesus is coming...and every knee will bow.

ENCOUNTER #8
3 A.M.

I shared my Arcadian home with four other residents in a three-story complex. I never really spoke to any of them since everyone kept to themselves, but I didn't mind at all since I always kept to myself too. Our landlord also had strict rules to follow, including a no-guest and a no-noise policy after 10 p.m. I couldn't complain though since I had early morning calls in order to cut through the LA traffic to get to work on time.

One night, I awoke to check the time on my phone in the middle of the night. This was common, since I could never sleep for an uninterrupted six or eight hours. It was around 3 a.m. when suddenly three loud knocks banged on my back wall. I shot up in the dark and fell quiet. These knocks were loud….and I mean LOUD. There is no way that anyone asleep would not hear them.

My first thought was that it had come from the resident behind me since we shared walls, but as I thought this, four LOUDER knocks banged on my wall on my left. I kept the light off as I got out of the bed and tried to listen, wondering if any of my housemates would get up. There's no way I can be the only one hearing this.

These were the loudest bangs I've ever heard, and there was nobody on the other side of my left side wall. I sat there for about ten minutes and listened in silence. Nobody got up or made a noise. The house was completely quiet. How was that possible? There's no way anyone could sleep through that. After a while, I returned to bed and tried to go to sleep.

Chapter 15

THE BREAKING OF THE SEALS

Then I saw in the right hand of him who sat on the throne a scroll with writing on both sides and sealed with seven seals. And I saw a mighty angel proclaiming in a loud voice, "Who is worthy to break the seals and open the scroll?"

Revelation 5:1-2

During Jesus' revelation to John, he was taken to the throne room of God to be shown the things that must come to pass at the end of the age—it must've been quite the sight since very few on earth have ever seen it or been in its presence. God was sitting on His throne and was holding a scroll in His right hand, one sealed with six seals. This scroll held the deed and judgements of the earth. However, there is none in the throne room worthy of opening them until the slain Lamb appears:

Now when He had taken the scroll, the four living creatures and the twenty-four elders fell down before the Lamb, each having a harp, and golden bowls full of incense, which are the prayers of the saints. And they sang a new song, saying:

*"You are worthy to take the scroll,
And to open its seals;
For You were slain,
And have redeemed us to God by Your blood
Out of every tribe and tongue and people and nation,
And have made us kings and priests to our God;
And we shall reign on the earth."*

Revelation 5:8-10

Like the rapture theories, the timing of the breaking of the seals is also contended. There are many interpretations as to when the seals are broken and what those seals actually are. Some proclaim that some of the seals have already been broken, while others hold fast that they have yet to be fractured. In either case, the seals mark the beginning of a series of judgements on the earth that lead to the harvest and final day of judgement. Once again, I will provide the most common interpretations of the seals, while also including my personal perspective. The seals begin with what you may have heard of: the four horsemen of the apocalypse.

The White Rider

I watched as the Lamb opened the first of the seven seals. Then I heard one of the four living creatures say in a voice like thunder, "Come!" I looked, and there before me was a white horse! Its rider held a bow, and he was given a crown, and he rode out as a conqueror bent on conquest.

Revelation 6:1-2

The first horseman is white, leading many to think that this is the Jesus that Revelation 19 refers to. This cannot be true though, since Christ wears many crowns (Revelation 19:12) and Christ will come with a sword, not a bow. Additionally, the timing of the first seal is too early for Christ's return on a horse. Many other interpreters turn to the antichrist as a possibility for this rider. This also seems unlikely since the antichrist doesn't come as a conqueror bent on conquest; he comes as a sly solution the world craves for and is accepted freely by the world.

Still though, believers of this interpretation attest that because the rider has no arrow, then this rider or antichrist will conquer through diplomacy. Another supporting theory is that the antichrist will bring a false peace under the authority of the crown he is given. Another interesting interpretation is that the first rider is a false rendition of Christ, directed by false prophets. This argument uses Matthew 24:4-5 to affirm that Jesus warned us not to be deceived for many false Christs will arise before the end.

But if the rider is not Jesus or the antichrist, then who is it? It would be dishonest of me to confirm a direct interpretation as truth. The scripture is not detailed enough to make a definitive claim to who or what this first rider is. All we know is that he holds a bow and was given a crown with which he rides forth to conqueror.

The Red Horse

When the Lamb opened the second seal, I heard the second living creature say, "Come!" Then another horse came out, a fiery red one. Its rider was given power to take peace from the earth and to make people kill each other. To him was given a large sword.

Revelation 6:3-4

The second seal is the red horseman who takes away peace and makes people on earth kill each other. This seal is more straightforward in its message, but it has also been the cause of additional interpretations. Many believers interpret this to be a time of great warfare on earth. While this is possible, it is worth noting that Jesus used the terminology of "nations against nations" in Matthew 24:7 in addition to the rumors of war that would be presented in the last days. This verbiage is more detailed in how it portrays people, falling more in line with the "heart of many growing cold" mentioned in Matthew 24:12.

This more localized perspective can mean an increase in crime and violent disputes across the world, something similar that can be seen in the *Kingsman* film. Whichever the case, I understand the second seal to be a confiscation of peace. Perhaps times of continual war and the darkening of the hearts of all peoples across the earth are what constitutes the second seal. In any case, both markers are definitely occurring now. Such turmoil in the world, and truly the most heinous of crimes and evil deeds are being performed in our times. I marvel at the thought of this seal being already opened.

The Black Horse

When the Lamb opened the third seal, I heard the third living creature say, "Come!" I looked, and there before me was a black horse! Its rider was holding a pair of scales in his hand. Then I heard what sounded like a voice among the four living creatures, saying, "Two pounds] of wheat for a day's wages, and six pounds of barley for a day's wages, and do not damage the oil and the wine!"

Revelation 6:5-6

The third horse is black and brings scarcity and inflation on earth. The voice proclaims that a quart of wheat is equivalent to a Denarius. To understand this, we must go back to the time in which John wrote the scrolls. In the time of John's revelation (approximately 90 AD), one Denarius was equivalent to a day's work. Translating this into our modern time, we can speculate that global hyperinflation is the third seal.

Sadly, this bringer of famine is being experienced in some areas of the world today. We who live in a metropolis have not experienced this yet, but many of our fellow brothers and sisters suffer from starvation and famine. When this seal is broken though, famine will be felt all over the earth and no one will be exempt from this (except the elites who might be hiding underground at this time…more on that later).

This is something that we will all most likely see when the U.S. dollar collapses, and the beginning of a global currency is being initiated. We haven't experienced this globally, so it's safe to say that this seal has not been broken. When it does though, the troubles for you and your family will begin. Shortage of food will cause many to commit crimes in order to feed their loved ones, and worse yet, this will mark the beginning of government dependence for all which paves the way for the Beast's system.

The Pale Horse

When the Lamb opened the fourth seal, I heard the voice of the fourth living creature say, "Come!" I looked, and there before me was a pale horse! Its rider was named Death, and Hades was following close behind him. They were given power over a fourth of the earth to kill by sword, famine and plague, and by the wild beasts of the earth.

Revelation 6:7-8

The final horseman is the pale horse who brings death over a quarter of the earth through the sword, famine, plague, and wild animals. As the seals intensify, the numbers of those killed and affected by the judgements increase. At the time of this writing, the world population currently sits at 7.8 billion. While this horseman brings death to a quarter of the earth, a large portion of people will be included in the final death count. Large amounts of people die daily, that's true. But this magnitude of death will not be able to be ignored and will leave a dent in the human population (and that's not counting animal species). If you haven't received Christ by this point, there is a chance you may die during this time depending on where you are when this seal is broken. While the world panics, find solitude to pray to God and develop your faith for the times ahead.

The Martyrs' Cry

When he opened the fifth seal, I saw under the altar the souls of those who had been slain because of the word of God and the testimony they had maintained. They called out in a loud voice, "How long, Sovereign Lord, holy and true, until you judge the inhabitants of the earth and avenge our blood?" Then each of them was given a white robe, and they were told to wait a little longer, until the full number of their fellow servants, their brothers and sisters, were killed just as they had been.

Revelation 6:9-11

There are two things to note about the fifth seal. The first is that this seal activates the distribution of white robes for all martyrs that have died for proclaiming faith in Jesus from the foundation of the church up to the moment of the seal. The second is that the full number of martyrs remains incomplete as well as the judgment against those who killed the saints.

This seal can feel a bit sad because it promises that more martyrs are coming. This is to be expected though because persecution against the followers of Christ heightens during the Great Tribulation, and many will be added to the Kingdom during this time. We are not promised relief from suffering during this time, but we are promised a new name and the Crown of Life if we endure. This is why it is critical that you ground yourself in faith, because the times ahead are going to require it in order to cross that finish line.

The Heavens Unleashed

I watched as he opened the sixth seal. There was a great earthquake. The sun turned black like sackcloth made of goat hair, the whole moon turned blood red, and the stars in the sky fell to earth, as figs drop from a fig tree when shaken by a strong wind. The heavens receded like a scroll being rolled up, and every mountain and island was removed from its place.

Then the kings of the earth, the princes, the generals, the rich, the mighty, and everyone else, both slave and free, hid in caves and among the rocks of the mountains. They called to the mountains and the rocks, "Fall on us and hide us from the face of him who sits on the throne and from the wrath of the Lamb! For the great day of their wrath has come, and who can withstand it?"

Revelation 6:12-17

The cosmic disturbances that arrive with the breaking of the sixth seal come during a time when people couldn't think of anything worse happening. After all, remember that a quarter of the earth has been decimated at this point. Now, a huge earthquake, the darkening of the sun, the bloodening of the moon, and the falling of stars obliterate the earth with cataclysmic magnitude.

With earthquakes increasing every year, seismologists have alerted that a great earthquake from the San Andreas fault line is inevitable and bound to occur at any time. The earthquake of the sixth seal has the power to shift islands and mountains. What is curious about this seal is that it specifically makes mention of kings, generals, the rich and mighty, and all inhabitants of earth hiding under rocks. Believe it or not, we are seeing preparation for this event by governments and wealthy people even now. We are already seeing the construction and selling of underground bunkers for such a catastrophic event in many countries like Germany and New Zealand. These are not just any bunkers either; they are luxurious bunkers that only the wealthiest can afford. This status symbol is exactly to what the seal is referring. If you live to see this day, take solace. For no one can hide from the wrath of God, and justice will be served for all who reject Jesus as the son of God.

The Fiery Censer

When he opened the seventh seal, there was silence in heaven for about half an hour.

And I saw the seven angels who stand before God, and seven trumpets were given to them.

Another angel, who had a golden censer, came and stood at the altar. He was given much incense to offer, with the prayers of all God's people, on the golden altar in front of the throne. The smoke of the incense, together with the prayers of God's people, went up before God from the angel's hand. Then the angel took the censer, filled it with fire from the altar, and hurled it on the earth; and there came peals of thunder, rumblings, flashes of lightning and an earthquake.

Revelation 8:1-5

The final seal is one of preparedness and atmospheric judgment on the earth. First, the angels are given each a trumpet, a clear foreshadowing of the upcoming trumpet judgements. Second, an angel prepares prayer-filled incense and throws it upon the earth to cause thunder, lightning, and an earthquake. This final seal is the calm before the storm that is the sounding of the seven trumpets. If you live to see this day, then be prepared for the trumpet blasts that are about to sound. Refer to scripture if available and do your best to stay safe if possible. Regardless of where you are on the earth, your salvation remains intact if you are a follower of Christ.

The Scroll Is Opened

These seals mark only the beginning of God's wrath on earth. While these may sound harsh, remember that God is patient...and just. There will come a day in which God will repay and avenge all who have transgressed the law and are uncovered by the blood of Jesus. Remember those questions in chapter one: Why does evil exist in the world? Why do bad things happen to good people? These judgements are the culmination of justice finally served to a world deserving of it. As God's children, we must accept this and rejoice in it—not in the fact that many will die, but in the fact that the time in which we will finally be with our Creator and our Savior has come. He is finally coming to retrieve us, and there is nothing more hopeful than that.

Chapter 16

THE 144,000

After these things I saw four angels standing at the four corners of the earth, holding the four winds of the earth, that the wind should not blow on the earth, on the sea, or on any tree. Then I saw another angel ascending from the east, having the seal of the living God. And he cried with a loud voice to the four angels to whom it was granted to harm the earth and the sea, saying, "Do not harm the earth, the sea, or the trees till we have sealed the servants of our God on their foreheads." And I heard the number of those who were sealed. One hundred and forty-four thousand of all the tribes of the children of Israel were sealed...

Revelation 7:4

Across the various conversations I've had with fellow believers, I am often surprised at how individualized the interpretations for the 144,000 are. Some believers are completely unaware of the subject (perhaps because it is only found in Revelation), and some have inherited a belief from an external explanation. Before delving into common explanations, first understand the characteristics of the 144,000. The 144,000 are servants of God and comprised of the twelve tribes of Israel:

*Of the tribe of **Judah** twelve thousand were sealed;*
*of the tribe of **Reuben** twelve thousand were sealed;*
*of the tribe of **Gad** twelve thousand were sealed;*
*of the tribe of **Asher** twelve thousand were sealed;*
*of the tribe of **Naphtali** twelve thousand were sealed;*
*of the tribe of **Manasseh** twelve thousand were sealed;*
*of the tribe of **Simeon** twelve thousand were sealed;*
*of the tribe of **Levi** twelve thousand were sealed;*

> *of the tribe of* **Issachar** *twelve thousand were sealed;*
> *of the tribe of* **Zebulun** *twelve thousand were sealed;*
> *of the tribe of* **Joseph** *twelve thousand were sealed;*
> *of the tribe of* **Benjamin** *twelve thousand were sealed.*
>
> Revelation 7:5-8

First, it is important to note that there were originally thirteen tribes of Israel. While Jacob had twelve sons, according to Genesis 48:5, when he reunited with Joseph in Egypt, he adopted Joseph's two sons, Manasseh and Ephraim as his own. We can confirm that Jacob's grandsons became two tribes and were counted under Joseph in Joshua 14:4 and Numbers 1. Secondly, notice that the tribe of Dan is missing and that the tribe of Ephraim has been renamed. Dan's abstention is most likely due to the idolatry and wickedness the tribe of Dan committed in 1 Kings 12:28-30. The renaming of Ephraim is likely included under the tribe of Joseph This restored list of the twelve tribes of Israel is comprised of "the children of Israel," meaning that they are most likely dispersed Jewish people from all over the world. Later on, they are also revealed to be virgin men:

> *Then I looked, and there before me was the Lamb, standing on Mount Zion, and with him 144,000 who had his name and his Father's name written on their foreheads. And I heard a sound from heaven like the roar of rushing waters and like a loud peal of thunder. The sound I heard was like that of harpists playing their harps. And they sang a new song before the throne and before the four living creatures and the elders. No one could learn the song except the 144,000 who had been redeemed from the earth.* **These are those who did not defile themselves with women, for they remained virgins.** *They follow the Lamb wherever he goes. They were purchased from among mankind and offered as firstfruits to God and the Lamb. No lie was found in their mouths; they are blameless.*
>
> Revelation 14:1-5

While the text is clear in describing that these are men who did not defile themselves with women and remained virgins, I should note that this is a literal interpretation and that a metaphorical one exists for this scripture. Some attribute the defilement of women to be the fulfillment of the great harlot, meaning defilement with idolatrous religion. The timeline of the appearance of these 144,000 is critical and is the cause of various interpretations. First, they are introduced after the sixth seal is broken and before the first trumpet is blared. Secondly, they are followed by another great multitude:

After these things I looked, and behold, a great multitude which no one could number, of all nations, tribes, peoples, and tongues, standing before the throne and before the Lamb, clothed with white robes, with palm branches in their hands, and crying out with a loud voice, saying, "Salvation belongs to our God who sits on the throne, and to the Lamb!" All the angels stood around the throne and the elders and the four living creatures, and fell on their faces before the throne and worshiped God, saying:

"Amen! Blessing and glory and wisdom,
Thanksgiving and honor and power and might,
Be to our God forever and ever.
Amen."

Then one of the elders asked me, "These in white robes—who are they, and where did they come from?"

I answered, "Sir, you know."
And he said, "These are they who have come out of **the great tribulation;** *they have washed their robes and made them white in the blood of the Lamb. Therefore, they are before the throne of God*
and serve him day and night in his temple
and he who sits on the throne
will shelter them with his presence.

*'****Never again will they hunger;***
never again will they thirst.
The sun will not beat down on them,'
nor any scorching heat.

> *For the Lamb at the center of the throne*
> *will be their shepherd;*
> *'he will lead them to springs of living water.'*
> *'And God will wipe away every tear from their eyes.*
>
> Revelation 7:9-17

Notice that these in white robes are separate from the 144,000 and specifically come from the Great Tribulation. We can also confirm this because the elder states that they will never hunger, thirst, or face scorching heat. These conditions fit the previous judgement of the seals and the future trumpet and bowl judgements that every person alive on earth will experience during the Great Tribulation.

But what makes the 144,000 so special? After all, they have the honor of having God's seal on their foreheads. Not only will they be protected during the Great Tribulation but they will seemingly also evangelize many during the worst of times. This perspective derives from the definition of "firstfruits" in Leviticus:

> *Speak unto the children of Israel, and say unto them, When ye come into the land which I give unto you, and shall reap the harvest thereof, then ye shall bring a sheaf of the firstfruits of your harvest unto the priest: And he shall wave the sheaf before the LORD, to be accepted for you: on the morrow after the sabbath the priest shall wave it*
>
> Leviticus 23:10-11

While this is my interpretation (so far) of what I deem to be the 144,000, there are a myriad other interpretations and explanations that exist today across believers and denominations. Unfortunately (and I mean no disrespect), the most popular interpretation is that of Jehovah's Witnesses, which believe that literally only 144,000 will enter heaven while everyone else will live on earth (in paradise).

The Jehovah's Witnesses interpretation is unfortunate, because there are many flaws in this interpretation. As previously stated, if the 144,000 are the only ones in heaven, then they will all be Jewish male virgins. This would mean Peter, any women, or even the founder of Jehovah's

Witnesses, Charles Taze Russel, would not be in heaven. Secondly, Jesus never mentions or alludes to separate flocks or groups of people. One Bride and one Body of Christ is His remnant. Even in simpler terms, the only separation mentioned are those whose names are and aren't in the Book of Life.

Regardless of this interpretation, this is another topic that should not divide the church. If you have a different interpretation, then great. It's okay. Whichever interpretation you have, keep a lookout for this as it unfolds. I am sure we will know which one is correct when we see it.

ENCOUNTER #9
PINK SKY

Living alone can be tough sometimes, so I always enjoyed visiting my family back home in the Central Coast. Being back felt like I had never left, and it felt great to return to my "real" room.

During a weekend visit, I awoke around 6 a.m. to what I saw was a normal view of my room. Something was off though. The colors were different. The lighting seemed "shimmery" or "moving." I got up as I usually do to begin my morning routine and sat on my desk chair. I noticed an odd color coming through the window curtains. I opened the curtain and saw a pink, glimmering sky with moving lightning streaks. It was beautiful, but not normal.

I was confused and thought maybe I was just seeing a beautiful pink sunrise, but I wasn't completely convinced. As I prepared to get my supplies, I turned to my bed and saw myself sleeping. In an instant, I realized I was out of body.

At this point, these experiences were common, so I wasn't as bewildered as I used to be. I immediately thought, "Oh no! I need to get back." I started to panic because I didn't know how and just ran to my bedside. As soon as I did, I awoke. No shimmering colors, no pink sky…all normal colors. I went straight to my window to make sure and looked at my chair and my bed. Did I just unintentionally come out of my body again? What is happening to me?

Chapter 17

THE SOUNDING OF THE TRUMPETS

Then the seven angels who had the seven trumpets prepared to sound them.

Revelation 8:6

Now that the seals have been broken and the scroll is ready to be read, the judgements on earth really begin. If you thought the seals were bad, the trumpets sound quickly and increase in intensity. In fact, many pastors don't spend much time covering these judgements because they are frightening and scare even believers.

Like Jesus has instructed though, these things must come to pass before His coming. During the prelude of the trumpets, the world is already in disarray and a quarter of the earth has been completely depleted by the Pale Horseman. Unlike the seals, some trumpets specifically target unbelievers, leading many to think that the church is no longer on earth. It definitely is possible, but while the majority of the world continues to be unrepentant despite the wrathful catastrophes, there will still be those who will accept Christ and repent during this time. Regardless, if you are present during this time, remember to ground yourself in faith and fully devote yourself to Christ. It is the only way that you are going to make it through this.

The First Trumpet

The first angel sounded his trumpet, and there came hail and fire mixed with blood, and it was hurled down on the earth. A third of the earth was burned up, a third of the trees were burned up, and all the green grass was burned up.

Revelation 8:7

Just as the scripture describes, the first trumpet brings forth hail and fire mixed with blood to bombard the earth heavily. So much so, that a third of the earth is completely burned up as well as a third of the trees and grass. To put this into perspective, there were 3.04 trillion trees in the world in 2015.[25] A loss of a third of that would change the landscape of the earth, and suddenly, all those apocalyptic depictions of the end of the world easily become a reality. With famine from the black horseman already in effect, this would devastate whatever is left of food production and resources.

Warfare Tip

People in the world would most likely be anxious and hysterical during this judgement. All laws and code of ethics would probably be thrown out the window with everyone fending for themselves. You should stay close with any believers and loved ones if you can find any. You will need to empower one another and survive as long as possible. Because you know scripture, you can then prepare for the next trumpet.

The Second Trumpet

The second angel sounded his trumpet, and something like a huge mountain, all ablaze, was thrown into the sea. A third of the sea turned into blood, a third of the living creatures in the sea died, and a third of the ships were destroyed.

Revelation 8:8-9

When reading the depiction of the third trumpet, one can easily determine that this "huge mountain" is most likely an asteroid hurled at the sea. We haven't experienced a large asteroid impact on earth yet, but thanks to digital rendering, we can deduce that it would be catastrophic, killing many creatures in the marine ecosystem as well as destroying any ships that lie in its tidal aftermath (if it lands on the sea).

In May of 2019, the Federal Emergency Management Agency (FEMA) and the European Space Agency (ESA) conducted a simulated experiment in which a 200-foot asteroid hit the earth at the speed of 43,000 miles per hour over the city of New York.[26] The results of the impact would release up to 20 megatons of energy—1,000 times stronger than the Hiroshima bomb released on Japan. The large fireball, or "megabolide," would devastate a 15-kilometer radius, completely destroying Manhattan in the process.[27] While we cannot definitely say that these verses speak of an asteroid, we can assume that "something like a large mountain" could be a description John used when describing what he saw in the vision—after all, the word asteroid or meteor had not yet been coined in John's day. Either way, this blazing mountain will directly hit the sea and destroy maritime commerce and marine ecosystems in particular.

Warfare Tip

Since this trumpet will hit the sea, this means there will most likely be large tsunamis depending on the point of impact. If you are alive, try to pinpoint the location of the forecasted impact. There may be radio broadcasts or media that might speculate on it or know the impact coordinates. In any case, search for high altitude and keep yourself and loved ones close if possible. If this event will take your life, ask God to receive your spirit...for your time has come.

The Third Trumpet

The third angel sounded his trumpet, and a great star, blazing like a torch, fell from the sky on a third of the rivers and on the springs of water—the name of the star is Wormwood. A third of the waters turned bitter, and many people died from the waters that had become bitter.

Revelation 8:10-11

Similar to the second trumpet, the third trumpet lunges a burning star from the sky and directs it to the rivers and the remaining source of potable water. The effect of this is that the waters turned "bitter," and many people die from attempting to drink it. With the increased knowledge we have today, we know that waters can become radiated if a radioactive source has enough concentrated radiation to pollute it.

A cosmic meteor or comet can be a possible depiction of what John saw being thrown into the rivers. When reading the description of the third trumpet, it's easy to just focus on the blazing torch falling from the sky. However, the primary intention of this trumpet is what the "Wormwood " star does to the earth's water supply: to poison it. This is not the first time God has made waters bitter as a form of judgement. Jeremiah and Lamentations demonstrate that this is a divine form of judgement God utilizes:

Therefore thus says the LORD of hosts, the God of Israel: "Behold, I will feed them, this people, with wormwood, and give them water of gall to drink.

Jeremiah 19:5b

He has filled me with bitterness,
He has made me drink wormwood.
He has also broken my teeth with gravel,
And covered me with ashes.
You have moved my soul far from peace;
I have forgotten prosperity.
And I said, "My strength and my hope
Have perished from the LORD."
Remember my affliction and roaming,
The wormwood and the gall.
My soul still remembers
And sinks within me.
This I recall to my mind,
Therefore I have hope.

Lamentations 3:15-21

This judgment specifically destroys many people by eliminating the drinkable source remaining on earth—shortening the days ahead and ramping up the intensity of the coming trumpets and bowls.

Warfare Tip

The times would be truly difficult at this point. Being alive would be a miracle, and as such a miracle, rely on God with all your strength and heart. Remember, if the Father feeds the birds of the air, then will He not feed you who are much more valuable (Mathew 6:26)?

The Fourth Trumpet

The fourth angel sounded his trumpet, and a third of the sun was struck, a third of the moon, and a third of the stars, so that a third of them turned dark. A third of the day was without light, and also a third of the night. As I watched, I heard an eagle that was flying in midair call out in a loud voice: "Woe! Woe! Woe to the inhabitants of the earth, because of the trumpet blasts about to be sounded by the other three angels!"

Revelation 8:12-13

The fourth trumpet is a cosmic premonition in anticipation of the remaining three trumpets. The sun, moon, and stars will inexplicably diminish by one third, and darkness will envelop the earth. I use the word inexplicable, because this is not an eclipse.

Even the day is affected and will be without light. While it doesn't seem as destructive as the previous trumpets, one can only imagine what prolonged darkness would do to the remaining agriculture on earth. This would eliminate large food resources quickly and devastate an already destroyed earth. Worse yet, an eagle laments, "WOE! WOE! WOE!" to all the people on earth that are left, for what the rest of the three angels with trumpets are about to bring. How can these judgements get any worse?

Warfare Tip

If you haven't yet, consider evangelizing during such a time. Surprisingly, there are going to be many people that will still not believe that these are judgements from God. The great delusion is just as Paul described in Romans 1 and clouds the truth for many people.

However, there are also some who will know that this is God's wrath on earth and are seeking answers. Many will have questions on how to accept Jesus and what they need to do to be saved. This is where you come in. The revival isn't solely the responsibility of the 144,000 and the two witnesses—it rests upon believers like you and me. If you are alive on earth at this time, then you are the light amidst the darkness over the world. Even if you spread the Gospel and one person hears it to be saved, then you have aided in adding one member to the Kingdom—a priceless and honorable purpose fulfilled in your life.

The Fifth Trumpet

The fifth angel sounded his trumpet, and I saw a star that had fallen from the sky to the earth. The star was given the key to the shaft of the Abyss. When he opened the Abyss, smoke rose from it like the smoke from a gigantic furnace. The sun and sky were darkened by the smoke from the Abyss. And out of the smoke locusts came down on the earth and were given power like that of scorpions of the earth. They were told not to harm the grass of the earth or any plant or tree, but only those people who did not have the seal of God on their foreheads. They were not allowed to kill them but only to torture them for five months. And the agony they suffered was like that of the sting of a scorpion when it strikes. During those days people will seek death but will not find it; they will long to die, but death will elude them.

The locusts looked like horses prepared for battle. On their heads they wore something like crowns of gold, and their faces resembled human faces. Their hair was like women's hair, and their teeth were like lions' teeth. They had breastplates like breastplates of iron, and the sound of their wings was like the thundering of many horses and chariots rushing into battle. They had tails with stingers, like scorpions, and in their tails they had power to torment people for five months. They had as king over them the angel of the Abyss, whose name in Hebrew is Abaddon and in Greek is Apollyon (that is, Destroyer).

The first woe is past; two other woes are yet to come.

Revelation 9:1-12

Similar to the other trumpets, a star falls on earth, but this one carries a special key. This description leads many to believe that this star is actually an angel due to the fact that he is holding something that opens the "shaft of the abyss." This is likely compared to Revelation 20:1-3 in which an angel is described as the holder of the key to the abyss.

Regardless of the identity of the star, its purpose is clear. It opens the abyss. One can immediately think that this abyss is a "deep hole," and while that is correct, this abyss has another function. It is a prison for evil and demonic forces; so much so that Satan himself will be chained and be thrown into it in the future. We first hear of this abyss when Jesus casts out Legion out of a man in Luke 8:

Jesus asked him, saying, "What is your name?"

*And he said, "Legion," because many demons had entered him. And they begged Him that He would not command them to go out into the **abyss**.*

Now a herd of many swine was feeding there on the mountain. So they begged Him that He would permit them to enter them. And He permitted them.

Luke 8:30-32

We can see clearly that God has control and authority over demons and decides who He allows freedom to traverse the earth and who is imprisoned into this prison. The demons (over 4,000 to 6,000 of them in that man alone) were so terrified of being sent to the abyss that they begged Jesus to be instead sent into swine.

During the sounding of the fifth trumpet though, this prison is finally opened, and when it is, a dark smoke rises to engulf the sky, bringing darkness over the earth. Out of this smoke comes the judgement: the release of locusts, which are given the power to sting with the intensity of scorpions.

The following description of them has caused some division among believers with how literal the translation can be. We have to remember that John saw these creatures around 90 AD and describes them to the best of his ability. We must also realize that many people on this earth have never seen a demon in their life. I, for one, have seen a variety of them, and truly they are grotesque creatures—many with horrid faces and disfigured body types. So when I read John's description, I take it literally.

These locusts are coming from the abyss, which means that they are most likely going to be hideous things. I can easily believe that they indeed look like horses ready for battle, having human-like faces with lion's teeth, breastplates, noisy wings, and tails of a scorpion. As hideous as they are and as free as they will be once the abyss is opened, they will not be able to do anything they wish.

The angel gives them clear directions that they are not to harm anything green on earth, but only the people who do not have God's seal on their foreheads. This passage is commonly used as further reference to the church not being present during this time, but there are definitely believers (the 144,000 and new believers) present during this trumpet.

We can attest to this when we see what these locusts actually do. They will harm and torture all who do not have God's seal on their foreheads for a totality of five months. And just as the directive that the angel gave, they will not be allowed to kill any man, woman, or child. In fact, those afflicted by their stings will not be allowed to die or commit suicide. God's power is amazing, and He truly has ownership of the breath of life in all of us. While we have free will to do with this life on earth as we please, God has ultimate ownership of the soul. In torture, those who are attacked by these locusts will not be able to die and escape the torment. This is the first Woe.

 **Warfare Tip**

As a believer in Christ, you will not suffer this trumpet. If anything, feel joyful that these locusts are not harming you. This means you have God's seal on your forehead. REJOICE! The end is closer, and you will see Jesus very soon!

The Sixth Trumpet

The sixth angel sounded his trumpet, and I heard a voice coming from the four horns of the golden altar that is before God. It said to the sixth angel who had the trumpet, "Release the four angels who are bound at the great river Euphrates." And the four angels who had been kept ready for this very hour and day and month and year were released to kill a third of mankind. The number of the mounted troops was twice ten thousand times ten thousand. I heard their number.

The horses and riders I saw in my vision looked like this: Their breastplates were fiery red, dark blue, and yellow as sulfur. The heads of the horses resembled the heads of lions, and out of their mouths came fire, smoke and sulfur. A third of mankind was killed by the three plagues of fire, smoke and sulfur that came out of their mouths. The power of the horses was in their mouths and in their tails; for their tails were like snakes, having heads with which they inflict injury.
The rest of mankind who were not killed by these plagues still did not repent of the work of their hands; they did not stop worshiping demons, and idols of gold, silver, bronze, stone and wood—idols that cannot see or hear or walk. Nor did they repent of their murders, their magic arts, their sexual immorality or their thefts.

Revelation 9:13-21

The sixth trumpet continues the release of evil as punishment on the world. The sixth angel releases four imprisoned fallen angels to kill one third of mankind. With a mounted army of 200 million, the horsemen will eviscerate a third of what is left of mankind. Once again, these riders seem to be as supernatural as the locusts are, and they are described as having the resemblance of a lion's head. Unlike the locusts though, these riders kill using fire, smoke, and sulfur that come out of their mouths—as well as killing with their snake-like tails.

What's even more incredulous is that, despite these awful creatures and the massive killings, the survivors of this trumpet still do not repent. They continued in their idolatry and sin. So much is the hatred of God and the love for their pleasure that they continue to be blind to the time and wrath they are living in.

The Two Witnesses

Before the second woe is completed, something monumental happens in Jerusalem:

I was given a reed like a measuring rod and was told, "Go and measure the temple of God and the altar, with its worshipers. But exclude the outer court; do not measure it, because it has been given to the Gentiles. They will trample on the holy city for 42 months. And I will appoint my two witnesses, and they will prophesy for 1,260 days, clothed in sackcloth." They are "the two olive trees" and the two lampstands, and "they stand before the Lord of the earth." If anyone tries to harm them, fire comes from their mouths and devours their enemies. This is how anyone who wants to harm them must die. They have power to shut up the heavens so that it will not rain during the time they are prophesying; and they have power to turn the waters into blood and to strike the earth with every kind of plague as often as they want.

Now when they have finished their testimony, the beast that comes up from the Abyss will attack them, and overpower and kill them. Their bodies will lie in the public square of the great city—which is figuratively called Sodom and Egypt—where also their Lord was crucified. For three and a half days some from every people, tribe, language and nation will gaze on their bodies and refuse them burial. The inhabitants of the earth will gloat over them and will celebrate by sending each other gifts, because these two prophets had tormented those who live on the earth. But after the three and a half days the breath of life from God entered them, and they stood on their feet, and terror struck those who saw them. Then they heard a loud voice from heaven saying to them, "Come up here." And they went up to heaven in a cloud, while their enemies looked on. At that very hour there was a severe earthquake and a tenth of the city collapsed. Seven thousand people were killed in the earthquake, and the survivors were terrified and gave glory to the God of heaven. The second woe has passed; the third woe is coming soon.

Revelation 11:1-14

Two prophets will be appointed and prophesy God's Word for two months. In a world full of unrepentant people, they will be hated tremendously and attacked—only to discover their death through the literal fire that comes out of their mouths. After they complete their testimony though, a beast from the abyss (or the antichrist) will have the power and authority to kill them, and their bodies will be left on display in a public place of Jerusalem. The global population will cheer and gloat in celebration of their deaths for a total of three and a half days until God returns the breath of life into the witnesses. This resurrection will fill the people with terror, and God will call his witnesses to heaven once more as the woe closes.

The identity of these witnesses is not revealed. However, many predict that they will be Elijah and Enoch, since they never experienced death on earth. There is also an interpretation that the two men will be Moses and Elijah. Whoever they are, their purpose is to prophecy what is to come and reveal God's truth to all who will not listen.

What is astonishing is how much of a discomfort these witnesses of God are for these unrepentant people—not just the lack of rain during these 42 months, but a constant preaching and prophesying to an unbelieving world. I see a sample of this today in our world. Street evangelists are increasingly suffering from violent attacks because the message is such a discomfort for unbelievers and their lifestyles. The two witnesses are going to be an amplification of this, only they will be unstoppable until their testimony is completed. And then, while the world celebrates their death, God uses their resurrection to affirm and glorify His power and

His identity as the only true God. If you live to see these two men, listen clearly, and take hope that time is drawing nearer.

The Seventh Trumpet

The seventh angel sounded his trumpet, and there were loud voices in heaven, which said:

"The kingdom of the world has become
the kingdom of our Lord and of his Messiah,
and he will reign for ever and ever."
And the twenty-four elders, who were seated on their thrones before God,
fell on their faces and worshiped God, saying:
"We give thanks to you, Lord God Almighty,
the One who is and who was,
because you have taken your great power
and have begun to reign.

The nations were angry,
and your wrath has come.
The time has come for judging the dead,
and for rewarding your servants the prophets
and your people who revere your name,
both great and small—
and for destroying those who destroy the earth."
Then God's temple in heaven was opened, and within his temple was seen the ark of his covenant. And there came flashes of lightning, rumblings, peals of thunder, an earthquake and a severe hailstorm.

Revelation 11:15-19

The final trumpet is one of worship in the heavens—a moment to be grateful that the day of the Lord has finally come, a moment of thanksgiving that the Lord has begun to reign on earth, a moment to finally see justice across millennia and time, and a moment for rewards given to the prophets and all who revere His name. While the woe does not end until the final trumpet sounds in Revelation 20, the time is short, and the covenant promised is now coming to fruition.

THE SOUNDING OF THE TRUMPETS

ENCOUNTER #10
NO!

At this point in my life, these attacks were becoming so frequent that I could never sleep or get rest. People don't realize that those who suffer from demonic attacks face torture and have to pretend to the world that everything is okay. I was beginning to become agitated and angry at these things because I could never get a time of peace. Because of this, I feared less and was angered more.

One night in Arcadia, a beastly face hovered above me as I went into sleep paralysis. Already knowing that I couldn't move even if I tried, I was fed up. I was so exhausted after a long day of work that I began to shout at the thing in my mind, "GET OUT IN THE NAME OF JE—!" And immediately I was interrupted by a horrid shout: "NO!"

I was petrified and completely caught off guard that I used all the energy I could ever use to try to break free from this paralysis. I fought and fought until I could move my neck a little and finally break free. I was terrified. The thing had shouted back at me. This wasn't in my head. That demon was real, and it had yelled back at me.

I turned on the light until I calmed myself down again. That voice...was horrible. It really was a voice one would think a monster has.

What do I do?

Chapter 18

THE ANTICHRIST REVEALED

Now, brethren, concerning the coming of our Lord Jesus Christ and our gathering together to Him, we ask you, not to be soon shaken in mind or troubled, either by spirit or by word or by letter, as if from us, as though the day of Christ had come. Let no one deceive you by any means; for that Day will not come unless the falling away comes first, and the man of sin is revealed, the son of perdition, who opposes and exalts himself above all that is called God or that is worshiped, so that he sits as God in the temple of God, showing himself that he is God.

2 Thessalonians 2:1-4

Many have heard of the term "antichrist" at some point in their lives, and many deem him to be a man. But how much do people know about who he is and what he will do? The antichrist has a great role to play during the last seven years of the Great Tribulation. I am confident in the future relevance he must play. However, I must disclose that there are multiple interpretations of exactly what the antichrist is.

The first is that he is not a human, but an emotional or sense of spirit that comes upon a man or upon the world. It is a spirit that contradicts or goes against Who Christ Jesus is or teaches. This "spirit" is often attributed to more conceptual or broad aspects, like societal morality, media, social programs, or societal consensus. The second interpretation of the antichrist is that it is any human being who opposes Christ (hence anti). You are either for or against Yeshua as Christ, so anybody in opposition of Him is automatically an antichrist.

Antichrist as an Adjective

John, the author of revelation, reveals in his own letters a description of the antichrist, but not of a future world leader:

*Little children, it is the last hour; and as you have heard that the **Antichrist** is coming, even now many antichrists have come, by which we know that it is the last hour.*

1 John 2:18

*Who is a liar but he who denies that Jesus is the Christ? He is **antichrist** who denies the Father and the Son.*

1 John 2:22

*And every spirit that does not confess that Jesus Christ has come in the flesh is not of God. And this is the spirit of the **Antichrist**, which you have heard was coming, and is now already in the world.*

1 John 4:3

*For many deceivers have gone out into the world who do not confess Jesus Christ as coming in the flesh. This is a deceiver and an **antichrist**.*

2 John 1:7

These verses reveal the antichrist as the spirit or characteristic of someone who denies Jesus as the Christ. John also likens this sentiment as a spirit that inhabits people and the world. In this sense, this spiritual condition is derived from the literal term "anti" or "against." Some use this as evidence that the antichrist is only limited to this spiritual sense. However, the reason for this is because the term John uses in these letters is literally the term "antichrist," but the antichrist of Revelation and Daniel use other names, such as the "son of perdition," "the man of lawlessness," and the "beast." All of these names describe one man, which is the man that will be discussed further.

The Beast and the Dragon

Following the sounding of the seventh trumpet, John sees the following:

*Then I stood on the sand of the sea. And I saw a **beast** rising up out of the sea, having seven heads and ten horns, and on his horns ten crowns, and on his heads a blasphemous name. Now the beast which I saw was like a leopard, his feet were like the feet of a bear, and his mouth like the mouth of a lion. The **dragon** gave him his power, his throne, and great authority. And I saw one of his heads as if it had been mortally wounded, and his deadly wound was healed. And all the world marveled and followed the beast. So they worshiped the dragon who gave authority to the beast; and they worshiped the beast, saying, "Who is like the **beast**? Who is able to make war with him?"*

Revelation 13:1-4

It is important to note first that this beast is of evil origin and receives his power from Satan. The dragon is defined as Satan within the same book of revelation. This "dragon" John saw directly gives power, authority, and his throne on earth to this beast to do his bidding. But who is this beast? In order to be certain of what John is describing, we need to decipher the beast's identity. Luckily, we can extract more detail and explanation from Daniel:

Daniel spoke, saying, "I saw in my vision by night, and behold, the four winds of heaven were stirring up the Great Sea. And four great beasts came up from the sea, each different from the other. The first was like a lion, and had eagle's wings. I watched till its wings were plucked off; and it was lifted up from the earth and made to stand on two feet like a man, and a man's heart was given to it.

"And suddenly another beast, a second, like a bear. It was raised up on one side, and had three ribs in its mouth between its teeth. And they said thus to it: 'Arise, devour much flesh!'

> "After this I looked, and there was another, like a leopard, which had on its back four wings of a bird. The beast also had four heads, and dominion was given to it.
>
> "After this I saw in the night visions, and behold, a fourth beast, dreadful and terrible, exceedingly strong. It had huge iron teeth; it was devouring, breaking in pieces, and trampling the residue with its feet. It was different from all the beasts that were before it, and it had ten horns. I was considering the horns, and there was another horn, a little one, coming up among them, before whom three of the first horns were plucked out by the roots. And there, in this horn, were eyes like the eyes of a man, and a mouth speaking pompous words."
>
> Daniel 7:2-8

The above descriptions may seem difficult to understand, but Daniel was as perplexed as you were when you first read them. Fortunately, he asked for an interpretation:

> *Those great beasts, which are four, are four kings which arise out of the earth.*
>
> Daniel 7:17

Something occurs hereafter though. Daniel becomes highly interested in the fourth beast. And we indeed get a thorough interpretation of who and what he is:

> *Then I wished to know the truth about the fourth beast, which was **different from all the others**, exceedingly dreadful, with its teeth of iron and its nails of bronze, which devoured, broke in pieces, and trampled the residue with its feet; and the ten horns that were on its head, and the other horn which came up, before which three fell, namely, that horn which had eyes and a mouth which spoke pompous words, whose appearance was greater than his fellows.*

I was watching; and the same horn was making war against the saints, and prevailing against them, until the Ancient of Days came, and a judgment was made in favor of the saints of the Most High, and the time came for the saints to possess the kingdom.

Thus he said:
'The fourth beast shall be
A fourth kingdom on earth,
Which shall be different from all other kingdoms,
*And shall **devour the whole earth**,*
Trample it and break it in pieces.
The ten horns are ten kings
Who shall arise from this kingdom.
And another shall rise after them;
He shall be different from the first ones,
And shall subdue three kings.
He shall speak pompous words against the Most High,
Shall persecute the saints of the Most High,
And shall intend to change times and law.
Then the saints shall be given into his hand
For a time and times and half a time.
'But the court shall be seated,
And they shall take away his dominion,
To consume and destroy it forever.
Then the kingdom and dominion,
And the greatness of the kingdoms under the whole heaven,
Shall be given to the people, the saints of the Most High.
His kingdom is an everlasting kingdom,
And all dominions shall serve and obey Him.'

Daniel 7:19-27

This fourth beast will be a kingdom (or a nation) that will produce an eleventh king after the ten seen in the horns. This king will persecute Christians, subdue three other kings, and change God's law and times for a period of three and a half years. When you compare the beast to that of which John saw in the book of Revelation, you can begin to see the connection:

And he was given a mouth speaking great things and blasphemies, and he was given authority to continue for forty-two months. Then he opened his mouth in blasphemy against God, to blaspheme His name, His tabernacle, and those who dwell in heaven. It was granted to him to make war with the saints and to overcome them. And authority was given him over every tribe, tongue, and nation. All who dwell on the earth will worship him, whose names have not been written in the Book of Life of the Lamb slain from the foundation of the world.

Revelation 13:1-8

There are more identifiers that point to the beast being a man. He will be given authority over all nations across the globe and unbelievers will worship him (freely), and in his reign, he will specifically persecute and kill those who believe in Jesus and succeed in doing so. We can see the beginning of this given authority in our world today as political and economical leaders push for a one world government. Many famous ideological and political leaders have already set the groundwork and propagated their plan to enact a one world government:

"Each of us has the hope to build a New World Order." [28]

Richard Nixon

"Some even believe we are part of a secret cabal working against the best interests of the United States, characterizing my family and me as 'internationalists' and of conspiring with others around the world to build a more integrated global political and economic structure – one world if you will. If that's the charge, I stand guilty, and I am proud of it."[29]

David Rockefeller

"By the end of this decade (2000 AD) we will live under the first One World Government that has ever existed in the society of nations, a government with absolute authority to decide the basic issues of human survival. One world government is inevitable."[30]

Pope John Paul II

"The New World Order cannot happen without U.S. participation, as we are the most significant single component. Yes, there will be a New World Order, and it will force the United States to change its perceptions."[31]

Henry Kissinger

"The new world order that is in the making must focus on the creation of a world of democracy, peace and prosperity for all,"[32]

Nelson Mendela

"We have before us the opportunity to forge, for ourselves and for future generations, a New World Order. A world where the rule of law, not the law of the jungle, rules all nations. When we are successful–and we will be–we have a real chance at this New World Order. An order in which a credible United Nations can use its peacekeeping forces to fulfill the promise and vision of its founders."[33]

George H.W. Bush

In a world of economic collapse and global catastrophe, the world will accept the antichrist as a savior. And while he provides them a false peace, an event will occur that will mark the final three and a half years of the age: the Abomination of Desolation.

The Abomination of Desolation

This event is important because Jesus Himself declares that His second coming cannot come until this abomination of desolation occurs:

*Therefore when you see the '**abomination of desolation**,' spoken of by Daniel the prophet, standing in the holy place" (whoever reads, let him understand), "then let those who are in Judea flee to the mountains. Let him who is on the housetop not go down to take anything out of his house. And let him who is in the field not go back to get his clothes. But woe to those who are pregnant and to those who are nursing babies in those days! And pray that your flight may not be in winter or on the Sabbath. For then there will be great tribulation, such as has not been since the beginning of the world until this time, no,* *nor ever shall be. And unless those days were shortened, no flesh would be saved; but for the elect's sake those days will be shortened.*

Matthew 24:15-22

Before continuing, I must preface by mentioning that many believe that this abomination of desolation has already occurred during the destruction of Jerusalem in 70 AD and not during the Great Tribulation. The clearest reasoning for this is that the entirety of Matthew 24 begins in response to the disciples inquiring about Jesus' reference that no stones of the temple would be left on another. While Jesus' description did indeed come to pass, Daniel's prophecy regarding the abomination of desolation have led many scholars and Christians to believe that this event can happen multiple times. Around 168 B.C., Hellenestic King Antiochus Epiphanes invaded Jerusalem to the point of erecting a statue of Zeus in the holy temple and "defiling" it by literally killing a pig on the altar of incense.[33] While the occurrence of the abomination of desolation may be a multiple repeating event, I believe the totality of the event has not occurred for the following reasons:

First, during His description in Matthew 24, Jesus tells the disciples that "then there will be great tribulation, such as the world has not seen since the beginning of the world…nor shall ever be…and unless those days were shortened, no flesh would be saved." While the destruction of Jerusalem was indeed violent and tragic, that does not compare to the horror and destruction of the Great Tribulation. We have already seen that the seals and the trumpets have eviscerated a large portion of the global population (and this is even before the bowls). Truly no flesh would survive unless the days were shortened during the Great Tribulation.

Second, Daniel defines and describes what the abomination of desolation actually is:

*And he will make a firm covenant with the many for one week, but in the middle of the week he will put a stop to sacrifice and grain offering; and on the wing of **abominations** will come one who makes **desolate**, even until a complete destruction, one that is decreed, is poured out on the one who makes **desolate**.*

Daniel 9:27

*Forces from him shall appear and profane the temple and fortress, and shall take away the regular burnt offering. And they shall set up the **abomination** that makes **desolate**.*

Daniel 11:31

Both of these passages describe an end to offerings and the placement of abomination(s). Two things. First, regardless of it's historical reference, a temple must be present in order for this abomination of desolation to be complete. For those who believe that this has already occurred, they have reason to believe it has already happened since the second temple was already there before its destruction. Like mentioned previously, Antiochus Epiphanes could have very well fulfilled this requirement. Today, however, the temple does not exist. The Muslim mosque, the Dome of the Rock, is believed to be in its place now.

In order for the abomination of desolation to be possible today, a third and new temple must be erected for this prophecy to be fulfilled. This is a problem for many because it is literally almost impossible. I for one do not doubt the power of God. The world thought the prophecy that Israel would return as a nation would be impossible and God proved all wrong. So too, I believe, that a third temple will be built.

Another reason why I believe that a third temple must be erected is because Daniel 11:31 specifically mentions, "They shall set up the abomination that makes desolate." In 70 AD, Rome destroyed the temple and fulfilled Jesus' prophecy that "There shall not be left here one stone upon another, that shall not be thrown down" (Matthew 24:2). Romans did not "set up an abomination" anywhere in which a covenant was made with Jews before halting offerings and sacrifices. They destroyed everything. Another reason can be found in 2 Thessalonians:

Let no one in any way deceive you, for it will not come unless the apostasy comes first, and the man of lawlessness is revealed, the son of destruction, who opposes and exalts himself above every so-called god or object of worship, so that he takes his seat in the temple of God, displaying himself as being God.

2 Thessalonians 2:3-4

Here, we see a very specific description of what will happen. The man of lawlessness (the antichrist) takes a seat in the temple of God and displays himself to be as God. This is the height of blasphemy. In the first temple, the Ark of the Covenant stood in the holy of holies. It was so holy that only the priest could enter once a year to provide sacrificial atonement on behalf of the nation. For any man to enter and declare that he is God and demand he be worshipped is the highest form of blasphemy. When this occurs, know that the man of lawlessness has finally revealed himself to the world.

False Christ

The identity of the antichrist is highly contested. Many denominations have their own interpretations of who and what he is. In my time, I've even heard that Barack Obama and Donald Trump are the antichrist—which is ludicrous, because neither of them match the identity of the beast that scripture describes. Whatever you believe, study to yourself approved. Look into scripture and ask God to reveal to you what you need to know. For me, knowing as many interpretations as possible is helpful. In the event I am wrong and I see a specific interpretation happening in real time, I will know how to act. If you see the world clamor and worship a man in the future, feel confident that he is the one Daniel and Jesus warned you about.

ENCOUNTER #11
THE MAN IN BLACK

One of the feelings I always had during these experiences was that there was always someone or something watching me. I could never see them up front or face to face like I wanted to. I was so fatigued and tired of this that I searched everywhere online to find an answer.

During a home visit, I awoke again in the middle of the night. I didn't move, but I could see the shape of a man in black. Pitch black. It was as if he was made of pure shadow. I moved slowly to get a clearer look, and as I began to move, the shadow began to run past my bedside. I shot forward to try to block him and get a full view of what it was, but he disappeared past the wall.

I thought over the incident because something was strange. The outline was clearly of a man. And it seemed as if he was watching me until he or "it" realized I was awake and aware of its presence. Once I was alert, he ran. I had researched online that some people purposefully astral project to travel all over the world, so maybe it was a projection of such an individual, but I don't know. To this day, I still don't know who or what that was.

Chapter 19

THE FALSE PROPHET

He performs great signs, so that he even makes fire come down from heaven on the earth in the sight of men.

Revelation 13:13

While the term or notion of the antichrist is more mainstream across Christian and secular circles, the false prophet is less known; despite being an essential asset to the antichrist in his rise to power. Many pastors and Christian evangelists have a variety of interpretations as to the identity of the false prophet, ranging from a broader perspective of a concept to the more specific aspect of an individual person alive during the same time as the antichrist. I will present the scripture as it stands and then provide one of the most common interpretations as to who this false prophet is.

*Then I saw another **beast** coming up out of the earth, and he had two horns like a lamb and **spoke like a dragon**. And he **exercises all the authority of the first beast in his presence**, and causes the earth and those who dwell in it to **worship the first beast**, whose deadly wound was healed. He **performs great signs**, so that he even makes fire come down from heaven on the earth in the sight of men. And he deceives those who dwell on the earth by those signs which he was granted to do in the sight of the beast, telling those who dwell on the earth to **make an image to the beast** who was wounded by the sword and lived. He was granted **power to give breath to the image of the beast**, that the image of the beast should both speak and cause as many as would not worship the image of the beast to be killed. He causes all, both small and great, rich and poor, free and slave, to **receive a mark** on their right hand or on their foreheads, and that no one may buy or sell except one who has the mark or the name of the beast, or the number of his name.*

Revelation 13:11-17

The Beast
Just as the beast that rises from the sea (the antichrist), another beast erupts from the earth. This beast with two horns speaks like a dragon. As we already know, references to a dragon are references to Satan. The false prophet speaks like a dragon, meaning that he speaks like a devil: full of lies and deceit. The next description is that he exercises all the authority of the antichrist, but only in his presence. This is interesting because the things that the false prophet will do in order to make all on earth worship the antichrist are only going to be possible by the authority given by the antichrist, who receives power from Satan. This shared authority allows the false prophet to deceive many by performing great signs, one of which will be calling down fire from the sky. This is not surprising though, as Satan is an imitator of God. God is the one who has rained down fire upon earth previously.

The Image
One of the key things the false prophet does is telling (certain) people on earth to create an image of the antichrist and breathe life into it. This image will be able to speak and cause all who do not worship it to be killed. This event is the reason why many believe this image is the abomination that makes desolate in the third temple at the midway point of the Great Tribulation:

> *Forces from him shall appear and profane the temple and fortress, and shall take away the regular burnt offering. And they shall set up the **abomination** that makes **desolate**.*
>
> Daniel 11:31

The Mark
Finally, the assistance of the image and the false prophet will incur a mandatory mark that all people on earth will be required to take. A detailed account of this mark will follow in the next chapter.

Who Is the Beast?

Before delving into what is likely the most common interpretation and my personal take as well of who the false prophet is, I want to be clear that the identity of the false prophet is impossible to pinpoint at the moment of this writing. The antichrist has not revealed himself (as I write this) and as such, his false prophet has not been called. I've heard and read that the Beast is one of the main religious leaders on earth, such as Pope Francis, but I have to be clear: that is speculation. It may or may not be true. Whether it is Pope Francis or a future pope, here are the reasons why the False Prophet will likely come from the Vatican.

Is the Papacy the False Prophet?
Many will likely stop reading here. There are many Catholics who are offended at the mere thought that the pope will be the false prophet of the antichrist, and I completely understand. I, myself, was raised Catholic and would become irritated when Catholicism was criticized or scrutinized. If you feel offended by this interpretation, I understand. I only ask that, after skipping or reading this, you begin your own research into the identity of this false prophet through scripture and provide a rebuttal to this claim.

First, we must first note that the false prophet is to the antichrist as John the Baptist was to Jesus. John paved the way for Jesus' first coming and ministry on earth. So too, the false prophet of Revelation will also pave the way for the antichrist to ascend to global power.

We must ask first what exactly is needed for the antichrist to implement his self-worship and mark upon the world. In order for the antichrist to gain power, he first needs control over all nations and tongues as Revelation 13 dictates. He needs a one world government and one world religion to unite all the people of the earth. While I do not know if he will be the false prophet, I believe a pope will be the one to set the stage for the antichrist.

Why do I believe this? For one, the current pope as of this writing, Francis, has made huge strides in uniting political leaders and religious leaders during his leadership—all under the guise that we all worship the same God. I want to be clear that I am not saying Pope Francis is the false prophet, but what I am saying is that he is certainly taking strides to unite the world under climate change and world peace initiatives.

One of the characteristics of the false prophet is that he is a global religious leader. With his help, the antichrist rises to power and, when the time comes, is the one who is responsible for the creation of the false image and getting people all over the world to worship the beast. In order to do that, the false prophet must unite the world. This means that all religions on earth today need to be united: Islam, Christianity, Buddhism, Hinduism, Judaism, and all smaller or denominations that fall under their systems.

Doing this is quite the feat, since none of these religions would seemingly ever coexist, and it is difficult to believe that they would ever agree to unite as one. The current Pope Francis, however, has made historic news when he met Russian Orthodox leader Patriarch Kirill in 2016, a meeting between their respective churches that had not happened in over 1,000 years.[35] In 2019, he met with over 700 religious leaders across 22 faiths in Abu Dhabi to discuss peace among themselves to better serve the world and said, "Today, we too in the name of God, in order to safeguard peace, need to enter together as one family into an ark which can sail the stormy seas of the world: the ark of fraternity."[36]

I must step in here to make an indication. First, Christians and other religions will never share the kingdom of heaven together. Nobody comes to the Father but through Jesus. The notion that all religions enter the ark together is preposterous and the antithesis of what Jesus taught and of the basis of the Christian faith. Secondly, he gave his speech at the Sheikh Zayed Grand Mosque.[37] What a self-proclaimed follower of Christ is doing there in the first place, I do not know. Being a follower of Yeshua is to make a clear distinction to the world that you do not follow and live as they do. Jesus is very clear about what describes a follower of Him:

If the world hates you, you know that it hated Me before it hated you. If you were of the world, the world would love its own. Yet because you are not of the world, but I chose you out of the world, therefore the world hates you.

John 15:18-19

And you will be hated by all for My name's sake. But he who endures to the end shall be saved.

Mark 13:13

You cannot double dip with Christ. Either you're in all the way or you're not. Remember what Jesus said about being lukewarm? What about not serving two masters? Another problem with Pope Francis' message is that he is promoting peace across all faiths. Once again, Jesus is clear regarding the peace He brings on earth:

Do you think I have come to bring peace to the earth? No, I have come to divide people against each other! From now on families will be split apart, three in favor of me, and two against—or two in favor and three against. Father will be divided against son and son against father; mother against daughter and daughter against mother; and mother-in-law against daughter-in-law and daughter-in-law against mother-in-law.

Luke 12:49-53

And also:

Do not think that I came to bring peace on earth. I did not come to bring peace but a sword. For I have come to 'set a man against his father, a daughter against her mother, and a daughter-in-law against her mother-in-law'; and 'a man's enemies will be those of his own household.' He who loves father or mother more than Me is not worthy of Me. And he who loves son or daughter more than Me is not worthy of Me. And he who does not take his cross and follow after Me is not worthy of Me. He who finds his life will lose it, and he who loses his life for My sake will find it.

Matthew 10:34-38

To think that the world is going to get better and to propagate world peace is to not know scripture, for Jesus Himself has proclaimed that He came to earth to cause division…not peace. This may sound surprising to some but let me explain. When I publicly came out as a Christian, many people and acquaintances immediately hated me for my message. Some unfriended me on social media, some asked other people what my problem was, and even a family member told my dad I needed mental health help. This is the division Jesus speaks of—especially in the world today. To stand in God's Word today is to be labeled a bigot and intolerant.

Again, I'm not saying that Pope Francis is the false prophet of Revelation, but I do question his behavior and his words as a proclaimed follower of Christ. Most importantly though is his recent change to the Lord's prayer. In 2017, Pope Francis approved the changing of the Lord's prayer from "lead us not into temptation" to "do not let us fall into temptation."[38] While his reasoning is that Satan is the one who leads us into temptation, the original Greek translation is quite literal in its vocabulary. Translating God's Word is a huge task to undertake, usually requiring a great number of expert scholars painstakingly reviewing each word, phrase, and context to produce the most accurate rendition—especially when you are translating Jesus' literal words. Even modern translations like the New International Version or the Queen James Bible are under heavy fire for modifying grammar and phrases outside of their native origin. For Pope Francis to publicly announce his logic for the change based off his reasoning of what he thinks it means (as opposed to what the actual Greek text says) is blasphemous at best. You do not ever change the Lord's Word. EVER. Under no circumstance do you have the authority or capacity to do so. Just reference Revelation 22:18-19 and Deuteronomy 4:2 to see what God and Jesus have to say about anyone who adds or changes His Word.

This (unsurprisingly) is another characteristic of the false prophet, for he will change God's times and laws. One of these changes has already been fulfilled with the changing of the Sabbath to Sunday worship (more on that later). Examples like these are reasons to believe that a pope has the capacity to become a unifier of people and religions across the earth. While it may or may not be Pope Francis, it is important to keep watch to see who the antichrist and the false prophet are. If you see a political and religious duo take prominence and change the world, rest assured that you know who they are. The world will love them. They will be saviors in their time of need. And while the antichrist will make a false peace for some time, he will show his true colors and betray everyone when he forces everyone to worship him and his image.

I included this interpretation as an aid so you can know what the most common interpretation of the false prophet is across Christendom. This does not mean its accurate. We do the best we can with the knowledge we have. I may be wrong. But it is important to know and prepare so you can identify the principals involved. Remember, Jesus warns that these false prophets are so good at deceiving that they will even deceive the elect. Research this topic further if you feel unsatisfied and keep watch. Because the events leading to the end are moving faster, just like the labor pains Jesus described 2,000 years ago.

Chapter 20

MARK OF THE BEAST

Then the beast was captured, and with him the false prophet who worked signs in his presence, by which he deceived those who received the mark of the beast and those who worshiped his image. These two were cast alive into the lake of fire burning with brimstone.

Revelation 19:20

This is the most important chapter in this book, and in my opinion, the most crucial piece of information in the book of Revelation for the last generation. If you get anything out of what you have read so far, please be attentive to this, because this piece of information and the choice you make directly affects your salvation.

You may have heard of this "mark of the beast" already, but many who have a vague perspective of it miss one crucial part. No matter what you think, no matter if you've been a Christian all your life, and no matter if you are ignorant of this information, if you take the mark of the beast, you will go to hell!

No questions asked. Do not pass Go. Do not collect $200. This may sound harsh, but I have to bring this with as much attention as possible, because the last generation is here, and the implementation of this mark is being realized today to the surprise of many.

More importantly, scripture is very clear about what the mark is and what happens to those that take it. Please read ahead attentively and consider what scripture has to say about the mark of the beast. If you disagree, by all means continue your research until you feel confident that you are sure (as I am) about the consequences of taking this mark. Whether or not we agree, one thing is clear: this mark is highly important in the end times and is the difference between salvation and condemnation.

Before moving forward and interpreting what the mark of the beast is, I will first provide a textual demonstration of what the scripture describes the mark of the beast to be.

The Mark According to Revelation

When discussing the mark of the beast, it is important to note that the mark is only described in the book of Revelation. Having said that, the book of Revelation is the final revelation of Jesus Christ and specifically describes the final events before Jesus' return to earth. The first mention of the mark of the beast is as follows:

Then I saw another beast coming up out of the earth, and he had two horns like a lamb and spoke like a dragon. And he exercises all the authority of the first beast in his presence, and causes the earth and those who dwell in it to worship the first beast, whose deadly wound was healed. He performs great signs, so that he even makes fire come down from heaven on the earth in the sight of men. And he deceives those who dwell on the earth by those signs which he was granted to do in the sight of the beast, telling those who dwell on the earth to make an image to the beast who was wounded by the sword and lived. He was granted power to give breath to the image of the beast, that the image of the beast should both speak and cause as many as would not worship the image of the beast to be killed. **He causes all, both small and great, rich and poor, free and slave, to receive a mark on their right hand or on their foreheads, and that no one may buy or sell except one who has the mark or the name of the beast, or the number of his name.**

Here is wisdom.

Let him who has understanding calculate the number of the beast, for it is the number of a man: His number is 666.

Revelation 13:11-18

We can see immediately that the mark of the beast comes from the partnership of the antichrist and the false prophet. Alongside the great signs and the creation of the image of the beast, he attempts to force ALL on earth to receive a mark on their right hand or on their forehead. This is literally all people on earth. Regardless of class, wealth, ethnicity, or freedoms, all will be mandated to take this mark.

The reason for this indiscriminate characteristic follows quickly and succinctly: you will not be able to buy or sell without it. This, of course, makes it clear as to why the vast majority of the global population chooses to take it. You won't be able to live as you do. No mark means no transactions for food, housing, and the necessities you need to live. Combine this scenario with the (already) killing of those who do not worship the beast, and you've got yourself the biggest temptation a person on earth can have during this time. Not taking this mark will most likely mean death by starvation or survival by means of hiding and living in the wilderness; or worse yet, captured and beheaded. Some may begin to think that the choice is easy: just take the mark. Why would you succumb to suffering? Well, the angel has the answer:

Then a third angel followed them, saying with a loud voice, **"If anyone worships the beast and his image, and receives his mark on his forehead or on his hand, he himself shall also drink of the wine of the wrath of God, which is poured out full strength into the cup of His indignation. He shall be tormented with fire and brimstone in the presence of the holy angels and in the presence of the Lamb. And the smoke of their torment ascends forever and ever; and they have no rest day or night, who worship the beast and his image, and whoever receives the mark of his name.**

Here is the patience of the saints; here are those who keep the commandments of God and the faith of Jesus.
Then I heard a voice from heaven saying to me, "Write: 'Blessed are the dead who die in the Lord from now on.'"
"Yes," says the Spirit, "that they may rest from their labors, and their works follow them."

Revelation 14:9-13

This is the reason why you must never, ever, under any circumstances receive the mark. From this point forward, anyone with the mark will suffer from God's wrath (more on that during the bowl judgements) and be eternally condemned. The third angel is clear when he says those with the mark will be tormented with fire and brimstone in the presence of Jesus.

He also adds that the smoke of their torment ascends forever and ever; and they have no rest day or night. There are some that interpret this torment to only the time of God's wrath before Jesus' second coming. However, the text is clear to note eternal terms. There is an emphasis on "forever" and "ever." In fact, the angel clearly says they will burn in the presence of Jesus, meaning that this torment comes after Jesus' second coming.

For those still unconvinced, read further to see that the angel makes a declaration for those who endure and do not take the mark. He states that blessed are the dead who die in Jesus from that point forward. God knows exactly that believers true in faith will likely die because of their refusal to take this mark. Whether through martyrdom, starvation, or other means, He provides us with hope that comes after our endurance to the end so that we can be confident and unafraid of the choice we made.

Even with this scripture though, there are still many that reject the condemnation of the mark. As an interpretation, the final evidence for eternal separation from God through this mark is as follows:

And I saw thrones, and they sat on them, and judgment was committed to them. Then I saw the souls of those who had been beheaded for their witness to Jesus and for the word of God, **who had not worshiped the beast or his image, and had not received his mark on their foreheads or on their hands.** *And they lived and reigned with Christ for a thousand years.*

Revelation 20:4

John saw the souls of those who were beheaded, who did not worship the beast, and did not take his mark on their foreheads or on their hands living and reigning with Christ for a thousand years. This is it. As clear as it can possibly be. John saw only those who did not receive the mark being in the presence of Jesus.

This is why not taking this mark is crucial to your salvation. It matters not if you repent after. If you take this mark, you will receive the judgment and condemnation of those who also bear it.

You cannot afford to make this mistake. Similar to God's seal, this mark will separate the sheep from the goats. I've heard people question, "What if you are forced to take it?" The angel in scripture makes strong assumptions that this mark will be a choice, since those who do not receive it (most likely) die. The language used states that those who were beheaded for their witness to Jesus and did not worship the beast or his image, and who had not received the mark lived with Christ. This implies that many will die for making this choice.

That's what makes this situation so difficult for people. It will take true faith and reliance on God to endure to the end. This is why it's so important to repent and get right with God today, because the technology of the mark is here, and its implementation is at our doorstep.

The Mark Revealed

While there is not a definitive mark of the beast today as of this writing, the advent of technology has made it possible for the mark to be created and implemented in our modern world today. I will present the two most common interpretations of the mark of the beast as they exist today and how they could be implemented on a world-wide scale: the RFID Chip and the Sunday Law.

The RFID Chip

For Christians a century ago, the realization of what the mark of the beast could be was very limited. Many thought the mark was a tattoo, leading critics to attack the idea that a tattoo could prevent one from buying or selling. Well, just as the visions of Daniel and John, they described possibilities based on their present time. Today, the advent of technology has provided a more sophisticated interpretation of the mark of the beast to include a sensical scenario of the mark's invention and implementation.

Radio frequency in our modern world has given us possibilities we deemed impossible. Commencing after World War II, this technology has been utilized in tracking assets and personnel, collecting data and access to restricted areas, and providing quick economic transactions. Many do not realize that this technology is in our hands now. From our debit cards to passports, we have begun to use such technology to ease our lives and protect our identities.

The radio-frequency-identification (RFID) chip takes this capability a step forward by implementing a small chip under the skin of your hand (as small as 1.25x7mm). This chip has the capabilities of all radio frequency technology to track personal, medical, and financial information, while also interacting with smart devices such as doors, cars, and phones. For those of us utilizing our current technologies, these capabilities sound like a modernist's dream come true.

While many would definitely opt into this, there are those who are skeptical that this can ever be installed into people willingly. Well, it's happening today as of this writing in 2020. Biohax, a Swedish company that supplies RFID chips, has implanted over 4,000 installations over five years since its launch.[39] In fact, Sweden has become a trendsetter in utilizing this technology to replace physical identification cards and train tickets. But what does this have to do with the mark of the beast?

The mark of the beast is clear on three things: One, that the antichrist and the false prophet will force everyone on earth to receive it. Two, that it will be implanted on a person's forehead or right hand. And three, that nobody will be able to buy or sell without it. Many believe the RFID will be the instrument and means for the mark of the beast because it has capability to track every person on earth while also holding a person's financial information. This chip has the capacity to enforce a society that only allows transactions by those who have this technology implanted in them. Imagine not being able to purchase food or basic necessities unless you had this chip.

We can see the beginnings of this with RFID credit cards and REAL ID's that are beginning to be required if you intend to travel. Another reason why many believe this to be the mark is that it is implanted in your wrist or in your hand. This is one of the main indicators that persuade many to this interpretation. It falls in line with the scripture in Jesus' revelation.

I share this interpretation because bearing the mark causes irreversible condemnation. You cannot risk making the wrong choice. The RFID may or may not be the mark, but you must be alert and have sharp discernment at the ready. If you begin to see that this is something being spoken about in society, then be on high alert. Read the scripture again and pray to God for discernment.

The Sunday Law

Another interpretation of the mark of the beast is not physical at all. Held primarily by Seventh Day Adventists, the mark is more similar to a metaphorical interpretation of God's seal on people's foreheads. It is invisible, being a mark borne by conduct. In short, the interpretation of the Sunday law is based on observance of the Sabbath in contrast to Sunday worshippers. To those who don't know, the Sabbath is observance (as dictated by God in creation and His fourth commandment) of God's holy day of rest. This day has been observed on Saturday and is still practiced today by Jews. Observance of Sunday then becomes the height of deception for Sabbath observers and thus, gives light into a Sunday Law interpretation of the mark of the beast.

Under this scenario, the antichrist and the false prophet will invoke a mandatory Sunday Law that requires all on earth to rest and worship (the new one-world religion) on Sunday. This essentially requires Sabbath observers to denounce the Sabbath as the day of rest and forcibly worship "the beast" on Sunday.

Many have criticized this view because of a few markers. The first is the bearing of the mark on the forehead or the right hand. If this "invisible" mark is so, then how is it implemented on the body? Similar to God's seal on the 144,000, those in favor argue that this mark is spiritual and invisible. And just as God has an invisible seal on His chosen, so do those who (knowingly or unknowingly) worship the beast.

The harshest criticism though is from the aspect of buying or selling. How does the Sunday Law prevent you from buying or selling? This is a tough and important notion to analyze, because this must be one of the conditions for the mark. Not many Seventh Day Adventist hold a popular or public stance on this portion of scripture. I have heard from a few that Sunday can possibly be the day that people "check-in" to receive their allotment of funds for the week (assuming that the government will only provide you funds if you have a built in chip or mechanism that tracks your attendance). This is, of course, being under the presumption that all people on earth are given living wages from the one-world government (similar to universal basic income).

The reason this interpretation is so unpopular is because if this is true, then that means that millions of Christians today (and from years past) would go to hell for not observing the Sabbath on Saturday and worshipping on Sundays. After all, how many of us believers worship on Sunday? Most Christians by far. But is there substance to this? There might be. The transfer of the Sabbath to Sunday is actually catalogued in writing by the Catholic Church:

> Q. Which is the Sabbath day?
> A. Saturday is the Sabbath day.
>
> Q. Why do we observe Sunday instead of Saturday?
> A. We observe Sunday instead of Saturday because the Catholic Church, in the Council of Laodicea (AD 336), transferred the solemnity from Saturday to Sunday.
>
> Q. Why did the Catholic Church substitute Sunday for Saturday?
> A. The Church substituted Sunday for Saturday, because Christ rose from the dead on a Sunday, and the Holy Ghost descended upon the Apostles on a Sunday.
>
> Q. By what authority did the Church substitute Sunday for Saturday?
> A. The Church substituted Sunday for Saturday by the plenitude of that divine power which Jesus Christ bestowed upon her!
>
> —*Rev. Peter Geiermann, C.SS.R., (1946), p. 50."*
> *Convert's Catechism of Catholic Doctrine*

> "The Church of God has thought it well to transfer the celebration and observance of the Sabbath to Sunday!"
>
> *p 402, second revised edition (English), 1937. (First published in 1566) Catechism of the Council of Trent*

Ron Wyatt

Ron Eldon Wyatt was a Christian anesthesiologist that resided in Tennessee, United States. An ardent follower of Christ, it was his passion to discover God's archeological remnants so the world could see and believe. Noted for discovering Mount Sinai in Saudi Arabia, Noah's ark in Turkey, and the Red Sea crossing location, Ron is well known today for the discoveries of some of the largest and most profound Biblical events in our history. One of these discoveries, however, is surprisingly the most unknown and the most controversial; and that is the discovery of the Ark of the Covenant in Jerusalem.

According to Ron, as he was walking near Golgotha with his friend in Jerusalem, he (uncontrollably) pointed his finger to some rubble underneath a cliff and said, "There is Jeremiah's Grotto; and the Ark of the Covenant is there." His friend was astounded and asked him to repeat what he had just said. Confounded, Ron repeated what he thought he just said. Not convinced, Ron went back to study the Bible to confirm if that location was even possible. After some research, Ron began excavating the location with his two sons and found large signs dating back to the Roman period. As he descended further, he also found four large constructed square holes plugged by a removable rock; which led Ron to believe this was a site for crucifixions that displayed the crimes committed by those crucified. In addition, he also found a cistern filled with round rocks and finger bones; leading Ron to believe that this was also a site where people were stoned to death.

As the excavation progressed deeper during a span of eight years, Ron and his Arab assistant made themselves into a deep cave underneath the site. Upon removing an astelakyte, his assistant went in and came running out, yelling, "I quit!" as he desperately escaped the cave. Ron made a wider opening for himself and went further in. Using his flashlight, he noticed a stone slab split in two pieces and a crack above. The space was so tight that Ron couldn't see inside the rock, but he began to notice what he presumed to be dried blood at the top of the rock and drippage on and under the crack of the stone slabs. Upon realizing this, he knew - that blood dripped from the top of the crucifixion site and into the cracked stone slabs. He knew the Ark was there. This realization is profound since that means that the earthquake that occurred at Christs crucifixion caused a rupture on the ground that split the container of the ark; and Christs blood dripped all the way down into the Mercy Seat.

Following his discovery, he informed Israeli government officials and went back into the chamber room; later finding other golden temple items like the seven-lamp Menorah, the Table of Showbread, the Golden Altar of Incense, a sencer, and a large sword (most likely Goliath's). In the rear of the Ark, Ron found scrolls that contained the Book of the Law; written on ancient animal skins. After collecting some of the blood found on the stone slabs, he had it analyzed in an Israeli laboratory. Ron recounts that the experts reconstituted the blood for 72 hours. At Ron's request, he requested that they take some of the white blood cells and place them in a growth medium and put them in body temperature for 48 hours. The lab technicians reluctantly agreed and informed Ron that it would do no good since the blood was dead. After the 48 hours passed Ron was present during the examination. Speaking in Hebrew, one of the lab technicians shuffled and called the boss to investigate as they looked into the microscope. They turned to Ron and told him, Mr. Wyatt, this human blood only has 24 chromosomes in it." (A normal human has 46 - 23 from your mother and 23 from your father; 22 autosomes from each and an x or a y chromosome) Ron explains that this blood has 23 chromosomes from the mother's side and one Y chromosome only. After this, the lab technician said, "This blood is alive. Whose blood is this?" to which Ron emotionally responded, "It's the blood of your Messiah".

On his fourth and final visit to the Ark's chamber, Ron found the chamber and tunnel completely cleared up of rocks and debris. The temple items were all arranged and organized along the walls of the chamber. In front of Ron he saw four angels, two on each side of the Ark of the Covenant; that now glowed brightly outside of its stone casing. They informed Ron they were assigned to protect the Ark and asked Ron to place his camera on a tripod and record. They lifted the Mercy seat and asked him to take out the Ten Commandments written on the tablets of stone. Ron held them and displayed them in front of the camera for some time. Lastly, they told Ron that this will be released and shown at God's appointed time. Before leaving, Ron left the camera and the tapes (along with the blood results) in the chamber and never saw this day time fulfilled.

Quite a remarkable story this is. Many are split in believing this story because of its enormous implications. But what does this have to do with the Mark of the Beast? Well, Ron knew and the angels confirmed it, the appointed time would be at the implementation of the Mark of the Beast. The Mark of the Beast is the execution of global manmade Sunday laws that require you to break one or more of God's Ten Commandments. This is why I share Ron's testimony. According to Ron, a person living in the time these Sunday laws get passed and enforced will receive the Mark of the Beast if they participate and choose to obey these Sunday laws. Ron simplifies this and says that if you keep God's Ten Commandments, you will have God's seal; however, soon there will be a set of man-made laws. These man-made laws will require that you break God's Ten Commandments. If you keep those man-made laws, then you will receive the Mark of the Beast.

Now many will believe and not believe Ron, but I think it is important to be as impartial and discerning as possible. It does nobody any good to be prideful and be absolute in their interpretation of what the Mark of the Beast is. After all, if Ron is right, then it will be too late for many; since the Ark would be revealed AFTER the Sunday laws are in place... meaning there would be no turning back for those who kept those set of man-made laws. I encourage you to discern this information and view Ron's video testimony and footage to come to your own decision. It is of my opinion that more information is better. In the event that you hear or live during a time that a set of Sunday laws are in effect, rest assured that Ron Wyatt was right.

If you are interested in learning more about Ron and his discovery, visit arkfiles.net or read Rebecca Tourniaire's King of the Ark.[40][41]

High Alert

Regardless of which interpretation you prefer, it is imperative that you are aware of this mark. You cannot afford to be wrong! It does not matter if you didn't know or you took it by mistake. The judgement of the first bowl and the reaping of the harvest does discriminate on those who bear the mark and those who do not. It matters not if you were a Christian for 30 years, if you take this mark you are eternally condemned to hell. This is why it is so important to read your Bible and have a personal relationship with Jesus Christ. Once a week worship for two hours is not enough to have a relationship with the Messiah and have the ability to discern the times.

I get frustrated sometimes when I see my social media feeds and see many of the people I grew up with, shared friendships with, and forged family bonds be completely oblivious to the time that we live in. The world crumbles and deteriorates and many seek to the government or social ideologies to cure and create a better future. In reality, the world degrades and will continue to degrade as these things must come to pass before the end.

I have sadly come to terms with the fact that not everyone I know will be saved in the end. I understand that. I don't have the power to save. But sharing this message of the mark is of the utmost importance. Because while you breathe and are alive, you can be saved today. But this mark is final and immediate. Even if you wanted to repent or regretted taking the mark, it would not matter. You literally are beyond salvation. The thought of this saddens me and I want to scream this message off the mountaintops. If you get anything out of this book, please remember this message. Read your Bible and watch the world as it unfolds. Be on the lookout for this mark.

Warfare Tip

Taking the mark of the beast or not is going to be the hardest decision for many who live to see it. Not taking this mark will mean that you are going to be forced to live in the wild or die from starvation or execution. This isn't supposed to be easy. But think of it this way. How many of the early church and the disciples died in horrid ways for their faith in Jesus? We are not exempt from that just because we live in comfort.

As an American, I acknowledge that I have suffered little persecution compared to my brothers and sisters in Syria and China for example—simply because I live in the United States. The mark is global though and will force all believers to make a choice. Take solace that you are in good company and that this final test will lead you into the presence of the Most High. Let's show our God that we stand for Him against an unbelieving world and that Satan has no power over us or His name. I find hope and purpose that many us will be a light or a boost of courage to those that face execution in this time. Think about it. Long lines of Christians waiting their turn to be executed for not renouncing Christ.Fear gripping their bodies causing some to fall out of line and take the mark because they can't bear to die or see their loved ones executed. You could be a force of faith and encouragement to our brothers and sisters and remind them that our redemption has come. We are finally going to be absent of the body and in the presence of the LORD. When the time comes be ready. WE ARE NOT TAKING THE MARK. For we are children of the Most High. and He is with us always. Let's show the enemy that no mark on earth will separate us from our Lord; and if not taking it requires that we lay down our life then we do it willingly. For He has laid His life for me; so too, I lay it down for Him.

ENCOUNTER #12
LAUGHTER

I was nearing my time to end my employment and move back home. I knew I wouldn't return. I had lost all my ambition to work in the entertainment industry. The more I read the Bible, the more I began to change. My values changed, and I couldn't wait to leave and start over. I think a part of me also thought that maybe these attacks would go away if I left too.

One night, I felt the buzzing feeling all over my body that accompanied every previous sleep paralysis experience. I tried to fight, but was slapped on my right cheek while a female voice laughed in my right ear. As I tried turning my head, the laughter followed me to my left ear, and I was hit again. I was too afraid to open my eyes to see what it was, and after some struggle, I was free. I wasn't as scared as much as I was humiliated. Humiliated that these things held power over me and mocked me because I couldn't do anything about it.

Chapter 21

THE WRATH OF THE BOWLS

Then I heard a loud voice from the temple saying to the seven angels, "Go, pour out the seven bowls of God's wrath on the earth."

Revelation 16:1

This is it. The final set of judgements against earth before Jesus' return. Just as the previous seals and trumpets, the culmination of God's wrath ends with a set of seven rapid-fire bowl judgements. These bowls increase in intensity and affirm Jesus' words when he forewarned that, if God had not put an end to these days, there would not be anyone left alive on earth. Unlike the seals and the trumpets, the bowls affect those remaining on earth directly and set the stage for the final battle of Armageddon. If you are somehow alive during this time, you are near the very end. Look up, for your redemption is near.

The First Bowl

The first angel went and poured out his bowl on the land, and ugly, festering sores broke out on the people who had the mark of the beast and worshiped its image.

Revelation 16:2

The first consequence of obtaining the mark of the beast is realized here. All bearers of the mark will break out in agonizing sores all over their body. Notice that this bowl does not affect believers during this time. If you are a follower of Christ, you will not suffer this judgement.

The Second Bowl

The second angel poured out his bowl on the sea, and it turned into blood like that of a dead person, and every living thing in the sea died.

Revelation 16:3

Unlike the second trumpet that killed off a third of all marine life, the second bowl completes the job to terminate every living thing in the sea.

The Third Bowl

The third angel poured out his bowl on the rivers and springs of water, and they became blood. Then I heard the angel in charge of the waters say:

*"You are just in these judgments, O Holy One,
you who are and who were;
for they have shed the blood of your holy people and your prophets,
and you have given them blood to drink as they deserve."
And I heard the altar respond:
"Yes, Lord God Almighty,
true and just are your judgments."*

Revelation 16:4-7

In complement to the previous bowl, the angel causes the remaining springs of water to become blood. We can see a similar judgement in Exodus when Pharaoh suffered the plague of the Nile turning to blood.

The Fourth Bowl

The fourth angel poured out his bowl on the sun, and the sun was allowed to scorch people with fire. They were seared by the intense heat and they cursed the name of God, who had control over these plagues, but they refused to repent and glorify him.

Revelation 16:8-9

This bowl is fascinating because despite the calamity of all the judgements, the deniers of God still do not repent and go beyond that to curse Him. Even in scorching heat that burns their skin, those who bear the mark of the beast continue to denounce God. Sometimes I wish God would show His might on the earth for then, surely, people would repent and turn to Him. But with the above verses in mind, I'm not so sure it would work. Surprisingly, people would still doubt or choose to hate Elohim. Some people have made their choice, and unfortunately, no circumstance would make them change their minds. After all, Jesus walked on earth amongst people teaching and performing miracles and people still didn't believe.

The Fifth Bowl

The fifth angel poured out his bowl on the throne of the beast, and its kingdom was plunged into darkness. People gnawed their tongues in agony and cursed the God of heaven because of their pains and their sores, but they refused to repent of what they had done.

Revelation 16:10-11

Another Egyptian plague falls over the kingdom of the antichrist. Darkness. And curiously, this fifth bowl illustrates the continuation of the other judgements. Bearers of the mark continue to sprout sores and the agony of the pain on their skin continues. It's no surprise why their hatred for the Lord continues. Let this be confirmation of the severity of taking the mark of the beast.

The Sixth Bowl

The sixth angel poured out his bowl on the great river Euphrates, and its water was dried up to prepare the way for the kings from the East. Then I saw three impure spirits that looked like frogs; they came out of the mouth of the dragon, out of the mouth of the beast and out of the mouth of the false prophet. They are demonic spirits that perform signs, and they go out to the kings of the whole world, to gather them for the battle on the great day of God Almighty.

"*Look, I come like a thief! Blessed is the one who stays awake and remains clothed, so as not to go naked and be shamefully exposed.*"
Then they gathered the kings together to the place that in Hebrew is called Armageddon.

Revelation 16:12-16

The sixth bowl begins to pave the way for the final battle. First, the angel dries up the Euphrates river for a specific purpose. This purposefully creates a route for the coming nations to get to the site of Megiddo, where Armageddon will take place. Second, three impure spirits come out, one each from Satan, the antichrist, and the false prophet. These demonic spirits perform signs to persuade the remaining leaders of the world to assemble and literally fight against God to try and put a stop to the judgements. I've seen the Megiddo site myself in Israel, and it is easy to imagine the number of armies all lined up across the expanse of the great field. This bowl paves the way for this moment. Jesus is near!

The Seventh Bowl

The seventh angel poured out his bowl into the air, and out of the temple came a loud voice from the throne, saying, "It is done!" Then there came flashes of lightning, rumblings, peals of thunder and a severe earthquake. No earthquake like it has ever occurred since mankind has been on earth, so tremendous was the quake. The great city split into three parts, and the cities of the nations collapsed. God remembered Babylon the Great and gave her the cup filled with the wine of the fury of his wrath. Every island fled away and the mountains could not be found. From the sky huge hailstones, each weighing about a hundred pounds, fell on people. And they cursed God on account of the plague of hail, because the plague was so terrible.

Revelation 16:17-21

The final bowl shows God's mighty power to those still living. Massive rumblings and flashes of lightning make the presence of God known across the earth. An earthquake like never before shakes the land with immense power—a quake off the Richter scale that destroys all the cities and breaks Jerusalem into three parts. Even islands succumb to the depths of the bloody sea and mountains cannot be found. Enormous 100-pound hailstones fall on the earth, mercilessly killing people, and those who worshipped the beast curse God—because so great is the seventh bowl.

What a sight to behold to see the mighty power of God. To date, I've been amazed at His creation, the fury of ocean waves, the anatomy of the human body, and the variety of life on the earth, but to see the unrelenting power of God—what a sight it must be. It will be so much power that it brings the earth to its knees. Even more poetic, it is an amazing way to pave the way for the incoming King. Jesus is here.

ENCOUNTER #13
THE MAN IN WHITE

During my last days in Arcadia, I began the moving process and packed some of my belongings to take home with me. Feeling tired, I decided to take a nap before I returned to packing. I knew there was a possibility I would see something or go into sleep paralysis. I had put the odds around 50/50.

Near the end of my nap, I awoke slowly and opened my eyes. I saw a very tall figure—most likely that of a man. The being was as tall as the ceiling and was completely hooded in white robes. I tried to seek its face, but I couldn't see past the hood. It stood there motionless at the corner of the bed, just standing there looking down.

I had this experience once more after a few weeks, but I never discovered who or what it was. Unlike the man in black or shadows, this was different. It was the first time someone was in white. Could it be? Well, I am (and remain to this day) very cautious to make assertions without truly knowing what something is and if it is biblical. But I cannot deny the thought of it possibly being an angel.

Chapter 22

THE FALL OF MYSTERY BABYLON

And on her forehead was written a name of mystery: "Babylon the great, mother of prostitutes and of earth's abominations."

Revelation 17:5

Many have heard of Babylon in some way, shape, or form. To some, Babylon is the ancient Mesopotamian city. To others, it is a reference to a satirical news site. And to still others, it is a media trope seen in entertainment as seen in award shows. But what is Mystery Babylon in Revelation and what does it have to do with the end of time? And why is it even important to me?

Mystery Babylon can affect you personally without you realizing it, because you may be living in it. To identify Mystery Babylon, one must first understand the first Babylon. Babylon (the Greek word means confusion) or "Bab-ilu" was the first ancient global city under one tongue. Genesis describes it as such:

Now the whole earth had one language and one speech. And it came to pass, as they journeyed from the east, that they found a plain in the land of Shinar, and they dwelt there. Then they said to one another, "Come, let us make bricks and bake them thoroughly." They had brick for stone, and they had asphalt for mortar. And they said, "Come, let us build ourselves a city, and a tower whose top is in the heavens; let us make a name for ourselves, lest we be scattered abroad over the face of the whole earth."

But the LORD came down to see the city and the tower which the sons of men had built. And the LORD said, "Indeed the people are one and they all have one language, and this is what they begin to do; now nothing that they propose to do will be withheld from them. Come, let Us go down and there confuse their language, that they may not understand one another's speech." So the LORD scattered them abroad from there over the face of all the earth, and they ceased building the city. Therefore its name is called Babel, because there the LORD confused the language of all the earth; and from there the LORD scattered them abroad over the face of all the earth.

Genesis 11:1-9

We can take away a few immediate notions from this broad description. First, Babel was a post-flood conglomeration of people under one language. Secondly, the inhabitants came to an agreement to build a tower to the heavens and make a name for themselves. Lastly, in anticipation, God takes action against them and confuses their language, causing the dispersion of peoples across the earth. You probably have questions regarding the reason for this (as did I), since the scripture does not delve into the specific cause for the confounding of language. Luckily, more exposition is found in the non-canonical book of Jasher:

And king Nimrod reigned securely, and all the earth was under his control, and all the earth was of one tongue and words of union.

And all the princes of Nimrod and his great men took counsel together; Phut, Mitzraim, Cush and Canaan with their families, and they said to each other, Come let us build ourselves a city and in it a strong tower, and its top reaching heaven, and we will make ourselves famed, so that we may reign upon the whole world, in order that the evil of our enemies may cease from us, that we may reign mightily over them, and that we may not become scattered over the earth on account of their wars.

And they all went before the king, and they told the king these words, and the king agreed with them in this affair, and he did so.

And all the families assembled consisting of about six hundred thousand men, and they went to seek an extensive piece of ground to build the city and the tower, and they sought in the whole earth and they found none like one valley at the east of the land of Shinar, about two days' walk, and they journeyed there and they dwelt there.

And they began to make bricks and burn fires to build the city and the tower that they had imagined to complete.

And the building of the tower was unto them a transgression and a sin, and they began to build it, and whilst they were building against the Lord God of heaven, they imagined in their hearts to war against him and to ascend into heaven.

And all these people and all the families divided themselves in three parts; the first said We will ascend into heaven and fight against him; the second said, We will ascend to heaven and place our own gods there and serve them; and the third part said, We will ascend to heaven and smite him with bows and spears; and God knew all their works and all their evil thoughts, and he saw the city and the tower which they were building. And when they were building they built themselves a great city and a very high and strong tower; and on account of its height the mortar and bricks did not reach the builders in their ascent to it, until those who went up had completed a full year, and after that, they reached to the builders and gave them the mortar and the bricks; thus was it done daily.

And behold these ascended and others descended the whole day; and if a brick should fall from their hands and get broken, they would all weep over it, and if a man fell and died, none of them would look at him.

And the Lord knew their thoughts, and it came to pass when they were building they cast the arrows toward the heavens, and all the arrows fell upon them filled with blood, and when they saw them they said to each other, Surely we have slain all those that are in heaven.

For this was from the Lord in order to cause them to err, and in order; to destroy them from off the face of the ground.

And they built the tower and the city, and they did this thing daily until many days and years were elapsed.

And God said to the seventy angels who stood foremost before him, to those who were near to him, saying, Come let us descend and confuse their tongues, that one man shall not understand the language of his neighbor, and they did so unto them.

And from that day following, they forgot each man his neighbor's tongue, and they could not understand to speak in one tongue, and when the builder took from the hands of his neighbor lime or stone which he did not order, the builder would cast it away and throw it upon his neighbor, that he would die.

And they did so many days, and they killed many of them in this manner. And the Lord smote the three divisions that were there, and he punished them according to their works and designs; those who said, We will ascend to heaven and serve our gods, became like apes and elephants; and those who said, We will smite the heaven with arrows, the Lord killed them, one man through the hand of his neighbor; and the third division of those who said, We will ascend to heaven and fight against him, the Lord scattered them throughout the earth.

And those who were left amongst them, when they knew and understood the evil which was coming upon them, they forsook the building, and they also became scattered upon the face of the whole earth.

And they ceased building the city and the tower; therefore he called that place Babel, for there the Lord confounded the Language of the whole earth; behold it was at the east of the land of Shinar.

And as to the tower which the sons of men built, the earth opened its mouth and swallowed up one third part thereof, and a fire also descended from heaven and burned another third, and the other third is left to this day, and it is of that part which was aloft, and its circumference is three days' walk. And many of the sons of men died in that tower, a people without number

Jasher 9:20-39

Immediately upon reading this, one can begin to understand that Nimrod and his people wanted to ascend to the heavens for conquest. Although this book is non-canonical, we can see that, just as Lucifer, pride to be above God was the sin and blasphemy committed by the earth's inhabitants under Nimrod's rule. This is interesting to know because this exposes the enemy's ultimate goal and why Mystery Babylon is deserving of the upcoming judgement at the end of the age.

Characteristics of the Mother of Harlots

Now that you know about the first Babylon, here are the characteristics of Mystery Babylon as described in Jeremiah and Revelation:

1. Mystery Babylon is a nation (Jeremiah 50:12).
2. Babylon is a young nation (Jeremiah 50:12).
3. Babylon has a mother (Jeremiah 50:12).
4. She has sinned against the Lord (Jeremiah 50:14).
5. She is the hammer of the earth Jeremiah 50:23).
6. She will be called "the lady of kingdoms" (Isaiah 47:5).
7. Babylon is the land of carved images (Jeremiah 50:38).
8. Babylon is insane with her idols (Jeremiah 50:38).
9. Other nations are drunk off her wine (Revelation 18:3).
10. Inhabitants are from other countries (Jeremiah 51:9).
11. She is surrounded by many waters (Jeremiah 51:13).
12. Babylon is rich in treasures (Jeremiah 51:13).
13. Babylon tried to reach Heaven (Jeremiah 51:53).
14. Babylon became a prison for demons (Revelation 18:2).
15. Merchants became rich off her (Revelation 18:3).
16. She glorified herself in arrogance (Revelation 18:7).
17. Other kings became rich off her (Revelation 18:9).
18. Merchants will weep because they won't be able to reap off her after her destruction (Revelation 18:11).

What nation or place comes to mind when you read these characteristics? For many, including myself, the closest answer is the United States of America.

Mystery Babylon Revealed

The United States was born from mother England, is a young nation that is an export of culture and commerce—often deemed as the greatest country on earth. A global superpower surrounded by many waters and inhabited by people of multiple nations, "lady liberty" gives all the freedom to live as the citizens please and is the hammer of the earth to other nations. The angel that speaks to John goes into detail about who and what this mysterious nation is:

Then one of the seven angels who had the seven bowls came and talked with me, saying to me, "Come, I will show you the judgment of the great harlot who sits on many waters, with whom the kings of the earth committed fornication, and the inhabitants of the earth were made drunk with the wine of her fornication."

So he carried me away in the Spirit into the wilderness. And I saw a woman sitting on a scarlet beast which was full of names of blasphemy, having seven heads and ten horns. The woman was arrayed in purple and scarlet, and adorned with gold and precious stones and pearls, having in her hand a golden cup full of abominations and the filthiness of her fornication. And on her forehead a name was written:

**MYSTERY, BABYLON THE GREAT,
THE MOTHER OF HARLOTS
AND OF THE ABOMINATIONS
OF THE EARTH.**

I saw the woman, drunk with the blood of the saints and with the blood of the martyrs of Jesus. And when I saw her, I marveled with great amazement."

> "But the angel said to me, "Why did you marvel? I will tell you the mystery of the woman and of the beast that carries her, which has the seven heads and the ten horns. The beast that you saw was, and is not, and will ascend out of the bottomless pit and go to perdition. And those who dwell on the earth will marvel, whose names are not written in the Book of Life from the foundation of the world, when they see the beast that was, and is not, and yet is.
>
> "Here is the mind which has wisdom: The seven heads are seven mountains on which the woman sits. There are also seven kings. Five have fallen, one is, and the other has not yet come. And when he comes, he must continue a short time. The beast that was, and is not, is himself also the eighth, and is of the seven, and is going to perdition.
>
> "The ten horns which you saw are ten kings who have received no kingdom as yet, but they receive authority for one hour as kings with the beast. These are of one mind, and they will give their power and authority to the beast. These will make war with the Lamb, and the Lamb will overcome them, for He is Lord of lords and King of kings; and those who are with Him are called, chosen, and faithful."
>
> Then he said to me, "The waters which you saw, where the harlot sits, are peoples, multitudes, nations, and tongues. And the ten horns which you saw on the beast, these will hate the harlot, make her desolate and naked, eat her flesh and burn her with fire. For God has put it into their hearts to fulfill His purpose, to be of one mind, and to give their kingdom to the beast, until the words of God are fulfilled. And the woman whom you saw is that great city which reigns over the kings of the earth.
>
> Revelation 17: 1-18

We can retrieve a few takeaways from this scripture. First, Mystery Babylon is considered the mother of harlots for her abominations and fornication with other kingdoms. This can be both literal and metaphorical. The United States, for example, is the largest exporter of online pornography in the world at a staggering 60%.[42] When making a metaphorical contextual comparison, fornication in the Old Testament is attributed to spiritual contamination. Worship of false pagan gods was considered as playing the harlot and fornicating. In both ways, the United States is a strong candidate for this.

The country may have begun under Christian appearances, but the passage of time has allowed for the worship of both false religions and the worship of idols (another characteristic of Mystery Babylon). The celebrity worship culture was born out of the United States and has been adopted globally. "Hollywood" has created a culture where celebrities are seen and worshipped as demi-gods and exist today as false images.

Regardless of Mystery Babylon's identity, one thing is clear: Ten kings will destroy this nation in a combined effort and will enable the antichrist to come forth and rule under a one-world authority. While no one today may know with 100% certainty the identity of Mystery Babylon, one has to agree that it is a compelling case that the United States is the whore Revelation describes. After all, the United States has many enemies across the earth, and the world would be stunned and shocked if the United States was ever destroyed. Certainly, merchants would weep because they would not be able to profit off her. Despite these similarities, other interpretations exist as to the identity of this harlot.

Other Interpretations

The Vatican

Probably the second most popular interpretation as to who or what the whore is, is that of the Vatican in Rome. There are a few reasons why. First, the woman is seen sitting on top of seven mountains. Rome is known as the "city of seven hills."[43] Secondly, the harlot is dressed in purple and scarlet and is adorned with gold and precious stones. Cardinals and bishops often wear purple and scarlet robes and the Vatican (and its priestly members) are adorned in gold and affluent trinkets. [44] Lastly, and probably the strongest evidence, is that the harlot is drunk off the deaths of the saints and martyrs of Jesus. While it's difficult to estimate the number of Christians killed by the papacy during the Roman Inquisition, we know that they persecuted and killed many protestants under the accusation of heresy while also forbidding the distribution of the Bible.

Not Yet Existing

Another interpretation is that Mystery Babylon has not come to existence yet. The reasoning for it is likely due to what you have probably seen by now—in that no one interpretation so far is completely accurate. The United States has not murdered many Christians (at least not directly or at least not yet). Would merchants weep if the Vatican was destroyed? Not likely, since it is not a commercial nation. For these reasons alone, it may be that we don't have enough information yet. Even if we don't though, we have to prepare because, as you read further, we are warned to come out of her…unless we share in her sins and destruction.

Babylon, No More

After the identity of Mystery Babylon is revealed to John, he is a witness to her destruction:

After these things I saw another angel coming down from heaven, having great authority, and the earth was illuminated with his glory. And he cried mightily with a loud voice, saying, "Babylon the great is fallen, is fallen, and has become a dwelling place of demons, a prison for every foul spirit, and a cage for every unclean and hated bird! For all the nations have drunk of the wine of the wrath of her fornication, the kings of the earth have committed fornication with her, and the merchants of the earth have become rich through the abundance of her luxury."

And I heard another voice from heaven saying, **"Come out of her, my people, lest you share in her sins, and lest you receive of her plagues.** *For her sins have reached to heaven, and God has remembered her iniquities. Render to her just as she rendered to you, and repay her double according to her works; in the cup which she has mixed, mix double for her. In the measure that she glorified herself and lived luxuriously, in the same measure give her torment and sorrow; for she says in her heart, 'I sit as queen, and am no widow, and will not see sorrow.' Therefore her plagues will come in one day—death and mourning and famine. And she will be utterly burned with fire, for strong is the Lord God who judges her.*

Revelation 18:1-8

This passage is why Mystery Babylon is important to you. The angel provides a warning for all who live there. Come out of her—unless you wish to share in her destruction. If Mystery Babylon is the United States and you live there, then the angel is warning you to come out! Come out of her likely means get out of her literally—as in moving away from the country least you also be killed. But the message has a deeper meaning as well. I'll explain.

A Christian living in Babylon at the time of her judgement will die, yes. But this warning can also mean to come out of her sinful culture and practices—to "come out" in a more spiritual sense. What does this mean? If you practice in her idolatry and fornication for example or if you worship celebrities, condone or practice her abominations and depravity, the angel warns you to repent and leave her lifestyle so that you are ultimately saved and not suffer the fate of hell from those who die in her judgement unrepented. The angel continues to declare a shocking revelation about the timing of her destruction:

The kings of the earth who committed fornication and lived luxuriously with her will weep and lament for her, when they see the smoke of her burning, standing at a distance for fear of her torment, saying, 'Alas, alas, that great city Babylon, that mighty city! For in **one hour** *your judgment has come.'*

"And the merchants of the earth will weep and mourn over her, for no one buys their merchandise anymore: 1merchandise of gold and silver, precious stones and pearls, fine linen and purple, silk and scarlet, every kind of citron wood, every kind of object of ivory, every kind of object of most precious wood, bronze, iron, and marble; and cinnamon and incense, fragrant oil and frankincense, wine and oil, fine flour and wheat, cattle and sheep, horses and chariots, and bodies and souls of men. The fruit that your soul longed for has gone from you, and all the things which are rich and splendid have gone from you, and you shall find them no more at all. The merchants of these things, who became rich by her, will stand at a distance for fear of her torment, weeping and wailing, and saying, 'Alas, alas, that great city that was clothed in fine linen, purple, and scarlet, and adorned *with gold and precious stones and pearls! For in **one hour** such great riches came to nothing.' Every shipmaster, all who travel by ship, sailors, and as many as trade on the sea, stood at a distance and cried out when they saw the smoke of her burning, saying, 'What is like this great city?'*

*"They threw dust on their heads and cried out, weeping and wailing, and saying, 'Alas, alas, that great city, in which all who had ships on the sea became rich by her wealth! For in **one hour** she is made desolate.'*
"Rejoice over her, O heaven, and you holy apostles and prophets, for God has avenged you on her!

Revelation 18:9-20

One hour. This city or nation will be destroyed in one hour. This moment will be so shocking to the world. Imagine if all the United States was destroyed to ruins and ashes. Now imagine if that happened in one hour. How incredulous and shocked the rest of the world will be. How many would mourn her destruction. How chaotic the world will be at the fallout of this event and that ten world leaders collaborated to destroy her. This is why Mystery Babylon is important, because her destruction is quick and unexpected. An unrepentant unbeliever will die quickly...without notice, meaning they would go to hell. THIS is why it's important to be aware of Mystery Babylon. If you live there, you will die. Believers should know this very well. Obviously, you shouldn't move if you are not able to, but even believers need to be aware and prepared for this. It is possible that you live in Mystery Babylon. If you see the signs of sudden destruction, then rest confirmed that Mystery Babylon's judgement is upon you.

ENCOUNTER #14
VICTORY

Finally back home, I was relieved and hopeful of starting over. I was confident that, despite not knowing what I would do now, God was with me to the very end. I had grown so much with Him in my time in the Los Angeles area that I realized God intended for me to have every opportunity I had in the entertainment industry for me to learn...and then return it back to Him as a lesson learned.

Laying down on my bed never felt better, and as I was nearing sleep, I felt the vibrations of sleep paralysis coming. Not this again...NO, I thought. I saw a group of black and red ligaments coming at me. It was a flood of disgusting creatures all gathering and coming toward me. Knowing what was coming next, I felt anger and a refusal to let this continue.

Remembering a passage in revelation, I shouted immediately, "I COMMAND YOU TO GO INTO THE ABYSS IN THE NAME OF YESHUA THE CHRIST!" My voice thundered like a storm and echoed all over my room. And immediately, I heard screams of horror. Screams of horror and agony filled the room. I was startled and did not anticipate this would happen. Multiple screams of pain, loud and in agony. It was something like the sound of many pigs shrieking in slaughter.

As this was all happening, I tried to get some control of the situation and just shouted "Jeeeeeeessssssssssuuuuuussss!" And in a slice of a moment—nothing. Like a black hole, everything got sucked up in an instant. Nothing. Absolute silence. Peace. There was a stillness in the air. I was awake and just stared at the ceiling thinking about what had just happened. Is this what it feels like to be free? I felt a huge smile on my face and a sense of victory filled my body. This was it. It's over.

Chapter 23

GLORIOUS COMING

Behold, He is coming with clouds, and every eye will see Him, even they who pierced Him. And all the tribes of the earth will mourn because of Him...

Revelation 1:7

This is it—the moment countless souls have been waiting for. It's been over 2,000 years since His presence on earth. It is the reason for our hope and the fulfillment of His promise. His coming. In an act of glory, He finally returns. Yeshua the Messiah, the King of kings. Believers both dead and alive will finally rejoice in His presence. Oftentimes, I've imagined this moment and the sight that it will be to behold. Though He has always been here with me, there is still something glorious about finally seeing Him face to face. How incredible it will be to join my brothers and sisters in Christ and rejoice. When I imagine this moment, every pain, suffering, and ridicule fades into darkness, for our Savior is here. And after several millennia of mockers and scoffers, He is finally here to reign. While former texts prophecy about His second coming, Revelation details the magnificence of this event, first unfolding what happens in the Third Heaven:

After these things I heard a loud voice of a great multitude in heaven, saying, "Alleluia! Salvation and glory and honor and power belong to the Lord our God! For true and righteous are His judgments, because He has judged the great harlot who corrupted the earth with her fornication; and He has avenged on her the blood of His servants shed by her." Again they said, "Alleluia! Her smoke rises up forever and ever!" And the twenty-four elders and the four living creatures fell down and worshiped God who sat on the throne, saying, "Amen! Alleluia!" Then a voice came from the throne, saying, "Praise our God, all you His servants and those who fear Him, both small and great!"

And I heard, as it were, the voice of a great multitude, as the sound of many waters and as the sound of mighty thunderings, saying, "Alleluia! For the Lord God Omnipotent reigns! Let us be glad and rejoice and give Him glory, for the marriage of the Lamb has come, and His wife has made herself ready." And to her it was granted to be arrayed in fine linen, clean and bright, for the fine linen is the righteous acts of the saints.

Then he said to me, "Write: 'Blessed are those who are called to the marriage supper of the Lamb!'" And he said to me, "These are the true sayings of God." And I fell at his feet to worship him. But he said to me, "See that you do not do that! I am your fellow servant, and of your brethren who have the testimony of Jesus. Worship God! For the testimony of Jesus is the spirit of prophecy."

Revelation 19:1-11

After the destruction of Mystery Babylon, heaven prepares for the marriage of the Lamb. It is now time for Jesus to retrieve His bride. In shouts of worship and praise, an enormous multitude prepares the way for the Lamb. Those alive (and the dead if you do not believe in the rapture) will not see this moment as it takes place in heaven. But it is worth knowing because this is the prelude to the fulfilment of the promise. Here He comes.

HE IS HERE

Now I saw heaven opened, and behold, a white horse. And He who sat on him was called Faithful and True, and in righteousness He judges and makes war. His eyes were like a flame of fire, and on His head were many crowns. He had a name written that no one knew except Himself. He was clothed with a robe dipped in blood, and His name is called The Word of God. And the armies in heaven, clothed in fine linen, white and clean, followed Him on white horses. Now out of His mouth goes a sharp sword, that with it He should strike the nations. And He Himself will rule them with a rod of iron. He Himself treads the winepress of the fierceness and wrath of Almighty God. And He has on His robe and on His thigh a name written:

KING OF KINGS AND LORD OF LORDS.

Revelation 19:11-16

There's a reason why this moment is not often seen in any form of visual media. No film or special effects could ever capture this glorious moment. Heaven opens and all the earth looks above at the Truth and the Light. Jesus, on a white horse, appears in the clouds accompanied by innumerable armies in heaven, all clothed in white linen and mounted on horses. With eyes like flame and many crowns on His head, He is clothed in a white robe dipped in blood, and He has the WORD OF GOD as His name.

In wonder and splendor, He opens His mouth to reveal a sharp sword and strikes the nations below. Remember the sixth piece of armor? The sword of the spirit? The WORD OF GOD is the ultimate weapon. This is what Jesus uses to defeat the nations of the earth. His TRUTH and His WORD is all that is needed to obliterate the enemy. In fact, Revelation details what is happening down on earth as His glorious appearance is occurring:

Then I saw an angel standing in the sun; and he cried with a loud voice, saying to all the birds that fly in the midst of heaven, "Come and gather together for the supper of the great God, that you may eat the flesh of kings, the flesh of captains, the flesh of mighty men, the flesh of horses and of those who sit on them, and the flesh of all people, free and slave, both small and great."

And I saw the beast, the kings of the earth, and their armies, gathered together to make war against Him who sat on the horse and against His army. Then the beast was captured, and with him the false prophet who worked signs in his presence, by which he deceived those who received the

> *mark of the beast and those who worshiped his image. These two were cast alive into the lake of fire burning with brimstone. And the rest were killed with the sword which proceeded from the mouth of Him who sat on the horse. And all the birds were filled with their flesh.*
>
> Revelation 19:17-21

As ludicrous and insane as it sounds, the antichrist and the false prophet have gathered all the armies left on earth to conspire against God and His judgements and actually fight Him. This is insane and the height of deception that anyone (including Satan) could ever damage or even touch the Most High. But this is what will happen.

Armies lined up aiming all their firepower at the sky—at Jesus above. What happens next is fascinating because the antichrist and the false prophet are captured and judged before the destruction of the armies. The highest ranks of the enemy are condemned for all to see without so much as a fight or struggle. They are captured and cast into the lake of fire burning with fire and brimstone. The evil they committed is finally being repaid. Following their judgement, Jesus destroys the armies with His mouth—the sword of the Word of God—allowing for the birds to feed on the remaining flesh of the dead. And just like that, with the simple opening of Jesus' mouth, they are destroyed.

This moment of Jesus appearing in the clouds mounted on a white horse is what we believers long for. We know of this moment, and I am sure, that as I do, you imagine and hope for this day as well. In my estimation, the secular world also knows about the event. Perhaps not the specifics with the armies and the method in which Jesus defeats them, but the world certainly knows about Jesus appearing in the clouds.

Unlike the hope for us, this moment is a moment of terror and regret for many unbelievers. The hope for us is the realization of condemnation for them because they did not repent and believe. It is fascinating that such a moment is felt in such emotional extremities depending on your relationship with Christ. This is why I find it astonishing that many will still not believe. Even if you scoff or mock that Jesus isn't real and that He hasn't come in thousands of years, everyone, both dead and alive, will see this day fulfilled. Regardless of your position, what comes next is known to all: Judgement Day.

GLORIOUS COMING

Chapter 24

JUDGEMENT DAY

For we must all appear before the judgment seat of Christ, that each one may receive the things done in the body, according to what he has done, whether good or bad.

2 Corinthians 5:10

Judgement day or the "day of the Lord" has curiously created fear and anxiety in the many people I've discussed this topic with. Even some believers, secure in their faith, tend to be afraid of this day. The idea that you stand alone at the throne of God, in the presence of Jesus, to give an account of all that you have said and done is enough to bring one to their knees. For unbelievers, it is a day of terror, for they know their destination is crystal clear.

But why is this day a day of fear? For me, it is a day that must come to pass and for all my hidden secrets to be exposed. I am saved, yes, and I am a baptized believer of Yeshua, but I must also stand alone and account for my sins. While I know that the blood of Jesus covers them, just like death, this day must still come to pass. Sins that I know and sins that I have forgotten are to be brought up as evidence that I have broken the law. Believers will wonder why they have to go through this if their names are in the Book of Life. Well, Revelation explains the details of that day and what exactly is going to happen for all the dead:

Then I saw a great white throne and Him who sat on it, from whose face the earth and the heaven fled away. And there was found no place for them. And I saw the dead, small and great, standing before God, and books were opened. And another book was opened, which is the Book of Life. And the dead were judged according to their works, by the things which were written in the books. The sea gave up the dead who were in it, and Death and Hades delivered up the dead who were in them. And they were judged, each one according to his works. Then Death and Hades were cast into the lake of fire. This is the second death. And anyone not found written in the Book of Life was cast into the lake of fire.

Revelation 20:11-15

All the dead stand in front of God on this day. No matter the position, small or great, all stand before God when the books are opened. This is an important notion because we usually see injustice here on earth where people of stature or money often circumvent justice. But from tyrant kings of old to modern elites or celebrities, we all face judgement as individuals regardless of our position on earth. This probably scares some people, but this is the great reminder that we are the creation of our Father. We return to Him who bore our soul and gave us breath of life. Interestingly, death and hades (hell) deliver the dead who are in it, which implies that people are currently in hell now. This means that all of them are brought up to the throne of judgement as well. Once attendance is complete, judgement based off the books begins.

Opening the Books

Revelation 20 mentions that the "books," plural, were opened before the judgement of the dead. These books appear across the Bible and are as follows:

Book of Remembrance

> *Then those who feared the LORD spoke to one another,*
> *And the LORD listened and heard them;*
> *So a **book of remembrance** was written before Him*
> *For those who fear the LORD*
> *And who meditate on His name.*

> *"They shall be Mine,"* says the LORD of hosts,
> *"On the day that I make them My jewels.*
> *And I will spare them*
> *As a man spares his own son who serves him."*
> *Then you shall again discern*
> *Between the righteous and the wicked,*
> *Between one who serves God*
> *And one who does not serve Him.*
>
> Malachi 3:16-18

While many believe that the book of remembrance contains a list of all the deeds every person has committed, the only scripture that describes this book does not support such a claim. The book of remembrance is only mentioned in Malachi 3 and describes it as a book written before God that contains the names of those who fear and meditate on His name. Essentially, those who believe and follow God's commandments. In reference to judgement day, this book will contain the names of the righteous as evidence that those who truly feared and meditated in the Lord are remembered by God. Another promise fulfilled.

Book of Life

The most important book and one that Jesus referenced, the Book of Life is a book you want to make sure your name is in:

> *"And I urge you also, true companion, help these women who labored with me in the Gospel, with Clement also, and the rest of my fellow workers, whose names are in the* **Book of Life.***"*
>
> Philippians 4:3

> *"Charge them with crime upon crime; do not let them share in your salvation. May they be blotted out of the* **book of life** *and not be listed with the righteous."*
>
> Psalm 69:27-28

> "And I saw the dead, small and great, standing before God, and books were opened. And another book was opened, which is the **Book of Life**. And the dead were judged according to their works, by the things which were written in the books."
>
> Revelation 20:12

> "All who dwell on the earth will worship him, whose names have not been written in the **Book of Life** of the Lamb slain from the foundation of the world."
>
> Revelation 13:8

> "The beast that you saw was, and is not, and will ascend out of the bottomless pit and go to perdition. And those who dwell on the earth will marvel, whose names are not written in the **Book of Life** from the foundation of the world, when they see the beast that was, and is not, and yet is."
>
> Revelation 17:8

In short, this book is confirmation of your salvation. The status of your name in this book is what is going to determine your destination: heaven or hell. Jesus is very clear about the difference between those whose names are and are not in the book:

> "And anyone not found written in the **Book of Life** was cast into the lake of fire."
>
> Revelation 20:15

> "He who overcomes shall be clothed in white garments, and I will not blot out his name from the **Book of Life**; but I will confess his name before My Father and before His angels."
>
> Revelation 3:5

We can discern two things from this pair of passages. First, that clearly anybody not found in the book will be cast into the lake of fire. And secondly, that Jesus makes a promise to those who endure in the faith to the end. He will clothe them with white garments and never blot out their names from the book. The last sentence of Revelation 3:5 is vital. Jesus will confess our names under Him before God and the angels. An interpretation exists that believers will not face judgement, that only the wicked and condemned will be judged. This verse, however, serves as definitive proof that such a belief is not true. Jesus serves as our mediator in court in front of our Father and confesses our names on His behalf.

Book of the Law
Finally, the Book of the Law serves as the basis by which our actions are judged:

If you do not carefully observe all the words of this law that are written in this book, that you may fear this glorious and awesome name, THE LORD YOUR GOD, then the LORD will bring upon you and your descendants extraordinary plagues—great and prolonged plagues—and serious and prolonged sicknesses. Moreover He will bring back on you all the diseases of Egypt, of which you were afraid, and they shall cling to you. Also every sickness and every plague, which is not written in this **Book of the Law**, *will the LORD bring upon you until you are destroyed.*

Deuteronomy 28:58-61

Contextually, the Book of the Law mentioned in Deuteronomy is addressed to Israelites, in early memory of the exodus prior. As previously mentioned though, the "Law" is the codified commandments God has set for us. John reminds us of this and affirms that the Law transcends the old covenant:

Whoever commits sin also commits lawlessness, and sin is lawlessness.

1 John 3:4

And this I say, that the covenant, that was confirmed before of Yahweh in the Messiah, the law, which was four hundred and thirty years after, cannot disannul, that it should make the promise of none effect."

Galatians 3:17

Like in any courtroom, there needs to exist a set of laws by which the judge will rule on and the defendants abide by. The ten commandments are those laws by which our actions are judged by. So, if God brings up my false worship of graven images or my theft, He judges based on laws He created for us to live by. In this way, the Book of the Law is the standard that all are judged against. All our sins are cross-examined according to the breaking of any of the given commandments. To many, this is a given, as the ten commandments exist for that sole purpose. However, the Book of the Law may go beyond the commandments and include other laws mentioned in scripture. For example, drunkenness, fornication, or sorcery (although some of these may fall under the ten). Regardless, rest assured that the Book of the Law is what our actions will be judged by. After judgement based on the books, the separation begins:

When the Son of Man comes in His glory, and all the holy angels with Him, then He will sit on the throne of His glory. All the nations will be gathered before Him, and He will separate them one from another, as a shepherd divides his sheep from the goats. And He will set the sheep on His right hand, but the goats on the left. Then the King will say to those on His right hand, 'Come, you blessed of My Father, inherit the kingdom prepared for you from the foundation of the world: for I was hungry and you gave Me food; I was thirsty and you gave Me drink; I was a stranger and you took Me in; I was naked and you clothed Me; I was sick and you visited Me; I was in prison and you came to Me.'

"Then the righteous will answer Him, saying, 'Lord, when did we see You hungry and feed You, or thirsty and give You drink? When did we see You a stranger and take You in, or naked and clothe You? Or when did we see You sick, or in prison, and come to You?' And the King will answer and say to them, 'Assuredly, I say to you, inasmuch as you did it to one of the least of these My brethren, you did it to Me.'

"Then He will also say to those on the left hand, 'Depart from Me, you cursed, into the everlasting fire prepared for the devil and his angels: for I was hungry and you gave Me no food; I was thirsty and you gave Me no drink; I was a stranger and you did not take Me in, naked and you did not clothe Me, sick and in prison and you did not visit Me.'

"Then they also will answer Him, saying, 'Lord, when did we see You hungry or thirsty or a stranger or naked or sick or in prison, and did not minister to You?' Then He will answer them, saying, 'Assuredly, I say to you, inasmuch as you did not do it to one of the least of these, you did not do it to Me.' And these will go away into everlasting punishment, but the righteous into eternal life.

Matthew 25:31-46

Conditions for Judgement

If you will be judged by the books, then I'm sure you must be thinking how you can get your name in the Book of Life, especially if you are being judged by the Book of the Law and Remembrance. The conditions for judgement are simple, yet have become confounding due to misinformation and doctrines of men. Luckily, scripture has preserved Jesus' teachings over thousands of years.

Entry to Heaven

Everybody wants to go to heaven. Even unbelievers and false prophets want to go to heaven. I find it comical that many people have the desire to go to heaven solely based on the idea that they are good people. Most people think, "Well I'm not a murderer, so I must be a good person that deserves to go to heaven." Or perhaps they'll say, "I don't follow the Bible, but God knows my heart." This deception is frightening, because when you break down who God (or god) is for these people, you realize they have created their own version of God.

I used the term "frightening" for a reason because of how dangerous this mentality is. The God of the Bible is not a God who allows you to sin freely without retribution. This is important to note because entry to heaven is based on certain conditions instructed by Jesus and affirmed by not only the four Gospels but also from early testament writings. The four conditions set forth by Jesus are:

Belief in Yeshua the Christ

And as Moses lifted up the serpent in the wilderness, even so must the Son of Man be lifted up, that whoever believes in Him should not perish but have eternal life. ***For God so loved the world that He gave His only begotten Son, that whoever believes in Him should not perish but have everlasting life.*** *For God did not send His Son into the world to condemn the world, but that the world through Him might be saved.*

He who believes in Him is not condemned*; but he who does not believe is condemned already, because he has not believed in the name of the only begotten Son of God. And this is the condemnation, that the light has come into the world, and men loved darkness rather than light, because their deeds were evil. For everyone practicing evil hates the light and does not come to the light, lest his deeds should be exposed. But he who does the truth comes to the light, that his deeds may be clearly seen, that they have been done in God.*

John 3:14-21

The most famous and known scripture, John 3:16, sets the basic condition for salvation. Belief in Jesus. It's that simple. A belief in Him as God's Son of Man sent purposefully to be slain in order to pay the debt of our sins. That's how much God loves us. True belief in Jesus as the Savior is the primary requirement for salvation.

I used the word "true" specifically to highlight the importance of belief in Jesus as accurately to His teachings and writings. A vast amount of people all over the earth claim to be "Christians," but unfortunately, that means many things today. Some Christians don't practice baptism, some worship images and idols, some worship on Sundays, some only go to church services once a week, and so forth. Jesus means different things for many people.

I'm always curious as to which "Jesus" people believe in. The most common version I've encountered is the all forgiving Jesus. While it is true that He forgives all sins (except the unpardonable one), He expects you to repent and change your behavior. These notions are important, because there is only one Jesus, and that is the Jesus from the Bible and historical records. This is why it's important to be sure that you are actually believing in the real Jesus of the Bible, because on that day of judgement, Jesus is going to say the most horrible words ever said:

Not everyone who says to Me, 'Lord, Lord,' shall enter the kingdom of heaven, but he who does the will of My Father in heaven. Many will say to Me in that day, 'Lord, Lord, have we not prophesied in Your name, cast out demons in Your name, and done many wonders in Your name?' And then I will declare to them, 'I never knew you; depart from Me, you who practice lawlessness!'

Matthew 7:21-23

<u>Repentance</u>

Like previously stated, Jesus forgives on the basis of repentance. Repentance means you do two things. First, ask for forgiveness of your sins and, second, to change your behavior. The latter step is what many people fail to realize. It isn't enough to ask for forgiveness. You must depart from your sin. I first realized this when Jesus spoke to the adulterous woman:

Now early in the morning He came again into the temple, and all the people came to Him; and He sat down and taught them. Then the scribes and Pharisees brought to Him a woman caught in adultery. And when they had set her in the midst, they said to Him, "Teacher, this woman was caught in adultery, in the very act. Now Moses, in the law, commanded us that such should be stoned. But what do You say?" This they said, testing Him, that they might have something of which to accuse Him. But Jesus stooped down and wrote on the ground with His finger, as though He did not hear.

So when they continued asking Him, He raised Himself up and said to them, "He who is without sin among you, let him throw a stone at her first." And again He stooped down and wrote on the ground. Then those who heard it, being convicted by their conscience, went out one by one, beginning with the oldest even to the last. And Jesus was left alone, and the woman standing in the midst.

> *When Jesus had raised Himself up and saw no one but the woman, He said to her, "Woman, where are those accusers of yours? Has no one condemned you?" She said, "No one, Lord." And Jesus said to her, "Neither do I condemn you; go and sin no more.*
>
> John 8:2-11

Notice He reassures her that He doesn't condemn her, but He also instructs her to go and sin no more. I remember reading that and realizing that He expects the same of me. He forgives me, yes, but He expects me to sin no more. I have failed and backslid sometimes, and after each recovery, I remember the above verses. This is the follow up to believing in Him. He cannot mold us and correct us if we don't take this first step of repentance. After all, He has said:

> *From that time Jesus began to preach and to say, "Repent, for the kingdom of heaven is at hand."*
>
> Matthew 4:17

> *Then Peter said to them, "Repent, and let every one of you be baptized in the name of Jesus Christ for the remission of sins; and you shall receive the gift of the Holy Spirit."*
>
> Acts 2:38

> *In those days John the Baptist came preaching in the wilderness of Judea, and saying, "Repent, for the kingdom of heaven is at hand!"*
>
> Matthew 3:1-2

Baptism

This is curiously controversial because denominations disagree on various aspects of baptisms. Some denominations practice infant baptism, where similar to the Catholic Church, babies are baptized in shallow or sprinkled water, while other denominations do not practice it at all or deem it unnecessary for salvation. What does Jesus say about baptism?

And He said to them, "Go into all the world and preach the Gospel to every creature. He who believes and is baptized will be saved; but he who does not believe will be condemned."

Mark 16:15-16

We can deduce immediately that baptism is indeed a requirement. But what type of baptism is necessary?

And this water symbolizes baptism that now saves you also—not the removal of dirt from the body but the pledge of a clear conscience toward God. It saves you by the resurrection of Jesus Christ.

1 Peter 3:21

And now what are you waiting for? Get up, be baptized and wash your sins away, calling on his name.

Acts 22:16

But when they believed Philip as he proclaimed the good news of the kingdom of God and the name of Jesus Christ, they were baptized, both men and women.

Acts 8:12

We can directly affirm that the disciples and the early church definitely practiced baptism and required it for new believers. Scripture clearly mentions and describes immersion in water, so why the different methods across ages?

Regarding infant baptism, there is no mention or description of any infants or children being baptized. All baptisms were of adults or people over the age of accountability. Secondly, all baptisms followed a public confession or confirmation that they believed in Christ first before they were immersed in water. Since this is the case, infant baptism is not the correct baptism Jesus is referencing as a requirement. An infant or a child has no knowledge of what is happening and is not capable of understanding or proclaiming their faith in Jesus. I myself, for example, was baptized as an infant in a Catholic Church. I remember nothing of the event and even became an atheist during and after my age of accountability. That baptism did nothing, because I was incapable of being a believer in Christ. Compare this to my baptism as an adult believer.

Because I was not a member of any church or denomination, I decided to travel to Israel and see the places I had read so often in the Bible for myself. Part of the trip involved visiting the Jordan River, along with the opportunity to be baptized if you wanted to. This was a big reason why I went. I was not baptized, and I felt in my gut that scripture told me I needed to.

I traveled alone and was nervous about the whole experience because I didn't know anyone, and it was the first time I traveled internationally. I was surprised at how loving and incredible my fellow group travelers were. They were all believers and were all there for the same reason I was: to be as close to Christ as possible.

When my turn came to walk into the river, my entire journey with Christ played over my head. The past suffering, the good that He has done in my life, and His unconditional love for me. I could not help but burst into tears. When the moment came, I confessed His name to all and was fully immersed.

The joy after was indescribable. The sharing of that moment with my new friends who were so happy for me is what I imagine will be the happiness we will all feel in the New Jerusalem. I tell you this story because that baptism meant something. It was a public confession of faith. I was very well aware of what I was doing and of the commitment I was making. There is no way a child can experience this. One must be aware of what they are being baptized for.

Born Again

I am sure you have heard of the term "born again," especially in reference to Christians. Most believers understand already that to be born again is to be reborn with the Holy Spirit and be a new person. While this is true, Jesus clarifies it and notes that it is a requirement to see the kingdom of heaven when He speaks to Nicodemus:

There was a man of the Pharisees named Nicodemus, a ruler of the Jews. This man came to Jesus by night and said to Him, "Rabbi, we know that You are a teacher come from God; for no one can do these signs that You do unless God is with him."

Jesus answered and said to him, "Most assuredly, I say to you, unless one is born again, he cannot see the kingdom of God."

Nicodemus said to Him, "How can a man be born when he is old? Can he enter a second time into his mother's womb and be born?"

Jesus answered, "Most assuredly, I say to you, unless one is born of water and the Spirit, he cannot enter the kingdom of God. That which is born of the flesh is flesh, and that which is born of the Spirit is spirit. Do not marvel that I said to you, 'You must be born again.' The wind blows where it wishes, and you hear the sound of it, but cannot tell where it comes from and where it goes. So is everyone who is born of the Spirit."

John 3:1-8

Notice that Jesus says "born of the water and the spirit" as a reference to the qualifications of entering heaven. Being born of water is your first birth; the birth Nicodemus could not understand happening once more (since how does a person go into a fetus again to be born "again"). Your birthdate is the moment you were born of water. But what Jesus refers to as being born again of the Spirit is a spiritual birth. Jesus continues His explanation to Nicodemus:

Jesus answered and said to him, "Are you the teacher of Israel, and do not know these things? Most assuredly, I say to you, We speak what We know and testify what We have seen, and you do not receive Our witness. If I have told you earthly things and you do not believe, how will you believe if I tell you heavenly things? No one has ascended to heaven but He who came down from heaven, that is, the Son of Man who is in heaven. And as Moses lifted up the serpent in the wilderness, even so must the Son of Man be lifted up, that whoever believes in Him should not perish but have eternal life. For God so loved the world that He gave His only begotten Son, that whoever believes in Him should not perish but have everlasting life. For God did not send His Son into the world to condemn the world, but that the world through Him might be saved.

"He who believes in Him is not condemned; but he who does not believe is condemned already, because he has not believed in the name of the only begotten Son of God.

John 3:10-18

This is what is needed to be saved and be born of the Spirit. When you believe that Jesus, the son of God, came to earth to bear the cost of your sins in death and accept Him as your Savior, this is your second birth. Being born again is a bolt of hidden electricity in your body when you receive Christ. You cannot inherit this. You cannot be born into it. You cannot receive this even if you grew up going to church. This is a once in a lifetime event that a Believer goes through.

For me, it was a moment of excitement, utter joy, and quite simply… being reborn. It feels like you're finally alive and you have finally discovered your purpose and your Father. It truly is a moment of discovery. Just like a child, you are born again and rely on Father God and Yeshua like a baby relies on his parents. Paul confirms this in 2 Corinthians:

Therefore, if anyone is in Christ, he is a new creation; old things have passed away; behold, all things have become new.

2 Corinthians 5:17

You must be born again. Take some time to reflect on this and ask yourself: are you born again today?

Condemnation to Hell

A topic that most don't like to discuss is judgement to hell. Nobody wants this. Not even the most evil of people desire going there. I don't like hell either, but it is a reality we must face head on. If we love one another, we must be truthful and warn each other of the qualifications that will send someone there. This is why I have decided to show you the scriptures that define these requirements unfiltered and directly from the source. Remember, I am not the one making the judgements or condemning anybody. This is what God, Jesus, and the apostles say about those condemned to hell:

But the cowardly, the unbelieving, the vile, the murderers, the sexually immoral, those who practice magic arts, the idolaters and all liars—they will be consigned to the fiery lake of burning sulfur. This is the second death.

Revelation 21:8

He will punish those who do not know God and do not obey the Gospel of our Lord Jesus. They will be punished with everlasting destruction and shut out from the presence of the Lord and from the glory of his might on the day he comes to be glorified in his holy people and to be marveled at among all those who have believed

2 Thessalonians 1:8-10

This is how it will be at the end of the age. The angels will come and separate the wicked from the righteous and throw them into the blazing furnace, where there will be weeping and gnashing of teeth.

Matthew 13:49-50

If your hand causes you to stumble, cut it off. It is better for you to enter life maimed than with two hands to go into hell, where the fire never goes out. And if your foot causes you to stumble, cut it off. It is better for you to enter life crippled than to have two feet and be thrown into hell. And if your eye causes you to stumble, pluck it out. It is better for you to enter the kingdom of God with one eye than to have two eyes and be thrown into hell, where "'the worms that eat them do not die, and the fire is not quenched.' Everyone will be salted with fire.'"

Mark 9:43-48

In a similar way, Sodom and Gomorrah and the surrounding towns gave themselves up to sexual immorality and perversion. They serve as an example of those who suffer the punishment of eternal fire.

Jude 1:7

Do you not know that the unrighteous will not inherit the kingdom of God? Do not be deceived. Neither fornicators, nor idolaters, nor adulterers, nor homosexuals, nor sodomites, nor thieves, nor covetous, nor drunkards, nor revilers, nor extortioners will inherit the kingdom of God. **And such were some of you**. *But you were washed, but you were sanctified, but you were justified in the name of the Lord Jesus and by the Spirit of our God.*

1 Corinthians 6:9-11

As you can see, Paul describes a list of the type of people that will not inherit the Kingdom of God. It seems harsh, but we have to accept the truth. This was difficult for myself when I first read those words, because I was and practiced many of those things. I bolded the words that followed, because those words changed my entire perspective: "And such were some of you," meaning that it is possible to change your behavior and repent. If you feel judged by this, good! That's conviction from God. It's better to feel it than to be immune to God's correction. I know that it's probably something you don't want to hear, but you must consider this carefully. Especially believers. On this day, Jesus will say the worst words to the people who thought they had a relationship with Him:

Not everyone who says to Me, 'Lord, Lord,' shall enter the kingdom of heaven, but he who does the will of My Father in heaven. Many will say to Me in that day, 'Lord, Lord, have we not prophesied in Your name, cast out demons in Your name, and done many wonders in Your name?' And then I will declare to them, 'I never knew you; depart from Me, you who practice lawlessness!

Matthew 7:21-23

Those are the most horrifying words we can hear. I never knew you… depart from me. How many who thought they were followers of Christ will hear this? A frightening thought. This is why you have to be sure you are correct in your faith and in your relationship with Him. This is the Word of God, and many other scriptures affirm these words. Romans 1, for example, is a strong and direct rendition of God's wrath:

For the wrath of God is revealed from heaven against all ungodliness and unrighteousness of men, who suppress the truth in unrighteousness, because what may be known of God is manifest in them, for God has shown it to them. For since the creation of the world His invisible attributes are clearly seen, being understood by the things that are made, even His eternal power and Godhead, so that they are without excuse, because, although they knew God, they did not glorify Him as God, nor were thankful, but became futile in their thoughts, and their foolish hearts were darkened. Professing to be wise, they became fools, and changed the glory of the incorruptible God into an image made like corruptible man—and birds and four-footed animals and creeping things.

Therefore God also gave them up to uncleanness, in the lusts of their hearts, to dishonor their bodies among themselves, who exchanged the truth of God for the lie, and worshiped and served the creature rather than the Creator, who is blessed forever. Amen.

For this reason God gave them up to vile passions. For even their women exchanged the natural use for what is against nature. Likewise also the men, leaving the natural use of the woman, burned in their lust for one another, men with men committing what is shameful, and receiving in themselves the penalty of their error which was due.

And even as they did not like to retain God in their knowledge, God gave them over to a debased mind, to do those things which are not fitting; being filled with all unrighteousness, sexual immorality, wickedness, covetousness, maliciousness; full of envy, murder, strife, deceit, evil-mindedness; they are whisperers, backbiters, haters of God, violent, proud, boasters, inventors of evil things, disobedient to parents, undiscerning, untrustworthy, unloving, unforgiving, unmerciful; who, knowing the righteous judgment of God, that those who practice such things are deserving of death, not only do the same but also approve of those who practice them.

Therefore you are inexcusable, O man, whoever you are who judge, for in whatever you judge another you condemn yourself; for you who judge practice the same things. But we know that the judgment of God is according to truth against those who practice such things. And do you think this, O man, you who judge those practicing such things, and doing the same, that you will escape the judgment of God? Or do you despise the riches of His goodness, forbearance, and longsuffering, not knowing that the goodness of God leads you to repentance? But in accordance with your hardness and your impenitent heart you are treasuring up for yourself wrath in the day of wrath and revelation of the righteous judgment of God, who "will render to each one according to his deeds": eternal life to those who by patient continuance in doing good seek for glory, honor, and immortality; but to those who are self-seeking and do not obey the truth, but obey unrighteousness—indignation and wrath, tribulation and anguish, on every soul of man who does evil, of the Jew first and also of the Greek; but glory, honor, and peace to everyone who works what is good, to the Jew first and also to the Greek. For there is no partiality with God.

For as many as have sinned without law will also perish without law, and as many as have sinned in the law will be judged by the law (for not the hearers of the law are just in the sight of God, but the doers of the law will be justified; for when Gentiles, who do not have the law, by nature do the things in the law, these, although not having the law, are a law to themselves, who show the work of the law written in their hearts, their conscience also bearing witness, and between themselves their thoughts accusing or else excusing them) in the day when God will judge the secrets of men by Jesus Christ, according to my Gospel.

Romans 1-2:16

I share the above scripture in full because it changed my life. I have never felt such conviction and guilt until I read it. Everything Paul said hit me like a truck because he was right. I finally understood that I deserved hell. I knew why I burned with lust and why I had forsaken God in my younger years. As damning as this was, it was important because I finally realized why Jesus came to earth and died. It was for what I had done.

I had always heard that Jesus had paid for my sins, but I never really understood it. It was so cliché to hear it over and over again that I never got the meaning behind it. Romans 1 is the epiphany that finally opened my eyes. I deserve to go to hell and Jesus lived a perfect life so that He could bear my sins on my behalf. He died so I could live. I couldn't believe it. I don't deserve it at all, and He still intervened for me. To this day, I never forget the moment I read that passage, because it marked a turning point for me. It is my hope that it does for you too.

Are You Ready?

Nobody can escape this day of judgment. This day will happen, and we will be judged according to what God and Jesus have revealed. This is why it is so important to be sure about your standing. Are you saved? Is your relationship with Jesus real? Do you believe the Bible is 100% the Word of God? The answers to these questions can potentially condemn you to eternal fire.

Even if you disagree with what I have written or demonstrated, please research on your own! Reflect on what you actually believe and to what it holds up to. Remember, it matters not what we think, but what is. I pray that you think this through, because time is short. We are the last generation...and we are running out of time.

ENCOUNTER #15
I AM HIS

The year after I left Arcadia, California, was a year of change and further growth in the Lord for me. Some sins were easier to leave than others, and some new difficulties and tests arose in my new workplace.

During my vacation in Texas, on July 9th, I had a very different experience. Not knowing how I got there, I was invisible and laying down on shallow, still waters. I looked up and I saw a vast number of stars across a black landscape. This place was so calm. It felt like I was inside a dome. After a few moments, I thought, God...are You there?

A voice replied, "I am here, My child."

The voice was a male voice with reverb and something I can't describe—like the voice of a lion and thunder, yet calm and serene at the same time. Immediately after that, my body began to rise upward into an opening of white light above. As I began to reach the white light, I thought, Wait—I'm not ready. As the light engulfed me, all I saw was pure white.

I awoke in the hotel bed and remained there frozen. Did that just really happen? It can't be. I recalled the event over and over and tried to remember as much as I could before it turned to memory. I thought through it over and over to be sure. I was highly skeptical of people who said they talked to God or had heavenly visions because I thought many of them were fake or just dreams.

This wasn't a dream though. I had an invisible body like the times when I went outside my body. The waters...the dome...it was all so real. And His voice...once I was sure of what had happened, I realized I didn't need to have this experience to know that God was real. I knew very well He existed before but hearing His voice was...timeless. He was always there with me and is still there despite my horrid sins. God is always present. When I am hard on myself or I stumble, I remember that moment. No matter what evil attempts to afflict me, my race is won. I am His.

Chapter 25

ETERNITY FULFILLED

I give them eternal life, and they will never perish, and no one will snatch them out of my hand.

John 10:28

Heaven...the aspiration and destination every human wants after death. For millennia, people from all nations and tongues have attempted to explain and direct many to this place. While many religions have their own version of the characteristics and prerequisites of heaven, the concept of heaven is one that most cultures are familiar with.

But in the difference between religions, one thing becomes clear: they can't all be correct. One of them has to be true, rendering the rest as false (or none at all). When Oprah Winfrey describes multiple avenues of religious beliefs that lead to the same place, she is wrong, because Muslims and Christians alone have stark contrasting beliefs about what heaven is and who goes there. It's important to face facts and make this distinction, because failure to face this topic head on leads to false hope and deception.

For example, the terms "rest in peace" and "they are in heaven now" are common descriptors during funerals when describing the deceased. However, this is highly deceptive. What if they were not saved? What makes us assume that they are resting in peace and in heaven? Biblically speaking, many (and I interpret this as the vast majority) do not go to heaven:

Enter by the narrow gate; for wide is the gate and broad is the way that leads to destruction, and there are many who go in by it. Because narrow is the gate and difficult is the way which leads to life, and there are few who find it.

Matthew 7:13-14

The way to heaven is narrow while the way to destruction is broad and large. When you begin to understand what bearing your cross is and that Jesus provided literal instructions to enter the Kingdom, then you can acknowledge that much of what the world deems as easy entry is wrong.

Another reason why it's important to have a foundation of heaven based on God's instruction is because heaven exists, but only in the way God wanted it—not in man's. What I mean is that heaven means different things to many people. Even secular people have their own renditions of heaven that range from empty positive space, frequencies, empty matter, all the way to nirvana or other new age interpretations. I am an example of this myself.

Before I was a follower of Christ, I spoke about my rendition of heaven during a discussion with my cousin (who at the time was Catholic). As I described heaven to be an earth where there was no evil or wars and where I would enjoy activities like playing video games, he interrupted and asked, "Wait—what do you think heaven is actually like? Do you really think you'll be playing video games in heaven?"

I never forgot this moment, because what my cousin was essentially asking me for was evidence for my beliefs. I was stunned, because he was right. I had created a fantasy in my head of heaven based on absolutely nothing—just my hopeful imagination.

Similar to my experience, many people create their own heaven bubbles. Fantasies of hope of something better to come after the "horrible" act of death. Secular people are not the only ones though. Even Christians have succumbed to this. I've often witnessed Christians supporting and comforting those who've suffered the loss of a loved one by confirming said loved one was in heaven or in a better place. In truth, the loved one may not be!

This sounds harsh, I know, but we must speak in truth as the Bible dictates. I am not the judge that decides who enters and who doesn't, but I do share God's Word about what He has instructed regarding it. Heaven is a real location offered to God's people and those who accepted Christ as the Messiah during their time on earth. Revelation explains the line of events that follow judgement day...and lead us there.

Satan's Judgement

Finally. After thousands of years, all the evil committed by Satan is finally repaid. Most believers and non-believers have some idea of what this judgement is: damnation into eternal hell. But what does that look like and is it actually biblical? Revelation takes us into a sequential timeline of exactly what will occur, and it's not quite what many people think:

Then I saw an angel coming down from heaven, having the key to the bottomless pit and a great chain in his hand. He laid hold of the dragon, that serpent of old, who is the Devil and Satan, and bound him for a thousand years; and he cast him into the bottomless pit, and shut him up, and set a seal on him, so that he should deceive the nations no more till the thousand years were finished. But after these things he must be released for a little while.

Revelation 20:1-3

Immediately, we see that Satan is not cast into hell. He is chained and thrown into a sealed bottomless pit for a period of 1,000 years. This may sound strange, because the end of time and what seemed to be the final fight has already been won. Even more curious is the last line of the passage that, after the 1,000 years have passed, Satan was allowed to be released for a short time. The answer comes later in the following verses.

The 1000 Year Reign

And I saw thrones, and they sat on them, and judgment was committed to them. Then I saw the souls of those who had been beheaded for their witness to Jesus and for the word of God, who had not worshiped the beast or his image, and had not received his mark on their foreheads or on their hands. And they lived and reigned with Christ for a thousand years. But the rest of the dead did not live again until the thousand years were finished. This is the first resurrection. Blessed and holy is he who has part in the first resurrection. Over such the second death has no power, but they shall be priests of God and of Christ, and shall reign with Him a thousand years.

Revelation 20:4-6

While Satan is in prison for 1,000 years, believers in Christ live under the reign of Jesus on earth. Not all believers though—only those who were martyred and those that did not take the mark of the beast during the Great Tribulation.

I must state that this topic is controversial. This segment of scripture details specifically the first and second resurrection. As you have read already, this can be problematic for certain rapture believers, as the first resurrection becomes impossible as a pre-tribulation possibility. Some pre-tribulation believers will assert that they are in Heaven while the 1,000-year reign is occurring on earth. This is a little strange, since Jesus promised us that we would be with Him in His Kingdom after judgement day.

Personally, the text here is clear about the sequence of events. I would not disregard it simply because it goes against an interpretation I hold dear. Regardless if disagreements exist¬¬, the text confirms that the rest of the dead do not get to live again until after the 1,000 years are finished. John continues to describe his vision to include that those who are a part of the first resurrection are blessed and shall be priests of God and Christ during that time. When the 1,000 years conclude, something interesting happens. Another battle occurs on earth, only this one will be definitive.

The Final Battle

Now when the thousand years have expired, Satan will be released from his prison and will go out to deceive the nations which are in the four corners of the earth, Gog and Magog, to gather them together to battle, whose number is as the sand of the sea. They went up on the breadth of the earth and surrounded the camp of the saints and the beloved city. And fire came down from God out of heaven and devoured them. The devil, who deceived them, was cast into the lake of fire and brimstone where the beast and the false prophet are. And they will be tormented day and night forever and ever.

Revelation 20:7-10

The verses above are incredible for a couple reasons. First, God allows Satan to be released from the bottomless pit after the 1000-year reign. And second, some people on earth (who were saved and devoted to Christ) would be tempted and swayed to betray God and Christ and battle them in physical warfare. For this reason, this passage is highly contentious across a multitude of pastors and believers.

I myself find it incredulous that one could do this. But I believe the text nonetheless, because through time, men (and Israelites) have done incredulous things and betrayed God and His instructions knowing full well Who He is. So it is possible that after 1,000 years, a portion of earth's inhabitants are tempted by Satan as was Eve.

Another interpretation of this event is that not all people of the last seven years will die. In this case, these non-believing survivors are the human population for which the saints will rule over. Through time, the children of these survivors and generations of these descendants are the people that Satan deceives when he is released from his prison. Regardless of who betrays Christ, Satan will tempt them, and they will all attempt to fight Christ in the New Jerusalem.

Similar to the fight at Megiddo, God destroys and devours the people through fire. Unlike after Armageddon though, Satan is cast into the lake of fire and brimstone where the antichrist and false prophet are. It is important to note one thing here. John uses active language in describing them, meaning that the antichrist and the false prophet have been and continue to be burning in the lake of fire. Some people interpret the lake of fire or the second death to be a cessation of existence, that the second death is not eternal torture, but rather oblivion. The verses above refute that notion completely because it demonstrates that both antichrist and false prophet have been burning in the lake of fire during all of the 1,000 years. The last line of the verses further affirms to include Satan in this when it mentions that they will be tormented day and night forever and ever.

The Golden City

But what happens to the dead that have not been raised? What about heaven? Is it not the gates of gold that have permeated imagery and description? John's vision continues:

Now I saw a new heaven and a new earth, for the first heaven and the first earth had passed away. Also there was no more sea. Then I, John, saw the holy city, New Jerusalem, coming down out of heaven from God, prepared as a bride adorned for her husband. And I heard a loud voice from heaven saying, "Behold, the tabernacle of God is with men, and He will dwell with them, and they shall be His people. God Himself will be with them and be their God. And God will wipe away every tear from their eyes; there shall be no more death, nor sorrow, nor crying. There shall be no more pain, for the former things have passed away."

Then He who sat on the throne said, "Behold, I make all things new." And He said to me, "Write, for these words are true and faithful."
And He said to me, "It is done! I am the Alpha and the Omega, the Beginning and the End. I will give of the fountain of the water of life freely to him who thirsts. He who overcomes shall inherit all things, and I will be his God and he shall be My son. But the cowardly, unbelieving, abominable, murderers, sexually immoral, sorcerers, idolaters, and all liars shall have their part in the lake which burns with fire and brimstone, which is the second death."

Revelation 21:1-8

A new genesis occurs here. Creation of a new heaven and a new earth—a reversal to the perfection of the Garden of Eden with a new addition: the New Jerusalem. I must say that I look forward to this with all my heart. I was fortunate to visit Jerusalem in 2018 and it remains the fondest memory of my life. Truly, it is God's city and something to be felt and experienced when you set your eyes on it for the first time. To see a new "golden" city descend from the sky will be marvelous.

John describes this city with a promise that God will literally be with us and we shall be His people. He will wipe away every tear from our eyes and there will be no more pain or heartache, as the former things have now passed. There are not words that can describe the magnitude of what the New Jerusalem will be, but John does his best in illustrating what he saw:

Then one of the seven angels who had the seven bowls filled with the seven last plagues came to me and talked with me, saying, "Come, I will show you the bride, the Lamb's wife." And he carried me away in the Spirit to a great and high mountain, and showed me the great city, the holy Jerusalem, descending out of heaven from God, having the glory of God. Her light was like a most precious stone, like a jasper stone, clear as crystal. Also she had a great and high wall with twelve gates, and twelve angels at the gates, and names written on them, which are the names of the twelve tribes of the children of Israel: three gates on the east, three gates on the north, three gates on the south, and three gates on the west.

Now the wall of the city had twelve foundations, and on them were the names of the twelve apostles of the Lamb. And he who talked with me had a gold reed to measure the city, its gates, and its wall. The city is laid out as a square; its length is as great as its breadth. And he measured the city with the reed: twelve thousand furlongs. Its length, breadth, and height are equal. Then he measured its wall: one hundred and forty-four cubits, according to the measure of a man, that is, of an angel. The construction of its wall was of jasper; and the city was pure gold, like clear glass. The foundations of the wall of the city were adorned with all kinds of precious stones: the first foundation was jasper, the second sapphire, the third chalcedony, the fourth emerald, the fifth sardonyx, the sixth sardius, the seventh chrysolite, the eighth beryl, the ninth topaz, the tenth chrysoprase, the eleventh jacinth, and the twelfth amethyst. The twelve gates were twelve pearls: each individual gate was of one pearl. And the street of the city was pure gold, like transparent glass.

Revelation 21:9-21

What a stunning sight of light and majesty the New Jerusalem will be. The size alone is enormous: 1,363 miles across all directions with 12 large gates on each side. With jasper walls and the city made of pure gold, it is also adorned by a variety of unique stones. Even the foundations are made of the most beautiful stone minerals ever seen on earth with streets of gold that lead to gates made of pearls. I can only imagine the glory that John saw in his vision. But most importantly is what stands in the center of the city and what is most holy: the temple:

But I saw no temple in it, for the Lord God Almighty and the Lamb are its temple. The city had no need of the sun or of the moon to shine in it, for the glory of God illuminated it. The Lamb is its light. And the nations of those who are saved shall walk in its light, and the kings of the earth bring their glory and honor into it. Its gates shall not be shut at all by day (there shall be no night there). And they shall bring the glory and the honor of the nations into it. But there shall by no means enter it anything that defiles, or causes an abomination or a lie, but only those who are written in the Lamb's Book of Life.

Revelation 21:22-27

There is no physical temple in this new city. So holy and glorious is God that He and Jesus are the temple. Such is the light that emanates from them that we don't need a moon or a sun anymore. The glory of God illuminates the city and Jesus is the light. Those saved will get to experience this and walk the streets in the light, and kings on earth will come and honor it. There will be no light there, and nothing will ever enter that defiles it. Only those whose names are in the Book of Life may enter. Finally, John concludes the description by exposing the holiest of sites and objects that have not been seen in millennia:

And he showed me a pure river of water of life, clear as crystal, proceeding from the throne of God and of the Lamb. In the middle of its street, and on either side of the river, was the tree of life, which bore twelve fruits, each tree yielding its fruit every month. The leaves of the tree were for the healing of the nations. And there shall be no more curse, but the throne of God and of the Lamb shall be in it, and His servants shall serve Him. They shall see His face, and His name shall be on their foreheads. There shall be no night there: They need no lamp nor light of the sun, for the Lord God gives them light. And they shall reign forever and ever.

Revelation 21:1-5

The river of life that Jesus promised us is there. No longer do we thirst. The Tree of Life is on the side of the river bearing twelve fruits with leaves that heal the nations from previous curses. Not only will we be servants of God but we will also finally be able to see His face and reign with Him forever. This is heaven for us according to John's vision and Jesus' revelation.

Admittedly, it is definitely different from what I had perceived it to be. The third heaven continues to exist, however, being as it is God's plane of residence. For us, we will inhabit the new earth and the New Jerusalem while being in His full presence. What a day that will be. This is what we as believers in Christ strive for. Every pain, suffering, or persecution on earth we faced on His behalf is finally worth it. This is our reward and the promise fulfilled He gives to us.

Jesus' Final Words

Eternity will be fulfilled for all who repent and believe in Yeshua the Christ. We are the last generation and His coming is near. For Jesus has declared it :

"And behold, I am coming quickly, and My reward is with Me, to give to every one according to his work. I am the Alpha and the Omega, the Beginning and the End, the First and the Last."

Blessed are those who do His commandments, that they may have the right to the tree of life, and may enter through the gates into the city. But outside are dogs and sorcerers and sexually immoral and murderers and idolaters, and whoever loves and practices a lie.

"I, Jesus, have sent My angel to testify to you these things in the churches. I am the Root and the Offspring of David, the Bright and Morning Star." And the Spirit and the bride say, "Come!" And let him who hears say, "Come!" And let him who thirsts come. Whoever desires, let him take the water of life freely."

Revelation 22:12-17

ETERNITY FULFILLED

CONCLUSION

You made it to the end. It is my hope and my prayer that God has released you from the enemy's strongholds and that your life is renewed through the blood of Jesus. Regardless if this is true for you today, I want to tell you that God has not forgotten about you. He accepts you today with open arms if you choose His Christ as your Saviour and are ready to repent and turn away from sin. We are so lucky to be alive today. We get a second chance at eternity with Jesus.

Think about that in the coming time. The time we have been chosen to live in is just that-time. While fear can grip and take a hold of you, remember that this is a time of faith. This is our chance to prove our faith in action. Yes, times will be tough and we will have to make eternity-changing choices that might cost us our flesh, but rejoice! Rejoice in the hope fulfilled that Jesus has finally come to pick up His remnant. Remember His words to you:

"And do not fear those who kill the body but cannot kill the soul. But rather fear Him who is able to destroy both soul and body in hell."

Matthew 10:28-29

We have nothing to fear. We are in God's hands and He has not forsaken us. Be strong. Be of good courage. Have faith. God is and will be there right with you...in the coming days....and to the very end.

"...And surely I am with you always, to the very end of the age."
Jesus

Matthew 28:20

I hope to meet you that day. See you on the other side...

Your brother in Christ,
Luis

ABOUT THE AUTHOR

Luis Lopez is a first-time author and member of the Body of Christ since 2014. During his walk, he has experienced over 60 demonic attacks. From sleep paralysis, out-of-body experiences, to supernatural manifestations, he has achieved victory with the help of Jesus. Now a free man, he enjoys reading scripture and traveling to Israel in his free time. Luis holds a M.S. in Technical Communication and is currently a Technical Writer.

NOTES

Chapter 1

1. Sun-tzu, and Samuel B. Griffith. 1964. The art of war. Oxford: Clarendon Press.

2. Mishkov, Aleksandar. "George S. Patton versus Erwin Rommel - The Tactician's Battle during World War II." DocumentaryTube, July 27, 2015. http://www.documentarytube.com/articles/george-s-patton-versus-erwin-rommel-the-tactician-s-battle-during-world-war-ii.

Chapter 2

3. Hearne, Kevin. The Demonization of Pan, 1998. https://www.mesacc.edu/~thoqh49081/StudentPapers/pan.html.

4. Dizdar, Russ. Expelling Darkness - Engaging Non Human Entities Now and IN The End of Days, 2017.

Chapter 3

5. Samuels, H. C., & O'Boyle, J. (2013). The Role of the Brain in Addiction. In Alive again: Recovering from alcoholism and drug addiction (p. 67). Hoboken, NJ: Wiley.

6. Ramirez, John. "The Real Battle Begins." Essay. In Out of the Devil's Cauldron: a Journey from Darkness to Light: Santeria, Spiritualism, Palo Mayombe, 195. New York: Heaven & Earth, 2012.

7. Bushak, Lecia. "A Brief History Of Yoga." Medical Daily, October 21, 2015. https://www.medicaldaily.com/brief-history-yoga-ancient-hindu-scriptures-modern-westernized-practice-358162.

8. Guy Donahaye and Eddie Stern, Guruji: A Portrait of Sri K. Pattabhi Jois Through the Eyes of His Students (New York: North Point Press, 2010), 7.

9. Ramirez, John. "Initiation." Essay. In Out of the Devil's Cauldron: a Journey from Darkness to Light: Santeria, Spiritualism, Palo Mayombe, 45–52. New York: Heaven & Earth, 2012.

10. Ramirez, John. Out of the Devil's Cauldron: a Journey from Darkness to Light: Santeria, Spiritualism, Palo Mayombe. New York: Heaven & Earth, 2012.

11. Crowe, Cameron. "David Bowie: Ground Control to Davy Jones." Rolling Stone. Rolling Stone, June 25, 2018. https://www.rollingstone.com/music/music-news/david-bowie-ground-control-to-davy-jones-77059/.

12. McQuarrie, Christopher. The Usual Suspects. United States: Gramercy Pictures, 1995.

13. Felson, S. (2018, October 26). Sleep Paralysis - Causes, Symptoms, Treatment, and Prevention. Retrieved August 06, 2020, from https://www.webmd.com/sleep-disorders/sleep-paralysis

14. The Exorcist. United States: Warner Bros, 1973.

Chapter 4

15. Barriot, David B., George T. Kurian, and Todd M Johnson. "The World by Countries : Religionists, Churches, Ministries." In World Christian Encyclopedia : a Comparative Survey of Churches and Religions in the Modern WorldI, I:16–18. Oxford, NY: Oxford Univ. Press, 2001.

Chapter 9

15. Laurie, Greg, and Jeff Lasseigne. "Angels in the Life of the Believer." Harvest, September 10, 2020. https://harvest.org/resources/devotion/angels-in-the-life-of-the-believer/.

16. Mecklin, John. "Current Time." Bulletin of the Atomic Scientists, January 23, 2020. https://thebulletin.org/doomsday-clock/current-time/.

Chapter 12

17. "Coronavirus: How Action Against Hunger Is Responding to the Pandemic." Action Against Hunger, March 19, 2020. https://www.actionagainsthunger.org/story/coronavirus-how-action-against-hunger-responding-pandemic.

18. Mailonline, Amelia Wynne For. "The World Faces 'Mega-Famines' That Could 'Impact Us on Biblical Proportions' Due to CoronaviruS." Daily Mail Online. Associated Newspapers, May 8, 2020. https://www.dailymail.co.uk/news/article-8300297/The-world-faces-mega-famines-impact-biblical-proportions-coronaviruS.html.

19. Hickok, Kimberly. "Tons of Major Quakes Have Rattled the World Recently. Does That Mean Anything?" LiveScience. Purch, August 23, 2018. https://www.livescience.com/63412-california-big-quake.html.

20. Karimi, Faith. "More than 500 Earthquakes Have Rattled the Puerto Rico Region in 10 Days. There May Be More to Come." CNN. Cable News Network, January 8, 2020. https://www.cnn.com/2020/01/08/us/puerto-rico-region-hundreds-of-earthquakes/index.html.

21. Payne, J. Barton. Encyclopedia of Biblical Prophecy: the Complete Guide to Scriptural Predictions and Their Fulfillment. Michigan: Baker Books, 1997.

22. "State of Israel Proclaimed." History.com. A&E Television Networks, February 9, 2010. https://www.history.com/this-day-in-history/state-of-israel-proclaimed.

23. History.com Editors. "Yom Kippur War." History.com. A&E Television Networks, November 9, 2009. https://www.history.com/topics/middle-east/yom-kippur-war.

Chapter 17

24. Imster, Eleanor. "Earth Has 3 Trillion Trees, Says Study." EarthSky. Accessed September 16, 2020. https://earthsky.org/earth/earth-has-3-trillion-trees-says-study.

25. Bowler, Jacinta. "Here's What Happened When The World's Space Agencies Simulated a Killer Asteroid Impact." ScienceAlert, May 6, 2019. https://www.sciencealert.com/sorry-new-york-city-you-ve-been-squashed-in-a-hypothetical-asteroid-impact.

26. Bowler, Jacinta. "Here's What Happened When The World's Space Agencies Simulated a Killer Asteroid Impact." ScienceAlert, May 6, 2019. https://www.sciencealert.com/sorry-new-york-city-you-ve-been-squashed-in-a-hypothetical-asteroid-impact.

27. Nixon, Richard. "Toast at the Hall of the People in Beijing." Speech, February 25, 1972.

Chapter 18

28. Rockefeller, David. Memoirs. Random House Trade Paperbacks, 2002.

29. McKenzie, Richard Neal. "Chapter 33." Essay. In We the People: A Christian Nation, 301–. AuthorHouse, 2010.

30. Kissinger, Henry, and Eric Dubay. "World Affairs Council Pres Conference." In The Atlantean Conspiracy: Exposing the Global Conspiracy from Atlantis to Zion, 20–20, n.d.

31. Greenhouse, Steven. "Mandela Says U.S. Must Aid World's Poor." The New York Times. The New York Times, October 7, 1994. https://www.nytimes.com/1994/10/07/world/mandela-says-us-must-aid-world-s-poor.html.

32. Knott, Stephen, Stephen Knott1.1.1.1.1.1.1.1.Professor of National Security AffairsUnited States Naval War College, Stephen Knott, and Professor of National Security AffairsUnited States Naval War College. "George H. W. Bush: Foreign Affairs." Miller Center, August 14, 2020. https://millercenter.org/president/bush/foreign-affairs.

33. Volkmann, Hans. "Antiochus IV Epiphanes." Encyclopædia Britannica. Encyclopædia Britannica, inc., November 13, 2019. https://www.britannica.com/biography/Antiochus-IV-Epiphanes.

34. Stanglin, Doug. "Pope, Patriarch Meet in Cuba Nearly 1,000 Years after Split." USA Today. Gannett Satellite Information Network, February 12, 2016. https://www.usatoday.com/story/news/2016/02/12/pope-francis-patriarch-kirill-roman-catholic-church-russian-orthodox-church-meet/80278172/.

Chapter 19

35. Bergoglio, Jorge Mario. "Apostolic Journey to the United Arab Emirates: Interreligious Meeting at the Founder's Memorial (Abu Dhabi, 4 February 2019): Francis." Apostolic Journey to the United Arab Emirates: Interreligious meeting at the Founder's Memorial (Abu Dhabi, 4 February 2019) | Francis, February 4, 2019. http://www.vatican.va/content/francesco/en/speeches/2019/february/documents/papa-francesco_20190204_emiratiarabi-incontrointerreligioso.html.

36. Dennehy, John. "Pope Francis Makes Historic Visit to Sheikh Zayed Grand Mosque." The National. The National, February 4, 2019. https://www.thenational.ae/uae/the-pope-in-the-uae/pope-francis-makes-historic-visit-to-sheikh-zayed-grand-mosque-1.821818.

38. "Lord's Prayer: Pope Francis Calls for Change." BBC News. BBC, December 8, 2017. https://www.bbc.com/news/world-europe-42279347.

Chapter 20

39. Savage, Maddy. "Thousands Of Swedes Are Inserting Microchips Under Their Skin." NPR. NPR, October 22, 2018. https://www.npr.org/2018/10/22/658808705/thousands-of-swedes-are-inserting-microchips-under-their-skin.

40. Tourniaire, Rebecca. King of the Ark. Ark Files. thirdangelsmessage.com/arkfiles.net. Accessed September 2020. https://thirdangelsmessage.com/Downloads/King_Of_The_Ark.pdf.

41. "THE ARK AND THE BLOOD – The Discovery of the Ark of the Covenant." ArkFiles.net, October 6, 2019. https://arkfiles.net/the-ark-and-the-blood-the-discovery-of-the-ark-of-the-covenant/.

Chapter 22

42. Richter, Felix. "Infographic: 60% of Porn Websites Are Hosted in the United States." Statista Infographics, August 21, 2013. https://www.statista.com/chart/1383/top-10-adult-website-host-countries/.

43. Hengel, Livia. "What Are The Seven Hills Of Rome?" Culture Trip. The Culture Trip, September 15, 2016. https://theculturetrip.com/europe/italy/articles/what-are-the-seven-hills-of-rome/.

44. King, Msgr. William J. "Colors Worn By Cardinals and Bishops." Simply Catholic, August 25, 2020. https://simplycatholic.com/colors-worn-by-cardinals-and-bishops/.

www.ingramcontent.com/pod-product-compliance
Lightning Source LLC
Chambersburg PA
CBHW071805080526
44589CB00012B/697